America's Philosophical Vision

D1557181

America's Philosophical Vision

JOHN E. SMITH

The University of Chicago Press
Chicago and London

John E. Smith is the Clark Professor of Philosophy Emeritus
at Yale University and author of many books on American
philosophy including *Purpose and Thought* published by
this press.

The University of Chicago Press, Chicago 60637
The University of Chicago Press, Ltd., London
©1992 by The University of Chicago
All rights reserved. Published 1992
Printed in the United States of America
01 00 99 98 97 96 95 94 93 92   1 2 3 4 5 6

ISBN (cloth): 0-226-76367-6
ISBN (paper): 0-226-76368-4

⊗The paper used in this publication meets the minimum
requirements of the American National Standard for Information
Sciences—Permanence of Paper for Printed Library Materials,
ANSI Z39.48-1984.

This book is printed on acid-free paper.

Library of Congress Cataloging-in-Publication Data

Smith, John Edwin.
    America's philosophical vision / John E. Smith.
        p.   cm.
    Includes bibliographical references and index.
    1. Philosophy, American.   2. Pragmatism.   3. Royce, Josiah,
1855–1916. I. Title.
B893.S62 1992
191—dc20   91-22376
                                                        CIP

Contents

Acknowledgments

I wish to express my gratitude to Christopher Dustin, presently completing graduate study in philosophy at Yale, for his invaluable assistance in preparing an earlier version of this book. My thanks also go to Angie Harder and Pat Slatter, who typed the Introduction, and to Gordon and Susan Marino for clerical assistance.

John E. Smith
New Haven, Connecticut

Introduction

America has often been described as being less a geographical entity than a state of mind embodied in a people committed to the realization of ideals through democratic institutions. These ideals together with the problems of bringing them into being have found expression in the thought of our classical American philosophers—Peirce, James, Royce and Dewey. There is at present a need to focus the vision that motivated these thinkers as a way of presenting the experience of America to those across the world and of bringing to those at home a new self-consciousness of what America is and means. It is not to be supposed that philosophers are the sole bearers of the meaning to be attached to the odyssey of the American spirit, but there is an advantage stemming from a synoptic reflection that aims at grasping general drifts and underlying tendencies often eluding those who concentrate on the details of the situation at hand. The thinkers whose ideas occupy the center of attention in the essays to follow were engaged in an original attempt to clarify and interpret the ideals upon which life in America has been founded. Aware of the novelty of the undertaking in which they were involved, each of them sought to portray and to understand the peculiarities of the American scene. They thought for themselves and were not concerned about the reception of their ideas in places where it was already assumed that the New World represented a decline, a falling away from the cultural norms of European civilization. The source of their independence was in their sense of having to set new standards and to articulate new ideals not to be judged in terms of old models which had already shown their inadequacies.

Freedom, experience, democracy, community, education, religion, the pursuit of knowledge, human dignity, and loyalty are among the ideals which guided the thinkers I discuss. Belief, moreover, in an intimate connection between purpose and thought and between belief and action, led these thinkers to define their ideals in the most concrete terms. Freedom, for example, was no abstrac-

1

tion but meant individual initiative, intelligent judgment, responsible action, and opportunities for self-fulfillment. Democracy signified not only a representative form of government, but mutual respect for others as persons and a commitment to the founding and sustaining of free institutions together with communities and the values they engender. Experience no longer meant merely the deliverances of the senses, but was seen as the living tissue of all that we encounter and undergo and as the source of habits that structure both thought and action. Experience, moreover, was not thought to be locked up in individual "minds," but was to be opened out in the sharing and comparing of the episodes through which we live. The pursuit and dissemination of knowledge were placed under the aegis of purposes and values with a proper concern for the relevance of what we know about ourselves and the world for the resolution of human problems. Education on the broad, public scale necessary for maintaining a democratic system was to embrace the twin purposes of introducing the young to the cultural resources of their heritage and of liberating the talents within them and their creative possibilities. Religion meant a living piety that sustains a meaningful life and finds its ultimate expression in a religious community. In a country where so many faiths abound, a principle of religious pluralism came to be seen as essential in order to avoid the intolerance and strife that have so often plagued nations where an established church holds sway.

While it has become customary, both at home and abroad, to identify American philosophy with Pragmatism, the cluster of ideas covered by that name by no means exhausts the insights of the classical American thinkers. It is true that Pragmatism clearly represents an indigenous and original philosophical outlook, especially in contrast to much previous thinking which was largely a reworking of the philosophy imported from Europe. America's philosophical vision must, of course, include Pragmatism, but the vision is larger than that, as can be seen in the evolutionary metaphysics of Peirce, the idealism of Royce, and especially his doctrine of community, the humanism of James and the concern of Dewey to establish the values of the democratic idea as a way of life and not only as a political form. These ideas and ideals, to be sure, show the influence of past thinkers from Plato and Aristotle to the philosophers of the nineteenth century; the important point, however, is that they were reshaped in the light of the experience of American life and aimed at the resolution of problems that arose within that experience. It is in this sense that one can speak of an American

2

philosophical vision as a native body of insights not to be confused with ideas borrowed from whatever source.

In order to focus that vision, I wish to call attention to a number of the basic ideas and beliefs that it embraces. To begin with, there is, as might be expected in a country that has always stressed the promise of the future over the significance of the past, an insistence on the reality of time, of change, of novelty and organic development. As James pointed out, we have a great stake in "the more to come." One of the first questions raised was, What are the implications of taking time seriously for the nature of knowledge and the conception of truth? How are we to do justice to the measure of truth to be found in traditional conceptions that emphasized the "timeless" character of truth and at the same time take into account the actual growth of knowledge and the existence of "schools" representing different opinions about disputed issues even in the exact sciences? No less a thinker than Kant had declared that where such schools exist there is no science. Peirce, James, and Dewey, each in his own way, faced these difficulties and responded, first, by abandoning all claims to certainty, and, second, by showing how, through appropriate methods, we can attain knowledge having evidential force.

The reality of time, however, had an even deeper significance for these thinkers; time is the medium through which we live and seek to realize ourselves, and consequently major emphasis was placed on the future in which some of the real possibilities ingredient in the present may come to be. The dominant belief was that the past, being over and done with, is beyond our influence; the future, however, is another matter. We can have a hand, through deliberation, judgment, and action, in the shaping of what is yet to come. In the rejection of determinism or the view that there are no real possibilities in the natural order, the way was now open for the exercise of the human will and its freedom. It is impossible to exaggerate the importance of this belief for the development of American culture. Santayana saw this truth many decades ago and proposed that Americans would best understand themselves if they would acknowledge how very important is the will in their outlook on life.

Much has been said about the central role played by science and its offspring, technology, in the development of the enormous resources of this country. Not nearly enough attention has been paid to the efforts of the classical thinkers in putting, so to speak, a human face, on the scientific enterprise and technological society. Science was seen as a human activity carried out under historical conditions by, as Peirce put it, "flesh and blood investigators." Long before the development of the history of science as a discipline that has helped us understand more clearly the long and arduous road to scientific discovery, Peirce was engaged in studying the patterns of actual scientific inquiry and the process whereby the research of individual scientists becomes incorporated into the scientific community. James's *Principles of Psychology* is a remarkable synthesis of a scientific approach and a depth of humanistic understanding. The idea that all intellectual and artistic endeavors are human activities guided by purposes has made it possible to overcome the conflicts between "the sciences" and "the humanities" which have arisen as the result of viewing the former as impersonal and machinelike in character and the latter as a matter of subjective, personal expression. Dewey, moreover, was greatly concerned to show that technology represents an extension of human powers in the formation of a secondary environment and, while technology, to be sure, needs to be controlled, it must, nevertheless, be seen as a human achievement.

It is generally agreed that the most important single influence on the course of Western philosophical thinking since the early eighteenth century was the appeal to *experience* as the touchstone for judging all claims to knowledge and the possession of power. Unfortunately, the understanding of experience at the hands of the classical British empiricists was quite limited and was, in fact, as Dewey claimed, largely "unempirical." On the older view, experience was confined to the deliverances of the senses in atomistic fashion; it was set in opposition to reason and, since what is sensed was taken to be certain and incorrigible, the result was that "experience" came to be a purely private domain standing between us and the so-called external world. The watchword was, What we experience is "experience" and the world is well lost. The American philosophical vision put an end to that way of thinking. The signal contribution of all the thinkers considered in the following essays was to provide an account of experiencing that is far more in accord with what actually happens in our encounter with the world. Experience, among other things, was shown to be intimately connected with "knowing how" to respond to situations and indeed with the entire range of habits formed in the interaction between the self and the world. Our ordinary sense of what it is to be "experienced" conveys the meaning very well. An experienced sailor is not someone who merely knows many facts about boats, sails, and currents, but a person who knows how to respond to a shift in the wind or a brewing storm, and knows what is to be done next. All of this comes to reside, as Peirce said, not only in the head but in the muscles as well.

4

There is no need to disguise the fact that a trend towards individualism has been a powerful factor in American life. And that was to be expected in a situation where people had to fend for themselves often under adverse circumstances and unsettled conditions. Self-reliance and independence came to be highly prized. Despite this trend, however, the force of cooperative endeavor, of many working together to achieve what could not be accomplished by the isolated individual, has made itself felt throughout the course of life in America. Here Royce and Dewey were the two major voices in showing the value of community and in underlining the role of shared experience in the enhancement of human life. Royce, especially, recovered the ancient insight of Aristotle with the idea that a community—a togetherness of many individuals united by bonds of loyalty—has a special sort of being in that it is neither an individual as its members are, nor a collection with no more cohesiveness than a pile of sand on a windy day. The beauty of the idea is that it places community in its many forms—religious, social, scientific, legal, ethnic—in their proper place; on the one hand, it underscores the shortcomings of a brittle *individualism* and the isolation of self from self, and, on the other, it exposes the evils of *collectivism* wherein the impersonal mass is the primary entity and the individual persons do not count.

It is not without significance that in the revival of classical learning by the humanists of the Renaissance, the watchword was, "Back to the sources," which meant study of the original texts. I am convinced that the same approach is needed today for the recovery of America's philosophical vision in the writings of our classical philosophers. The essays that make up this volume are meant to provide a perspective on this heritage and to signal its importance for our present situation.

In proposing a return to the sources for a second look, I am fully aware of not being alone in this effort. Among those at present whom we may call latter-day pragmatists, Rorty stands out as the most vocal and at the same time the most Quixotic. Whitehead once remarked that philosophy is not—or should not be—a ferocious debate between irritable professors; with this sage comment in mind, I welcome the opportunity for "conversation" even though I regard this identification of philosophy as somewhat bland. Since there is a real value in bringing philosophy down to earth, I would prefer to do it in Hegel's terms when he said in a rare, disarming moment that philosophy is just thinking things over.

Richard Rorty has written perceptively about the impact of Pragmatism on philosophy in America, and his contribution must certainly be taken into account. A full-scale treatment is in any case not possible in an Introduction of this sort. In addition, there is the inconvenience imposed by the existence of at least two Rortys—perhaps there are even more—and some effort is needed to sort them out. There is first the Rorty—I shall use "rorty" for this persona following his own device with the use of "philosophy" and "Philosophy"—who acutely captures the central drift of Pragmatism and brings it to bear on recent discussion in an illuminating way. The second Rorty—I shall use "Rorty" for this persona—is doing something quite different in latching onto Dewey and onto the idea of "overcoming the tradition" in order to get rid of Platonism and metaphysics or what he sometimes calls "Philosophy." My concern to distinguish these two personae stems from the definite sympathy I have for the position rorty takes and the doubts I have about what Rorty is proposing on the constructive side. Before I proceed further, a precautionary word is in order; it has to do with what Peirce would call the ethics of philosophical discussion. Everyone is at liberty to express philosophical views of his or her own, but if someone does this via the invoking of the views of others—Kant, Hegel, the Pragmatists as a body or Dewey in particular—that person incurs the obligation to express these other views as accurately as possible and not merely to enlist their support for notions of his or her own. G. E. Moore once began a seminar on Russell with the following comment made in his intimidating, wide-eyed manner: "Mr. Russell is at liberty to use words in any way he pleases, but he is not at liberty to do so and at the same time claim that this is what *other people* mean when they use these words."

Now, I am not about to say that rorty gets the philosophers he discusses all "wrong," for that would not be true; he knows a great deal about their writings and has read widely in them with obvious comprehension. I am, however, less confident about Rorty in this regard, especially when he attempts to sum up a thinker through some one idea or pronouncement—Hegel, for example, usually appears on stage saying the line that "Philosophy is its own time apprehended in thoughts"—or when, as sometimes happens with the Pragmatists, he singles out some idea that fits in well with his criticism of Philosophy and simply ignores their other views.[1]

1. A good illustration of this tendency is Rorty's emphasis on Dewey's "overcoming the tradition" and neglect of Dewey's attack on the classical conception of experience. See *Consequences of Pragmatism* (Minneapolis: University of Minnesota Press, 1982), p. xl. See also note 49 on p. xlvii where it is said that the sentence quoted from Hegel together with the famous "owl of Minerva" passage are not typical of his thought as a whole, but instead provide a basis for the historicism that followed in the aftermath of Hegel.

To return to the two personae, I regard rorty at his best when he sets out to apply to recent discussion some basic notions of the Pragmatists in order to see what contribution they can make. I should like to consider four examples with the understanding that they are no more than that since each involves further discussion that is beyond our scope here. The first of these concerns the idea of "natural starting points" for thought and the attack upon them made by Peirce in particular. The point is well focused by rorty when he writes: "(Candidates for such starting points include clear and distinct ideas, sense data, categories of the pure understanding, structures of pre-linguistic consciousness, and the like). Peirce and Sellars and Wittgenstein are saying that the regress of interpretation cannot be cut off by the sort of intuition which Cartesian epistemology took for granted."[2] I see this convergence of opinion as adding support to Peirce's rejection of the idea that one "must" begin somewhere, since, as he claimed, one can only begin where one is—in the midst of things and armed with a stock of beliefs that will retain their tenure until there appears some critical reason for questioning them or replacing them with other beliefs.[3]

My second illustration has to do with something that rightly runs throughout rorty's analyses, namely, a full appreciation of Dewey's attack on what he called "the epistemology industry." When the Pragmatists thought of truth, Rorty says, as being what we shall believe if we keep on inquiring, or as what it is better for us to believe, or, again, what can be asserted with a warrant, "(they) were making it something you could use, instead of something you could merely respect."[4] The point is well taken; Peirce, James, and Dewey, each in his own way, were claiming that a conception of the nature of truth or a theory of the purported nature of knowledge do not of themselves provide any test or recipe for inquiry whereby it is possible to achieve knowledge *in concreto*. And it was for this reason that they placed so much emphasis on method. One might sum up their point—it is actually *the* consequence of Pragmatism for rorty and he develops it well—by adapting the well-known saying of Berkeley that "we do not see with geometry" to read "we do not

---

2. *Consequences*, p. xx.

3. Peirce denied the claim that there "must be" a first in the *process* by which thought begins and maintained that the problem is the same as that expressed in the Achilles paradox. See "Some Questions Concerning Certain Faculties Claimed for Man," *Collected Papers of Charles Sanders Peirce*, ed. Hartshorne and Weiss, vol. 5 (Cambridge [Mass.], Harvard University Press, 1934).

4. *Philosophy and the Mirror of Nature* (Princeton, Princeton University Press, 1979), p. 308.

know with epistemology." I think, however, that Rorty does not take seriously enough the fact that Dewey's dissatisfaction with epistemology was based mainly on his belief that its main problems are not perennial but stem from the errors of the classical conception of experience. In short, Dewey's criticism of epistemology was only partly due to his rejection of "foundations."

Rorty, in his discussion of Dewey's metaphysics,[5] persistently interprets his attack on epistemology solely in terms of skepticism and the supposition that Dewey was getting rid of epistemological issues by "denying that justification must repose on something other than social practices and human needs."[6] I have no quarrel with the emphasis on skepticism in Dewey's account, but focusing on that alone leaves out what is most important not only in Dewey's view but in that of James and Peirce, namely, that the roots of this skepticism are found in the view of *experience* developed by the British Empiricists. According to that view, experience is confined to sense and stands, as a tissue of subjectivity, like a veil between us and the world so that the grand problem becomes how, confined to this inner world, we are to reach the "external world." In rejecting that conception of experience as the creator of "epistemology," Dewey was saying that the issues involved can be dissolved by developing a new conception of experience to replace the erroneous view. Although he refers to Dewey's "An Empirical Survey of Empiricisms"—Dewey's "Hegelian" way—Rorty does not mention the experience issue at all, and, in fact, it is surprising that given the importance of the topic for the Pragmatists, there is no entry for "Experience" in the index to *Consequences*.

Another point at which Rorty is exactly on the target is in his capturing the stance of the Pragmatists to skepticism. If, rorty says, you were to ask Dewey why he thinks that Western civilization has the slightest idea of what goodness is, he would ask you why you have *doubts* about it. And, as rorty sees it, Dewey would not have to offer verificationist arguments for his position; Dewey need "simply ask why (he) should worry about the skeptical alternative until (he) is given some concrete ground of doubt."[7] This response is entirely in accord with Peirce's attack on Descartes's program of universal doubt—what Dewey called "wholesale" doubt—and his insistence that genuine doubt must always be based on specific reasons and has no force if it is expressed merely in the form of "I doubt that" with no further illumination.

5. *Consequences*, pp. 72–89.
6. Ibid., p. 82.
7. *Mirror*, p. 311.

My fourth example of rorty on the right track as regards the Pragmatists also involves some ambivalence on his part. In the course of arguing against the need for metaphysical and epistemological justifications, Rorty proposes a most perceptive question that he says is engendered by Pragmatism, "In just what sense were there physical features of reality capable of being represented accurately by differential equations, or tensors, *before* people thought of so representing them?"[8] He declares this question "unanswerable," but goes on nevertheless to tell us that "our natural inclination" would be to say, "In the fullest possible and most straightforward sense," except that this answer will not help us to get rid of such questions if we still have the need to *justify* the answer by constructing a theory. Is it not peculiar, however, that a question should be "unanswerable" and yet have an answer—and a "robust" one at that—based on "natural inclination"? Why, moreover, should we want to get rid of such a question, especially in view of the fact that it is perfectly intelligible and has an "instinctive" answer? The idea behind the question is clear enough; someone wants to point out that, in the absence of evidence that the universe had changed its cosmic habits, there is no need for the Pragmatist to deny that it *could have been* accurately represented by differential equations before these were introduced. Or, taken from the other side, there is no need for the Pragmatist to claim that what is represented by these equations somehow came into being with them. I cannot say whether rorty would object to this way of putting it, but I take it that he would object if someone were to claim that some further *justification* is needed, for that would involve us at once in Philosophy. But why should more justification be needed in the face of rorty's "robust" answer, which seems to me correct? I am reminded of Peirce's comment on Hume's statement that he found his premises "perfectly satisfactory"—"he seems to have been dissatisfied with himself for being satisfied." The point in rorty's original question, nevertheless, is not insignificant because opponents of the Pragmatists have invariably claimed that they are forced to make the denial and the claim cited above. James discussed the point in *The Meaning of Truth,* where it figures among the "misunderstanders" of the pragmatic theory.

I wish now to consider the second persona, the one I am designating as "Rorty," whom I see as availing himself of ideas drawn from the Pragmatists, chiefly Dewey, for use in his own agenda, which includes "overcoming the tradition," "the end of Philosophy," "literature as the successor of Philosophy" and similar

8. Ibid., p. 234; italics added.

themes. I, for one, have no objection whatever to a philosopher's attempting to put creative ideas from the past to work in an ongoing discussion, and I would be the first to say that rorty understands the novel approach of the Pragmatists and also understands why anyone will go astray who supposes that they were engaged in finding "answers" to some set of "perennial" questions of philosophy. I become uneasy, however, when I see certain concerns of the Pragmatists either ignored or transformed in such a way that they become party to proposals about the future—if there is one—of philosophy which run counter to their own views concerning the importance and indispensability of philosophical thinking. James, for example, insisted that everyone "has a philosophy under his hat" and the only question is how it can become better informed, clearer, and more consistent. Peirce was fond of saying that the only thing worse than a scientist with a bad metaphysics—by which he usually meant "nominalism"—is one who thinks he has no metaphysics at all. And as for Dewey, his pages are filled with pleas for the need of critical, reflective thinking about issues that, though requiring scientific knowledge, go beyond the boundaries of particular sciences. I don't find much of this outlook in Rorty's appropriation of the Pragmatists.

Perhaps Rorty is omitting these features because he thinks they have had no "consequences," but this can hardly be the case when we consider some examples. What James and Dewey had to say about religion, for example, has had enormous consequences. James's *Varieties* was and remains a monumental work on the experiential dimension in religion, and his proposal for a "science of religions" furnished the beginning of what later became known as "comparative religion." Dewey's *A Common Faith*, despite Santayana's judgment, "a very common faith, indeed," sparked vigorous controversy when it first appeared and caused great uneasiness among his disciples because of his retention of the term "God." What Peirce had to say about hypothesis formation in relation to the development of science led to extended discussion about a so-called logic of discovery. James's idea, moreover, that novel insights in scientific inquiry must be incorporated into the body of scientific knowledge with maximum continuity and minimum jolt still expresses an opinion now widely held. Although Royce's philosophy went out of fashion in the decades after his death, no one has given a more exact analysis of the nature of community as an antidote to American individualism. Royce ingeniously adapted Peirce's theory of signs and interpretation and Peano's epsilon relation for inclusion as the means of laying bare the logical structure of a community. James's *Psychology* with its field theory of the self and layers of consciousness, its emphasis on the "fringes" of experience and its attack on the priority of the subject-object distinction had repercussions in many quarters, including creative literature and Phenomenology. The list could be multiplied, but perhaps I am guilty of changing the subject, and instead of focusing on what Rorty leaves out, I should be concentrating on how he treats what he includes. The issue is, obviously, a large one, but it might be sharpened by a representative example—Rorty's treatment of the distinction that Dewey makes between metaphysics and philosophy, including his ideas about how they are related to each other.

To begin with, in the opening chapter of *Experience and Nature,* Dewey set forth a conception of philosophy and its proper method in terms that do not yet make explicit the distinction between metaphysics and philosophy which appears later on. Philosophy is said to find its roots in primary experience as it arises out of the interaction between the one who experiences and the world; the appeal to experience obviates starting with "reflected products" that are themselves the results of analysis. Central to Dewey's idea of the task of philosophy—"analytic dismemberment and synthetic reconstruction of experience"[9]—is that the products of reflection must be brought back to primary experience for the purpose of seeing whether they render this experience in a luminous, intelligible, and coherent way. Following this introduction to his approach, Dewey writes: "If we follow classical terminology, philosophy is love of wisdom, while metaphysics is cognizance of the generic traits of existence."[10] This distinction is retained by Dewey throughout the work, and in the final chapter he makes an explicit attempt to show how the two are related. In the face of what Dewey actually says, I find myself baffled by several of Rorty's statements such as "[Dewey] sees no interesting future for a distinct discipline called 'philosophy' "[11] or "Dewey thinks of Philosophy, as a discipline, or even as a distinct human activity, as obsolete."[12] To make the situation even more puzzling, Rorty goes on to tell us that "[f]or Dewey, to go on talking about Thought is to insist that the end of metaphysics should not be the end of philosophy."[13] As regards the first statement, I can find no evidence in Dewey's writings for the claim that he saw no interesting future for "philosophy"; on the

9. *Experience and Nature,* 2d ed., (La Salle, Ill.: Open Court, 1929), p. 37.
10. Ibid., p. 46.
11. *Consequences,* p. 41.
12. Ibid., p. 52.
13. Ibid., p. 49.

contrary, Dewey argues for the indispensability of philosophy as the means of bringing about the connection between existence and value: "philosophy is inherently criticism, having its distinctive position among various modes of criticism in its generality; a criticism of criticisms, as it were. Criticism is discriminating judgment, careful appraisal, and judgment is appropriately termed criticism wherever the subject matter of discrimination concerns goods or values."[14] That is a typical statement and in it I can find no warrant for either the claim that Dewey saw no future in philosophy in this sense, or that he did not regard it as a distinct discipline having a distinctive function. When it comes to capital Philosophy, by which I take Rorty to mean the traditional quest for Being, for transcendental justifications, for the Truth, and the like and which he seems to equate with "metaphysics," there are grounds for saying, as he does, that Dewey thought this enterprise "obsolete." From this, however, it does not follow that Dewey regarded metaphysics in the sense of the generic traits of existence as obsolete or at an end. For Dewey the end of metaphysics in the pejorative sense designated by Rorty as Philosophy would not only fail to be the end of philosophy as criticism in the above sense, but it would also not be the end of metaphysics in the sense in which Dewey understands it. How can one fail to take into account Dewey's concerted effort in the final chapter of *Experience and Nature* to show the essential connections between metaphysics and philosophy, or, if one does take it into account, what sense does it make to say that he saw no future for philosophy? Such a claim goes against both the letter and the spirit of Dewey's entire thought. One has only to consider what Dewey says when he explicitly asks "what is to be said of the relation of philosophy to metaphysics?" Dewey begins his answer by saying that an account of the generic traits manifested by existences of all kinds may seem to have nothing to do with criticism and value. When metaphysics, he says,

> has revealed the traits and characters that are sure to turn up in every universe of discourse, its work is done. So at least an argument may run. But the very nature of the traits discovered in every theme of discourse, since they are ineluctable traits of natural existence, *forbids such a conclusion.* Qualitative individuality and constant relations, contingency and need, movement and arrest are common traits of all existence. This fact is source both of values and their precariousness . . . Barely to note and register that contingency is a trait of natural events has nothing to do with wis-

14. *Experience and Nature,* p. 322.

dom. To note, however, contingency in connection with a concrete situation of life is that fear of the Lord which is at least the beginning of wisdom.[15]

There is no need to go into further detail; Dewey's position is quite clear. Metaphysics as essentially the description of a network of pervasive categories provides an indispensable ground plan for the work of philosophy as criticism in the most comprehensive sense. If philosophy cannot get along without metaphysics, it is equally clear that civilized life is impossible without philosophy. In the light of Dewey's own statements it makes no sense to say that he did not believe in philosophy as a distinct activity and saw no future for it. It is not a matter of whether Dewey is "right" in these conceptions, but rather whether Rorty is right in the way he represents him. It makes no difference, moreover, whether Rorty still believes what he has written or not, because the damage has already been done.

I find ironic at the least the fact that while Rorty understands well enough what we may call Dewey's anti-epistemological stance—"philosophy does not begin and end with the theory of knowledge"—most of rorty's discussion about the "consequences" of Pragmatism centers on just that theme. This focus was probably not entirely of Rorty's own choosing, but stems rather from his concern to connect his interpretations with the work of Sellars, Quine, later Wittgenstein and Davidson, most of which has to do with questions about logic, language, and the nature of knowledge. There were, nevertheless, and still are, consequences of what the Pragmatists wrote for many other areas—the history of science, religion, ethics, social and political thought, not to mention the whole sphere of esthetics. To sum this all up in terms of "overcoming the tradition" or in trying to engender a "post-Philosophical culture" seems to me to leave out much that was valuable and still has resources for dealing with contemporary problems. Something at least of what is omitted by Rorty from the American philosophical tradition I am attempting to recover under the banner of "America's Philosophical Vision."

15. Ibid., p. 334; italics added.

I
Experience, Freedom, and the Pragmatic Outlook

1

The Reconception of Experience
in Peirce, James and Dewey

"The Reconception of Experience in Peirce, James and Dewey" was the opening address for a Conference on "American Pragmatism in Relation to Continental Phenomenology," held on August 3–5, 1984, sponsored by the Department of Philosophy at the Pennsylvania State University. I concentrated on the theme of experience as constituting an important link with Phenomenology; I did not draw comparisons because that was to be done in papers to follow. I regard the reconstruction of experience by the Pragmatists in opposition to classical Empiricism as their most important contribution. The essay appeared in The Monist, *vol. 68, no. 4 (1985), pp. 538–54. Copyright © 1985, The Monist, La Salle, Illinois 61301. Reprinted by permission.*

The attempts to interpret Pragmatism set forth in the writings of Peirce, James and Dewey as a continuation of British empiricism with a dose of action and American practicality thrown in, are not only misguided in their basic intent, but they have served as well to obscure the important fact that these philosophers, in different but related ways, were engaged in a full-scale critique of that empiricism because they regarded the conception of experience associated with Locke and Hume, especially, as inadequate, or, in Dewey's word, non-empirical. If a short formula is needed, no better can be found than to say that the American philosophers all appealed to experience but that they were not "empiricists" because they were developing a new and broader conception of experience based not on what experience "must" be if it is to serve the purpose of founding knowledge, but on what actual experiencing shows itself to be in the course of human life. This truth will be missed if one seeks to understand these thinkers by looking to their supposed answers to all the standard epistemological questions—the status of sense data, the conditions of verifiability, the relativity of perception, the problem of how to reach the "external world" and the like—which have been the stock in trade of British philosophy from Hume to Russell and beyond. On the contrary, not only did Dewey especially express serious doubts about the validity of the "epistemology industry," as he called it, but all three aimed at reconceiving experience in terms sufficiently broad and rich to provide a matrix for philosophy, science and ordinary human pursuits. Philosophy for them did not begin and end with the theory of knowledge.

The task at hand, then, is to provide some understanding of the new and reconstructed conception of experience to be found in the writings of Peirce, James and Dewey. In view of the great volume of material involved, however, it will be necessary to confine the present discussion within manageable limits; this can be done by starting with some general characteristics of the new conception and some brief comparisons with the classical view, followed by a more detailed account of the analyses set forth by the three thinkers in question. It is important to avoid at the outset the supposition that the Pragmatists were in complete agreement or had one single view of the nature of experience, for James, it is clear, accepted more of classical empiricism than either Peirce or Dewey and the position of the latter is the most radical of the three in the sense that it leaves little of the classical theory standing. On the other hand, as the sequel will show, there was a consensus, in the current idiom a "family resemblance," concerning what was deficient in the older empiricism and what new features must be taken into consideration in arriving at a more satisfactory account of what is involved when we speak of experiencing ourselves and the world, of having experience, and of being experienced.

For the philosophers representing modern empiricism, experience was construed as the domain of *sense* and the qualities of things in the world apprehended through the standard sensory organs. As such, experience was set in contrast to the understanding or reason so that the two were made to appear as occupying separate domains. Even Kant, who aimed to show that experience could not be correctly conceived as anything less than a synthesis of sensory material and conceptual form, still referred in many passages to "experience" as if it coincided with the sensory element alone. Because of the emphasis placed on the immediate perception or the first impressions of sense, the classical empiricists came to regard experience as a tissue of subjectivity or even as a veil somehow standing between the one who experiences and the so-called "external world." Accordingly, it was but a short step to the conclusion that what we really experience is only our own ideas — the experience of "experience." And indeed the long discussion that followed concerning how we are to reach the external world was initiated by the belief that, since we are supposed to know from the outset that the material of experience is internal to our consciousness, some way must be found to surmount or transcend this inner world and thus come into contact with the outer world of objects. In addition to thinking of experience in terms of sense and subjectivity, the classical empiricists saw it as a product of passivity on the part of the one who experiences, the result of adopting the stance of a spectator whose role is to record, if not exactly to copy, what experience writes on the mind regarded as a sheet of blank paper. Closely connected with the spectator view was the belief that experience is itself knowledge and must be analyzed in terms of what it would have to be in order to serve as a foundation for an edifice built upon it. The latter requirement placed a great strain on the interpretation of experience because attention was diverted away from the complexities of actual experiencing and directed instead to the analysis of the supposedly simple and atomic datum which is to supply the meaning for all conceptual thought. As a result, experience was construed as itself atomic and episodic; its ultimate constituents were taken to be sensible simples, hence the emphasis on the *term* as the basic unit of meaning, and episodic in the sense that it was not possible to think of a course, a growth, an internal development of experience, but only of a series of moments each clear and distinct both in themselves and in their relations to other moments.

By contrast, the Pragmatists expressed serious doubts about the validity of this entire picture and set out to develop a new conception of experience more in accord with the facts of the matter as they saw them. With the possible exception of James, whose thought is at certain points ambiguous, they rejected the identification of experience with sense taken as a clearly defined realm standing over against reason. The clearest indication of this rejection is found in the arguments advanced by Peirce and Dewey in support of the claim that experience has within it an "inferential stretch" which is inconsistent with the view that it is sealed off from reason and rational activity. They were, moreover, opposed to the belief that experience is a screen of subjectivity standing between us and the so-called external world since they regarded it as a public and reliable disclosure of that very world. Consequently, they could not subscribe to the thesis that what we experience is experience and not the world. Peirce laid the ground for this conclusion in his early anti-Cartesian papers where he showed that there is no intuitive certainty that what is immediately apprehended is wholly internal to the consciousness of the one who apprehends it. Thus if we do not start on the "inside," so to speak, the perennial empiricist problem of the external world is set aside. In addition, the Pragmatists did not accept either the spectator view of experience or the passivity of the one who experiences. For them the stance of the spectator or theoretical observer is, while of great importance, not *the* stance of experience itself but one approach, attitude or, in their language, a context, among others. As regards the matter of passivity, we find here what is the most basic point of contrast between the two views, namely, the emphasis laid by the Pragmatists on the activity and engagement of the subject in experience and especially on the close connection between experience and the formation of habits or patterns of behavior in response to the challenge of the situation. Finally, there is the refusal to accept the atomization of experience into singular moments or episodes and the insistence instead on the continuity and cumulative character of experience making up a course of life and the biography of an individual. As will become clear, it is the latter feature of experience together with the elements of habit and response which led the Pragmatists to think of an "experienced" person as one who has become familiar with the tendencies of people and of things to behave in certain ways and thus is prepared or "knows how" to respond appropriately according to the circumstances. The introduction of "know how" into the picture marks the appearance of a new dimension in the conception of experience, one which has no counterpart in the classical view.

Having indicated, albeit in general terms, the main drift of the two conceptions, I should like to consider in more detail some typical pronouncements by Peirce, James and Dewey on the nature of experience with the aim of clarifying further the positive features of their new position. For it is these features which, in addition to constituting a break with the older empiricism, provide significant points of contact with the phenomenological approach. In carrying out this part of my task, I must, as before, impose some limitations and hence I used the phrase "some typical pronouncements" as a way of dealing, within the confines of a relatively brief discussion, with the extensive literature at hand.

We are all familiar, in the case of Peirce, with the complaint that his views on any topic are spread over an enormous range of writings of various kinds and in different contexts so that it is a matter of some difficulty to determine what his views really were. I am not unaware of this difficulty, but I am convinced that, thanks to the efforts of many scholars and with help from Peirce's own insistence that we approach things experientially, a persistent reading of the relevant writings on a given topic results in the emergence of a consistent view. In the end it is the repetitions and recurrences which count and I am assuming that when Peirce says essentially the same thing five times that is a reliable indication of the position he is taking. Fortunately, throughout his numerous analyses and discussions of experience there are such recurrences and I intend to focus on them. I do not claim to have established an order of importance among the features to be singled out, but I do believe that Peirce's repeated insistence on the idea that experience is what is "forced" upon us has a claim to head the list and therefore I shall begin with that.

In the many passages where Peirce identified experience in terms of compulsion or constraint standing over against willfulness and prejudice on the part of the individual, he was careful to note that he was talking about a pervasive experience persisting over time for which he generally used the phrase "the course of life." It is not with a singular or isolated occasion that we are dealing but with something cumulative and lasting. "Experience," he wrote, "is that determination of belief and cognition generally which the course of life has forced upon a man" (2.138–39),[1] and in an account of the meaning of assertion, Peirce pointed out that the compulsion involved in experience is of a permanent sort in contrast to the temporary force exerted by individual "thises" encountered on singular occasions. The attachment of predicates to subjects in an assertion, Peirce claimed, continues in force on every relevant occasion so that experience assumes the character of law (3:435; 2:138–39; 7:437; 1:426; 7:391). In stressing the element of compulsion or force, Peirce was not supposing that the relation between the experiencer and what is encountered is that of the pure dyad, if such there be, but rather that in experience there is a direct awareness of something reacting against us which, though we may set our minds against it, cannot in the end be resisted. Hence he could speak of the "overwhelming rationalizing power of experience" (7:78) with the clear understanding that this power is shot through with thought and the interpretative activity of the one who experiences. Consequently, even when Peirce claims that experience is "brutally produced" (6:454), he hastens to add that the effect is conscious and contributes to a habit as something that is self-controlled. The point is reenforced in one of Peirce's analyses of consciousness (7:437) where experience is construed as a "sum of *ideas*" (Italics mine) distinguished by the fact that they "have been

1. All references are to *Collected Papers of Charles Sanders Peirce*, ed. Hartshorne, Weiss and Burks (Cambridge, Mass.: Harvard University Press, 1932–1958), vols. 1–8. Citations are by volume and section numbers (not pages).

irresistibly borne in upon us . . . by the tenor of our life." In summary at this point, we may say, first, that for Peirce experience is
essentially an invasion of the inner world of ideas by independent
reals which modify our ways of thinking in accordance with what is
really there. And, we must add, these reals are not confined to
things or objects since Peirce included propositions and truth
among the items which resist our efforts to ignore them. Secondly,
he attached great importance to the pervasive, continuing and cumulative character of experience as something general and poles
apart from the primitive simples of a sensory sort which were
thought to constitute experience on the classical view (2:138–39).

Closely connected with the compulsory nature of experience was
Peirce's repeated claim that experience is experience of the independent reals and not of representations; in short, he clearly rejected any form of the belief that what we experience is already
some form of "experience." "Nothing can be more completely
false," he wrote, "than that we experience only our own ideas. . . .
That is indeed without exaggeration the very epitome of *all* falsity"
(6.95). And to underline the point he went on to claim that "we
have direct experience of things in themselves" (Ibid.), clearly echo-
ing Hegel's rejoinder to Kant, except that in Peirce's view such
experience is relative and conditioned by the limited capacities of
fallible beings. In this connection, moreover, we must not lose sight
of the many points at which Peirce insisted that the reals to be
experienced are not themselves opinions, but what opinions are
about. Peirce's well known theory of reality and truth in terms of the
community and the convergence of opinion has often been misunderstood because of failure to take seriously his insistence that such
opinion must be under the constraint of both a proper method of
inquiry and the independent reals. In this sense Peirce did not
identify truth and reality.

On the all-important question of the relation of experience to
sense, I think it is fair to say that, taking a large number of discussions into account, Peirce not only refused to confine experience
within the bounds of sense, but he regarded it as wider than perception as well (1:335 ff.). In an important analysis of experience,
Peirce declared that he would not go so far as to say that all experience consists in sense perception, but only that every element of
experience is "in the first instance" applied to an external object.
That this qualification is important appears in the sequel where he
claimed that when a person wakes up in a bad humor the tendency
is immediately to project this state on the objects and persons with
whom one comes in contact, but that, whereas the persons and

objects are perceived, the bad humor is not perceived although it is *experienced*. This important distinction is given further confirmation in what we may call the "locomotive" example (1:336). There Peirce explicitly states that experience is "more particularly applied" to *events* and that these, as such, are not perceived. When a locomotive passes by with whistle sounding, says Peirce, the person perceives the whistle, but as the train passes the person the note is changed—for reasons not relevant to the point—and while, on Peirce's view, the change is experienced, it is not perceived. Experience is of changes and contrasts in perception from which it follows that experience is broader than perception and includes much that is not perceived. As he put the point in another section (1:358), secondness, limitation, conflict, restraint, "make up the teaching of experience," and not one of these features can be put down to perception alone. Obviously, much more would need to be said on this point, especially in connection with what Peirce has to say about the perceptual judgment, but I am focusing here exclusively on the point that experience goes beyond both sense and perception. Consider another instance, one taken from the Neglected Argument, in which experience is again construed as extending far beyond the boundaries set by traditional empiricism. In this discussion Peirce refers to the three "Universes of Experience" and describes them as (1) mere ideas whose being consists in their capability of being thought; (2) the brute actuality of things and facts manifesting the action and reaction of Secondness; (3) signs or the active power to establish connections not only between items in the same Universe but between those in different Universes as well. The fact that Thirdness is included within the scope of experience is sufficient to show that, for Peirce, experience cannot be exhausted by sense content. There is yet another example, one which I regard as very important in this connection especially because Peirce repeated it several times. I refer to his distinction between experiencing a *proof* and experiencing the *object* of a proof. Peirce, that is to say, was insisting on the difference between encountering a proof, actually tracing out the steps, particularly in the case of what he called Argumentations, and encountering its object in another context (3:35). It would, then, seem clear that the bounds of sense are too narrow to contain Peirce's conception of experience.

No account of Peirce's view can fail to include at least some indication of the way he conceived of general or universal experience as both distinct from and related to what he called special experience. Sometimes he expressed the distinction as that between familiar experience and recondite, the former being open and generally accessible while the latter, chiefly the minute observations of the sciences, obviously is not (6:560 ff.). To begin with, he regarded what is familiar, the most pervasive experiences, as very difficult to apprehend because, as he says, they surround us so completely with their constant presence that there is no background against which to contrast them. As long as our heart beats we do not know even that we have a heart, nor do we have any clear grasp of how our own voices sound. Consequently, familiar experience is likely to make little impression on us and comes to be neglected without being understood. On the other hand, recondite experience concerning particulars and details—Peirce is clearly thinking of experiment and controlled observation—will not, in the nature of the case, escape our notice, but he was concerned that the prominence and authority attached to special experience would lead to the subordination of general experience and the loss of its contribution.

To paraphrase his vivid expression of this point, we find him saying that "Young America" (6.564) will take familiar experience as if it were just so many squeezed lemons—whatever they had to teach has already been learned—whereas it will be dazzled by the recondite—gunpowder, the steam engine, the telephone—and will recall nothing else." Important as this observation is in the way of social commentary, its deeper significance is to be found in its serving as an introduction to Peirce's idea of the relation between science and philosophy. His thesis is that the great facts of nature, ultimately grasped and articulated through the medium of science, are all initially embodied in familiar experience also described as commonplace or universal. Such experience, he claimed, cannot "have their juices sucked out of them and be cast aside" (6.565) because they are both inexhaustible and indispensable. The history of the principle of the conservation of energy—"all that man has ever learned about force" (6:566)—shows that the entire investigation "rested almost exclusively upon familiar experiences" in which they served for scientists "as almost their sole premises" (6.567). Science as essentially special reasoning and experimentation always sets out from the matrix of familiar experience and is always dependent upon it for certain truths—for example, that there is a reason in nature and an affinity with the human mind—which are at the root of science but which at the same time surpass the power of science to support them. Here Peirce is arguing for the role played by general experience in the formation of common sense transmitted from each generation to the next and he even described general experience as a "far more valuable reservoir of truth than the aggregate of man's special experiences" (6:571). It should be obvious that Peirce was not engaged in disparaging science, but rather in securing a ground for philosophy which, as he says, must attend to normal and pervasive experience that otherwise goes unnoticed (1:241). By contrast with the special observational techniques of the sciences, philosophy has no experimental apparatus but must concern itself with the reflective elucidation of that universal experience from which the sciences abstract. Peirce's view is a bold one and perhaps only a philosopher with his credentials in science could sustain it; a purified, disciplined and consistent philosophy based as it must be on pervasive experience has a force of evidence which continually outstrips the power of special experience. Such is the price of precision and the vindication of vagueness.

Turning now to James, we must bear in mind that, despite his concern to broaden the classical conception of experience, he found that conception more congenial than either Peirce or Dewey and he was alone among them in allowing that there can be knowledge based on sense alone. On the other hand, it will not do to ignore, as have many who seem not to have made their way to the end of the second volume of the *Principles of Psychology*, the fact that in his discussion of the "house-born" ideas he came down on the side of the *a priori* and declared the failure of empiricism at this point. In what follows, I should like to concentrate on four focal points in an effort to elucidate James's conception of the nature of experience.

There is, first, his insistence on distinguishing within experience a central focus of attention from what he called the "fringe." Adopting a "field" theory, an approach which he described at the time as the most important advance to take place in psychology for decades, he claimed that there is always more in experience than is being attended to by what we may call the "spotlight" consciousness. Attention, as selective and hence abstractive, must in the nature of the case ignore the fringe but from that it does not follow that it does not exist. How seriously he took this conception can be seen in the *Varieties* where the "trans-marginal" consciousness plays a key role in the analysis of the phenomena of religion. There is far more in experience than is presented at any time since it has subconscious depths which may surface only on certain crucial occasions in the life of an individual. For James, the experience that figures in science and its accompanying theoretical stance is not experience *par excellence* but is rather the product of a special context, one among others. And the same holds true for everyday consciousness and experience which selects and retains only what is needed for practical purposes. One of James's main contentions in his analysis of experiences cited by mystics is that these do not occur unless the mundane consciousness has been surmounted and no longer commands the field.

Closely connected with this first point is James's insistence on analyzing actual *experiencing*—James was above all a thinker of participles—in order to grasp, as he liked to put it, the "particular go" of the thing. Consider the example of the clap of thunder. The experience of thunder is not exhausted as an instantaneous datum of sound, a sensible simple or impression, but is part of a temporal episode which James sought to represent by the use of hyphens. What is experienced is a sudden, sharp booming which breaks in upon a preceding silence making us vividly aware of the interruption and the contrast so that, if we may so say, we now "hear" the silence which was shattered since as part of the familiar, prevailing situation, we had no occasion to notice it before. The experience has the character of an event and belongs to the ongoing biography of the one who has it; to abstract from the total episode the bare sense quality of sound and call that the delivery of "experience" is, in James's view, to confuse the concrete experiencing with an abstraction and one which has been dictated by the demand that experience be preeminently sensory in character.

James's conception of "radical empiricism" follows in the same vein since it involves both a criticism and the expansion of the classical view, particularly that of Hume. Describing his own position as akin to Hume's in the sense that both are, in James's words, "mosaic" philosophies (presumably because both emphasize a putting together of facts), James maintained that Hume had not gone far enough in his inventory of the contents of experience. He did not get beyond the delineation of discriminable items, sensory impressions to be expressed as *terms,* and consequently he failed to take note of the connections, continuities, relations, transitions and tendencies which, according to James, are no less present in experience than the items they connect. Stated in other terms the point is that Hume gave priority to the relation of "other than" in his belief that what is distinguishable is also separable and in so doing overlooked the relation of being "with" which, on James's view, is a genuine feature of experience. The cover of the book is other than the pages, but it is quite obviously with the pages and belongs to the unity of the object. We need not go into James's underlying concern here which was to combat the view that, since relations and connectives are absent in experience as such, a supervening or transcendental subject is needed to supply what experience supposedly lacks. More important is his effort to expand the scope of experience by calling attention to all that it contains. Since, however, James included within his conception of the connective tissue in experience a number of items not all of which are the same, a word is in order concerning one that is of special importance, namely, the idea of tendency. The inclusion of relations in the doctrine of radical empiricism has been much discussed, but tendency as a factor has sometimes been overlooked. One of the reasons for the stress on the atomic in classical empiricism was the difficulty of not being able to find an acceptable "impression" answering to the directionality we encounter in processes of both the physical and organic worlds, to say nothing of the experience of change and growth in ourselves. James was aware of the problem as is evidenced by his use of the figure of the "stream" in his description of thought and consciousness. If the field of awareness is basically a flow or succession in which states interpenetrate each other and those which have passed leave traces on those yet to come so that at each point there are indications of what might or could come next, any analysis of these states into clear-cut and atomic units must result in the banishment of tendency from experience. The same point reappears in James's account of what he called the experience of effort or activity. In pushing a table from one place to another we are directly aware of the effort involved in the form of the weight, the friction between the table and the floor and we experience the continuity of our action and the tendency of the movement. If, however, we analyze the movement into a set of states complete and distinct in themselves, the continuity and tendency disappear.

We may summarize the radical empiricism doctrine by repeating James's own description of it as involving a postulate, a statement of fact and a generalized conclusion. The postulate is that only what is capable of being experienced is legitimate subject matter for philosophy; the statement of fact is that the connections are as real in experience as the items connected; the generalized conclusion is that since experience contains its own connective tissue there is no need for a supervenient reason to supply it.

The fourth focal point to be noted in presenting James's position is his notion of "pure experience." There is, of course, far more in this conception and its implications than we need to consider for our purposes; the main aim is to see what further light it throws on our central topic. The return to what James called "pure experience" means an attempt to recover what we actually live through and without the encumbrances of such habitual constructions as "mind," "body," "subject," etc. Such constructions, although they later develop from pure experience, are to be suspended at the outset so that the content can shine forth in its own light. Taking pure experience for a start, we can, James says, describe it "as subjective and objective both at once"[2] and this precludes our saying that it is exclusively one or the other. John Wild is, I believe, correct in calling attention to an ambiguity in James's account at this point.[3] On the one hand, James construed experience as having a generic structure which is neither exclusively subjective nor exclusively objective, but allows for both. On the other hand, and here I see the lingering influence of the classical conception in his thought, James described pure experience as composed of units which remain neutral to the subjective/objective distinction. "By the adjective 'pure,'" James says,

> prefixed to the word 'experience' I mean to denote a form of being which is as yet neutral or ambiguous, and prior to the object and subject distinction. I mean to show that the attribution either of mental or physical being to an experience is due to nothing in the immediate stuff of which the experience is composed—for the same stuff will serve for either attribution. . . .[4]

The question now arises whether this account is consistent with the view of the generic structure of experience set forth in the *Principles*. There he maintained that all experience belongs to a personal self; there is no thought or experience "which is nobody's thought"[5] and this would suggest that no experience is without the intentional structure ingredient in the personal stream to which it belongs. The question is whether James was not sacrificing the personal element upon which he had previously insisted by declaring the "neutrality" of pure experience in an effort to overcome the prevailing dualism. It is, moreover, curious that in *Essays in Radical Empiricism* where James was concentrating his argument on the defense of pure experience, he should have introduced the dualistic note himself. Referring to experience, he wrote, "It supposes two elements, mind knowing and thing known, and treats them as irreducible. Neither gets out of itself or into the other, neither in the way *is* the other,

2. William James, *Essays in Radical Empiricism* (New York: Longmans, Green & Co., 1912), p. 10.

3. John D. Wild, *Radical Empiricism of William James* (Garden City, NY: Doubleday & Co. 1969), p. 361.

4. Ralph Barton Perry, *The Thought and Character of William James*, 2 vols. (Boston: Little Brown & Co., 1936), vol. 2, p. 385.

5. William James, *The Principles of Psychology* (New York: Dover Publications, 1950 [authorized reprint of the original edition of 1890 in two vols.]), vol. 1, p. 226.

neither *makes* the other."[6] Without proposing to resolve the ambiguity, I would merely suggest that James was not in the end denying the validity of a subject-object distinction, but rather maintaining instead that it is not primordial and develops consequently as the result of reflection. In short, I take James to be defending the view that in actual experiencing the experiencer and the experienced are together and that, while one can distinguish them from each other conceptually, that distinction itself is not a constant and proper part of the concrete experience as it is undergone.

While James was working out the details of his doctrine of radical empiricism, Dewey was engaged in an even more radical reconstruction of the nature of experience in accordance with the biological orientation of a position he was to call by the name of instrumentalism. The shift in focus is by no means unimportant for, while Peirce's thought was shaped by his logical and speculative interests and James's by his humanistic psychology and moral and religious concerns, Dewey's philosophy was largely determined by his social and biological approach to problems. In considering Dewey's position, we have, of course, the concise comparison he set forth between his own conception of experience and that to be found in Aristotle and in Locke whom he took as the representative of British empiricism, to be found in his essay, "An Empirical Survey of Empiricisms." Since I have discussed that article at some length in other places, I shall, while not ignoring its contents, attempt a fresh approach not determined exclusively by the contrasts Dewey pointed out.

In describing Dewey's conception of experience as "radical" I meant first of all to point to a significant break with the tradition; many philosophers prior to Dewey had laid great stress on the need of experience to *conform* to antecedent fact or what he called antecedent being, whereas he made paramount the idea of *transformation* and construed experience in terms of its role in resolving problematic situations or in transforming the indeterminate, unsatisfactory situation into a determinate and non-problematic one. It is important to notice that, for Dewey, the intelligent attack upon any problem does not end with the correct theoretical explanation of the difficulty but only with the development, through experience, of the *means* whereby the difficulty is to be overcome. If I may avail myself of a nice ambiguity, Peirce was intent on "fixing" belief, while Dewey was aiming in the end at "fixing" the broken radiator! The emphasis on transformation itself transforms the dis-

6. *Essays in Radical Empiricism,* p. 218.

cussion, because experience appears no longer as a registry of finished fact but as the funded product of many interactions between the organism and the environment in which the former aims at overcoming the challenges presented by the latter. It was for this reason that Dewey was critical of the idea of experience as a kind of subject matter—the matter of sense—to be received by a spectator whose task is to copy it as closely as possible. On the contrary, as Santayana was among the first to see, experience has now become a weapon or a means for introducing such change as is necessary for transforming precarious human existence into something more stable.

Accordingly, Dewey attacked the idea that experience is coincident with the domain of the senses or even that it can be defined in any differential way whatever in terms of some subject matter, since experience embraces all that is encountered by an intelligent being in interaction with nature and the cultural world. Like James, Dewey maintained that there are numerous ways in which the things and events of experience can be taken or interpreted, many contexts—scientific, moral, social, political, aesthetic, religious— representing different interests and purposes from which these same things and events are viewed. In rejecting the coordination of experience with the deliverances of sense, Dewey was also denying the validity of the opposition between "experience" and reason or thought as envisaged by traditional empiricism. This opposition seemed to him mistaken on at least two grounds; first, there is the development of modern science made possible by the interpenetration of observation and rational construction so that any view according to which the two elements are totally distinct and opposed to each other would then have to account for their continuity and togetherness in bringing about the knowledge we actually possess. In the second place, Dewey, like Peirce, would not accept the view that experience is itself devoid of inference. Experience, he claimed, is shot through with clues that, in Peirce's term, "suggest" connections whereby thought is able to pass logically beyond the items presented to other items and to other features of the same item. Dewey even offered a biological argument in this connection, insisting that if experience were no more than the series of atomic sensations of the empiricist view, mankind would never have been able to infer and retain such knowledge as was needed for survival.

It is not necessary to do more than mention Dewey's rejection of the subjective bias inherent in the traditional conception of experience, because the point is so well known. The main consideration is that, for Dewey, experience, in virtue of its being the meaningful and funded result of many interactions between the individual and the environment, attains a *public* character evidenced, among other things, by the fact that it can be communicated, shared and compared. On Dewey's view, it was the psychologistic tendency and the belief that experience is what is exclusively connected with the "mind" that led to the idea of its being a private content which is not only immediately available to the one who has it, but, as was noted earlier on, is something of a screen standing between the individual mind and the external world. By contrast, Dewey held that experience is a genuine medium of disclosure, reaching down into nature and providing access to a real world. One might say that Dewey laid such stress on the objective and public nature of experience that there are grounds for questioning whether he did justice to its personal and individualized aspects. As I shall point out, he did not indeed omit this dimension of experience, but no reader of Dewey can entirely suppress the impulse to ask from time to time the question "Whose experience?"

Another significant feature of Dewey's reconstruction of experience concerns his refusal to equate experience and knowledge. This feature is more complex than any of the preceding and demands a lengthier discussion than is possible here, but at least the main point can be indicated along with the problem Dewey was trying to resolve. It is clear that the classical empiricists saw in the experience they acknowledged not only knowledge but a sure foundation capable of supporting a body of knowledge. Kant, who sought to broaden the empiricist conception, also took experience and knowledge as co-extensive as can be seen from the many passages in which *Erfahrung* is said to be *empirische Erkenntnis,* an expression customarily translated as "empirical cognition." Dewey rejected the identification for a number of reasons among which was his claim that knowledge is always mediated, the outcome or result of a critical process of inquiry, and hence is not something to be read off, as it were, from the direct course of experience. He sought to deal with the problem by distinguishing between "having" and "knowing," a distinction which at once expresses his refusal to identify "Being" and "Being known" and his claim that many experiences are simply "had" or undergone without the need for them to become matters of theoretical knowledge. If such knowledge is called for, then these experiences must become the material and set the conditions for the controlled inquiry which alone can issue in knowledge. It is clear that Dewey was trying to allow for the sort of thing which has been designated by others as "pre-thematic" experience or the ongoing encounters and interactions between individuals and the world, including the world of other individuals, which make up the course of human life. According to Dewey, were experience *ipso facto* knowledge the dimension of having, which he tended to identify with the esthetic, would be done away with and experience would become one with science. This view, of course, as has been pointed out by a number of critics, is thoroughly dependent on Dewey's identification of knowledge with science so that it is fair to raise the question whether there is any noetic element in what he called having, or, to put the question in another form, whether knowledge is exclusively an affair of the sciences. I cannot join that issue here; suffice it to say that Dewey was on the right track in seeking to liberate experience from its traditional identification with knowing and the spectator attitude which went along with that view. In this regard, Dewey has affinities with the attempts made by others to recover lived experience with all its vividness and import.

Perhaps I should have considered earlier in this discussion a feature of Dewey's view of experience which many have regarded not only as novel but as expressive of something distinctive on the American scene. I have in mind the connection between experience and intelligent activity and practical skill; in short, the role of experience in the development of "knowing how." This feature was little emphasized in the classical view because of its emphasis on the perceiving of sense qualities without regard to their dynamic meaning as manifest in the way in which things possessing those qualities would react in relation to other things. Like Peirce, Dewey asked what things "would do" if they possessed a certain character or belonged to a certain kind and then used these expectations as a basis for preparing the proper response to be made when we are in the presence of these things. The central point can be made by considering what we mean when we say that someone is "experienced" in dealing, for example, with horses.[7] To begin with, we do not mean primarily that such a person has "perceived" many horses since that will be taken for granted and, in any case, that fact alone would not qualify one as "experienced." What we mean is essentially that a person has come to understand the behavior of horses and to interpret signs of what they are likely to do under particular circumstances as a basis for "knowing how" to respond, knowing what to do in the presence, for example, of a frightened or unfriendly horse. It should be obvious that gaining experience in this

7. It is an interesting question whether and to what extent one can speak of someone as being "experienced" in languages other than English.

sense cannot be a matter merely of singular occasions when one perceives the qualities of horses, but requires a continuous and cumulative interaction with the animals in the course of which one becomes familiar with how they behave and how we are to respond in dealing with them. It is in this sense that experience for all three of our thinkers is essentially related to the formation of habits and skills which serve to direct our actions and shape the course of our lives.

Finally, we would do injustice to Dewey if we failed to take into account his conception of the esthetic and its expression in works of art as having their roots in those experiences where the present alone is significant, experiences which transcend instrumentalities and place us beyond direct concern for past and future. Dewey's attack on the "museum" conception of art according to which it is too "fine" to have grown out of or to be associated with ordinary experiences, is well known. The key to overcoming this conception is a new understanding of the experiential roots of art in all its forms, and, in turn, a new perception of the meaning bestowed upon experience when its esthetic dimension is taken fully into account. I know of no better passage in Dewey's writings for conveying his central contention about the relation between experience and art than the following from *Art As Experience:*

> It is mere ignorance that leads . . . to the supposition that connection of art and esthetic perception with experience signifies a lowering of their significance and dignity. Experience in the degree in which it *is* experience is heightened vitality. Instead of signifying being shut up within one's own private feelings and sensations, it signifies complete interpenetration of self and the world of objects and events.
> . . . Because experience is the fulfillment of an organism in its struggles and achievements in a world of things, it is art in germ. Even in its rudimentary forms, it contains the promise of that delightful perception which is esthetic experience.[8]

In addition to its reenforcement of the idea that experience cannot be confined to an internal world, this statement is noteworthy for its emphasis on experience as a matrix within which self and world interpenetrate, an actual overcoming of the subject-object dichotomy. I regard this way of viewing experience as a significant counter-balance to Dewey's tendency, especially evident in his discussions of the role of experience in science, to equate experience

8. John Dewey, *Art As Experience* (New York: Putnam, 1934; reprinted Capricorn Books, 1958), p. 19.

with method and thus bring it perilously close to becoming identified with *experiment*. The results of experiment, what Peirce called special experience, great as their effect may be on human life and welfare, are not what make up the substance of a worthwhile personal existence. Dewey was not unaware of this fact as can be seen in his perceptive account of what he called "an experience," to which I shall now turn.

Dewey's conception of having an experience points to the depth and value of certain fulfillments and accomplishments which are not only lasting in their significance but come to define our being as individual persons. Experience, says Dewey, is often inchoate and dispersed, lacking in any definite unity or form. By contrast, an experience, the sort of event or episode of which we say, "That *was an* experience," is marked by a consummation or fulfillment, a completion rather than a cessation. A piece of work satisfactorily finished, a vexing problem solved, an outstanding dramatic performance, living through a violent storm at sea are all, in Dewey's language, undergoings that have a unity because they are pervaded by a quality and have a closure which bestows upon them an individuality and self-sufficiency. Qualities which hold together many elements in a unity—joy, sorrow, hope, fear, anger—are not to be regarded as isolable "emotions" set over against thought and action, but rather as the significance of what is for us an experience. Taking an experience of thinking as an example, Dewey says that it is unified by the intent so that the conclusion when finally reached is not something separate but is the consummation of the process, an indication that thinking has its own esthetic character. Unfortunately, as Dewey well knew, experience is impoverished and becomes superficial when the pressures of events, our desire to be doing something coupled with impatience, lead to an unwillingness to let experience complete itself. The result is many experiences and the experience of many things, but little that attains the quality of an experience. The upshot of Dewey's account is that the esthetic dimension is no intruder in experience, nor is it a mere layer of refinement externally added to the ordinary and mundane; it is instead the essential character of complete experience—an experience. Dewey sums up the point in these words: "In short, art, in its form, unites the very same relation of doing and undergoing, outgoing and incoming energy, that makes an experience to be an experience."[9]

Given the extent of the ground to be covered, I could not attempt to correlate the views expressed with developments in the

9. *Art As Experience,* p. 48.

field of phenomenology. It should, nevertheless, be clear what the main points of contact are between the phenomenological approach and the efforts of Peirce, James and Dewey to arrive at a new conception of the nature of experience. There is first the emphasis on actual experiencing for the purpose of gaining a more accurate grasp of the intricacies and nuances; secondly, the broadening and deepening of the scope of experience and the refusal to identify it with atomic sensory data; thirdly, there is the concern to understand experience not only as material for knowledge but as the medium through which the individual person lives and develops; finally, there is the rejection of the spectator stance in favor of a self participating and acting throughout the entire range of what is there to be encountered in whatever way.

2

The Pragmatic Theory of Truth:
The Typical Objection

"The Pragmatic Theory of Truth: The Typical Objection," was written for a volume entitled, Contemporary Marxism. *These essays were concerned with, among other themes, the reception of American philosophy abroad. Since Marxist critics of Pragmatism, like realist critics, attacked the theory of truth as "subjectivism," it seemed to me wise to focus on this point which I am calling the "typical" objection to the theory. Accordingly, I have revised the title of the essay from its original, "Some Continental and Marxist Responses to Pragmatism."* Contemporary Marxism, *J. J. O'Rourke, ed., (Dordrecht, Holland: D. Reidel Publishing Company, 1984, pp. 199–214). Reprinted by permission of Kluwer Academic Publishers.*

Critical dialogue between different philosophical positions is as difficult to achieve as it is necessary. One must assume that the positions involved can be given a unified and consistent form of expression, and the whole enterprise presupposes a will to understand so that the discussion does not degenerate into a merely polemical exchange. A consideration of pragmatism, moreover, presents additional problems, first, because the classical representatives of the position, while sharing a core of common convictions, differ considerably in their emphasis and avenue of approach. Peirce's logical concerns play a major role in all of his thought, whereas James had definite reservations about the primacy of logic and laid great stress on direct experience and its interpretation from a psychological standpoint. Dewey's orientation was social and biological and, though like Peirce, he gave a central place to logic, that logic was more a structure of methodology than a formal system. The main consequence of this multiplicity in emphasis is that, although one may intend to be considering "pragmatism" as such, one may find that the focus is really on some dominant idea in one of the pragmatists. The difficulty is not, however, insuperable, especially if we are aware of its existence and are prepared to make the qualifications necessary for avoiding wholesale claims that are apt to be misleading. Secondly, until quite recently, the majority of

European critics and interpreters of pragmatism have not been acquainted with more than a very small portion of the primary literature and many of their judgments have been based largely on the vivid and popular slogans of James, notably his reference to the "success" supposed to be the reward of holding certain beliefs. There existed, moreover, antecedent biases of various sorts so that Horkheimer, for example, could declare that no "philosophical pedigree" at all would be accorded to pragmatism were it not for the fact that Peirce derived his philosophy from Kant! This is a curious criterion indeed, and its consistent application might make philosophical mongrels of us all!

Another set of problems involved in the assessment of pragmatism, especially for Marxist interpreters, is an unavoidable *ambiguity* stemming from the pragmatists' emphasis on the intimate connection that holds between meaning, thought, knowledge and *action*, a connection that makes it impossible to claim, as one might against some rationalistic idealisms, that the demands of *praxis* have been ignored. In short, as we shall see, Marxists are somewhat disconcerted if not confused in the face of pragmatism because standard criticisms of speculative philosophy as something divorced from both primary experience and the social matrix of thought will not apply to the pragmatic philosophy. Hence for some Marxists there arose the need to deal with pragmatism either by identifying it with positivism, a position generally uncongenial to Marxists, or by claiming that the central place accorded to action by the pragmatists is something quite different from *praxis* as they understand it.

I must confess at the same time to some ambiguity and ambivalence on my part. While I believe that there are as yet untapped resources in pragmatism for dealing with current issues, I am not unaware of difficulties posed by the position and hence I do not find it necessary to defend it at all costs and in the face of every objection. Horkheimer and others have made some acute criticisms that can and must be taken seriously. But, again, it is necessary to be sure that such criticism is based on an accurate understanding of the position and not merely on selected phrases intended to illustrate foregone conclusions. This sort of *ad hoc* criticism is easily made as is so well illustrated in Russell's essay, 'Transatlantic Truth'. There he makes no effort to get "inside" the pragmatic position, as it were, but is content instead to cite some slogans from James supposed to show that for pragmatism, truth is "made" or manufactured and thus provides a philosophical justification for believing what one wishes and for propaganda of all sorts.

In order to deal with a large topic in a quite limited space, it will be necessary to concentrate on some focal points in the hope that they will introduce the most important issues. I propose to discuss three such points, basing what I have to say on the writings of Horkheimer, Kołakowski and Habermas. The first is that pragmatism fostered the development of what Horkheimer calls "subjective" or formalized reason, and at the same time contributed to the erosion of objective ontologically grounded reason. The second is the charge that pragmatism is a form of positivism because it identifies meaning with the outcome of a process of verification.[1] The third is the claim that pragmatists, in contrast to Marx, abandoned the classical theory of truth in favor of the view that truth is "made" in accordance with processes whereby we "adapt" to the environment. In some ways this charge is the most important of the three, but it is also the most difficult to deal with in a limited space because it presupposes that there is *a* pragmatic theory of truth to be set side by side with other theories, and I regard this as a questionable assumption.[2] I regret, moreover, that space prevents me from dealing with Habermas' claim that pragmatism is essentially reflective account of scientific inquiry in "transcendental" terms.[3]

The first charge, to be found in Horkheimer's book, *The Eclipse of Reason,* is explicitly defined by the author as a treatment of pragmatism intended only to describe its role in what he calls the "subjectivization" of reason.[4] To begin with, I understand and sympathize with Horkheimer's interpretation of the development of the conception of reason in modern philosophy. Reason, on the classical view, was seen as objective structure, a force operative throughout the cosmos, and as a determiner of ends so that the degree of rationality in anything was a function of its harmony with a totality. This conception eroded as the result of a number of factors, not the least of which, I would add, was Kant's opting for the priority of understanding over reason in the sphere of knowledge, and sub-

1. On this head, see esp. L. Kołakowski, *The Alienation of Reason,* trans. N. Guterman, Garden City, N.Y.: Doubleday & Co., 1969, chapter 7. Cf. Horkheimer, *The Eclipse of Reason,* New York: Oxford University Press, 1947, p. 49, n. 29.
2. I have discussed the problem at some length in *Purpose and Thought: The Meaning of Pragmatism,* London and New Haven: Hutchinson and Yale University Press, 1979, pp. 50–77.
3. Jürgen Habermas, *Knowledge and Human Interest,* trans. J. J. Shapiro, Boston: Beacon Press, 1971, pp. 91–139. This discussion nicely illustrates what I pointed out previously about a treatment of pragmatism as such turning into an account of one aspect of the thought of one of its representatives, in this case Peirce's theory of scientific inquiry.
4. Horkheimer, pp. 42 ff.

sequently, reason came to be understood as no more than a subjective power of "reasoning", shorn of its former ontological reach
and totally at the mercy of subjective aims. Such reasoning came, in
turn, to be formalized in logic based chiefly on mathematical models with the almost inevitable result that reason came to be excluded
from the discussion of social, moral and religious concerns.
Horkheimer's account of the odyssey of reason seems to me essentially correct, and it has been reinforced in a recent book, *The Illusion of Technique,* by William Barrett in which the author astutely
asks how it happens that three such divergent philosophical views
as those represented by Russell, Whitehead and Wittgenstein could
all have emerged from the same formal or symbolic logic. What is
not so clear to me, however, is the validity of Horkheimer's interpretation of the way in which the pragmatists were supposed to
have helped bring about the subjectivity of reason. There are focal
points in Horkheimer's argument; one is the role played by the
concept of *purpose* and the other is the question whether a technical
or controlling reason can deal with the criticism of ends and goals.

As regards the first point, Horkheimer sees a total opposition
between an "objective" reason whose concepts refer to objects, and
a "subjective" reason that involves the relating of a concept or an
object to a purpose. Relying entirely on the statement of James that
an idea is "a plan of action", Horkheimer supposes that some private and purely personal interest or "purpose" on the part of the
knower is going to determine the truth of an idea as contrasted with
an "objective" concern for the "truth" of an idea in relation to an
object apart from any reference to purpose. What he fails to see,
however, is that for the pragmatists, *all* thought is guided by purposes, and that *one* of these purposes is that of gaining the purely
theoretical knowledge represented by science and objective reason.

Since the introduction of purpose was of central importance to
the development of pragmatism and at the same time causes concern on the part of critics, something further needs to be said on
the point. As I have already indicated, all the pragmatists recognized the legitimacy of the purely theoretical purpose of describing
and explaining the world through processes of empirical inquiry.
And they recognized the importance, the necessity in fact, of keeping this purpose free from all ulterior interests and purposes of
individual investigators. *In principle,* this purpose is unlimited by
any consideration other than the pursuit of truth and the acquisition of knowledge, although, as the history of science makes plain,
the contingent conditions under which the purely theoretical purpose must be carried out have had their own role to play. Pure

research is never independent of our ability to forge the necessary implements for experiment and it is no secret at present that what will become the subject of investigation, where and by whom is often dictated by the availability of funds, the interests of those who control them and public opinion concerning the relative importance of a line of inquiry.

Let me offer three examples of the appeal to purpose by the pragmatists, each of which is, in my view, entirely justified. First, James pointed out that in the attempt to answer a specific question or resolve a problem we must make judgments concerning the *relevance* of any information already available for dealing with the matter at issue. He was fond of pointing to an encyclopedia taken as a kind of model of pure knowledge about the world and asking, "*When* do I say the truths contained in these volumes?" I do not go about uttering true propositions starting with A and ending with Z, but rather I *select* from what is available just that information there is reason to believe is relevant or "counts" for answering the question. There can, of course, be no guarantee that our judgments of relevance will always be correct, but without them thought is without orientation and limitation, the sort of thing that happens on an examination when the specific question asked is ignored and the student attempts to record indiscriminately *all* he or she knows about whatever topic is mentioned.

A second form of appeal to purpose is to be found in Peirce's doctrine of vagueness. For Peirce, every idea we can frame is more or less vague and is subject to being made more precise depending on the purpose and context in which it appears. For ordinary purposes it will not be necessary to insist on a high degree of precision in meaning since "rough" conceptions will suffice and yield the desired results. If, for example, a hostess were to invite a guest to be seated in the "loveseat" whereas in fact the intended object is a "sofa", the vagueness need cause no problem because the guest will know that he is not to sit in the "ladder-back" chair which is clearly neither of the two. On the other hand, if we consider an auction of antique furniture, it would be absolutely essential that a high degree of precision be attained in the use of the relevant terms. No confusion between a "loveseat" and a "sofa" could be countenanced in that context because vagueness would be in fact a form of misrepresentation. The purpose in view determines the degree of precision in meaning necessary for achieving our aim.

A third example appears in the writings of Royce who claimed affinity with the pragmatists precisely because of the central role accorded to purpose in his conception of thought. If we consider what we mean when we speak of representations "corresponding" to their objects, we must also consider what sort of correspondence we intend. A photograph, an oil portrait, a caricature, an X-ray film and a silhouette all "correspond" to their objects, but they do not all do so in the same way. A relation of one-to-one mapping is meant to obtain in the case, for example, of the X-ray film and the silhouette, but not in the case of the caricature or the oil portrait. In short, the accuracy and adequacy of the correspondence between the representation and its object depend on the purpose controlling the sort of correspondence we seek to achieve. We expect the photograph to "look like" its subject in a sense that is inappropriate in the case of the X-ray or the caricature. The latter, for example, fails in its intent if it turns out to be no more than a "literal" drawing corresponding in a one-to-one relation to its object.

I must insist, however, that in all these appeals to purpose— selective relevance, degree of precision required, and our intent in representation—there is nothing "subjective" in a sense that would preclude "objectivity" as regards knowledge and truth. Presupposed throughout the writings of the pragmatists is the belief that the purpose of gaining purely theoretical knowledge remains intact, but that if such knowledge is not to be inert it must enter into all the contexts where it is used to shape belief and guide action.

Horkheimer (p. 46) is quite convinced that the pragmatists can have no place for such a theoretical interest, but this conviction is based largely on an exaggeration of James' "practicalism" or the demand for relevance in thinking and of Dewey's interest in closing the gap between scientific inquiry and technology. The fact is that Peirce thought of science as controlled inquiry into the "useless", and there can be no question that all three thinkers were careful to define the *context* of the theoretical knowing in terms of impersonal and intersubjective norms that have no place for personal interests and predilections. The contrast, therefore, between purpose and objectivity is misguided. Peirce, James and Dewey each argued for the superiority of empirical inquiry in gaining truth (in fact some critics said they went too far in this direction), but they also saw that we confront reality with more than one purpose in view and that the standpoint of the theoretical knower is not our only access to what there is. Stated in classical language, Being is not identical with Being known.

Horkheimer, like many other critics of pragmatism, is misled by James' language, and in fairness it must be said that James is not without some responsibility for putting his readers on the wrong track. His use of terms like "success", "satisfactory" and "satisfaction" (a term to which Peirce vigorously objected as an "incomplete predicate") led many to suppose that for him truth is "nothing but" some sort of personal, individual advantage gained by a knower who "successfully" uses an idea. Despite these problems of language, however, there need be nothing "subjective" in the pejorative sense about what James and the other pragmatists were maintaining. Where they referred to truth as a matter of "expectations" being fulfilled (or disappointed in the case of falsehood), they were legitimately introducing into their account of knowledge the *process* whereby ideas, propositions, theories are tested. The expectations involved are not the "interests" of individual thinkers, but references to objective *states of affairs* that *would* eventuate if the idea being tested were true. To take a simple but perfectly adequate example, we have a beaker before us containing a quantity of liquid and we want to know whether it is *true* to say that the solution is alkaline. It so happens that in this case we literally have a "litmus paper" test to determine the answer. If it is true that the solution is "alkaline", i.e., that the predicate *truly* applies, and we understand the nature of the test, we *expect* that the paper when dipped in the solution *would* turn blue. If *in fact* this happens, then our expectation is fulfilled *in the object* and we are justified in saying that the idea in question is true. I see nothing "subjective" in all this; our expectation based on the meaning of the terms involved obviously does not bring about the effect and if our expectation had been disappointed, i.e., if the paper had *not* in fact turned blue, we would have to conclude that the nature of the *object* in question was other than we had thought.

Horkheimer objects to this analysis, apart from the charge of subjectivity, on the ground that for pragmatism, "meaning" and "effect" become identical and this he takes to be an error because *present* meaning and *future* verification are not the same (p. 44). I do not deny the element of truth in this claim, but the issue is both ambiguous and too complex to be resolved satisfactorily here. All depends on whether the modalities—what Peirce called the "maybe's", the "would-be's", the "could-be's"—are taken seriously into account. Peirce rejected any theory of reality according to which it is reduced to the "is", "was" or "will be". These are all indicatives distinguished only by a temporal qualification and thus exclude all the conditional modalities that figure so largely in Peirce's thought. Thus, referring back to the previous example, Peirce would not say that the litmus paper "will" turn blue, but that under the circumstances it "would" turn blue if the objective character of the solution is of a certain kind. Peirce consistently refused to identify the meaning of a concept—"intellectual purport"—with any singular fact, and even less with an act (conduct) which was for him the most individualized reality there is. All concepts, on the other hand, embrace what is general and hence their "meaning" can never coincide with or be exhausted by singular instances. Horkheimer gives no indication that he is aware of this central point. Let us consider the familiar illustration of the diamond and what it means to say that it is "hard".[5] In accordance with what I call "dynamizing" the predicates, Peirce is asking how a given characteristic *manifests* itself in relation to other things encountered in experience. If something is "hard", it would have the *capacity* to affect other things in a certain way; that is, the diamond would scratch many other objects without being scratched by them in return. The central point, however, is that the meaning of "hard" is not identical with any particular occasion on which the diamond scratches something, nor even with a finite number of such occasions, but rather with the *habit* or general tendency of the diamond to behave in that way. As we shall see, it is characteristic of both nominalism and positivism to compress "meaning" into present, instantaneous and fully determinate fact. Whereas James had some tendency to fall in with that line of thinking, both Peirce and Dewey vehemently rejected it in favor of a more ancient tradition, according to which enduring objects are centers of continuing habits or potential behavior not exhausted by the singular occasions when their characteristics are manifested.

It is clear that what most troubles Horkheimer is the concern that the pragmatists reduced reason to an instrument serving "alien" ends and established not *rationality* but the "satisfaction" of the subject as the final criterion of thought. But surely there is a deep irony in the situation; the pragmatists were no less concerned than Horkheimer is to see that reason, thought, knowledge "make a difference" or have some actual bearing on the course of human affairs. The question is, of course, how reason is to exert this influence if it manifests itself in no form save a contemplative or reflective one and can maintain its integrity only at the cost of

5. Those who do not follow Peirce's writing too closely are apt to overlook the qualifications he made over periods of time. In the famous paper of 1878, 'How to Make Our Ideas Clear', Peirce had taken what he later rejected as a "nominalist" position with respect to the meaning of the predicate "hard". Earlier on he had maintained that, unless a test were actually made, it would make no sense to say that the diamond is hard. In footnotes, however, added later to 5.402 (*Collected Papers of Charles Sanders Peirce*, eds. Hartshorne, Weiss and Burks, Cambridge, Mass., 1934–1960, 8 vols.), Peirce rescinded the "nominalist view" just expressed in favor of the position indicated in the text here.

removing itself from the continuum of experience and the inter-play between means and ends.

The second criticism focused by Horkheimer comes in precisely at this point. On his view, an instrumental conception of reason taken over from experimental science must inevitably identify reason exclusively as a means, thus depriving it of the "depth" required for the selection and determination of ends. Here I agree with Horkheimer in principle; if reason is no more than formal, logical structure or an instrument for the expression of a purely "value-free", theoretical knowledge, then it is effectively cut off from the determination of values and ends, or what Whitehead called the sphere of "importance". There is, however, if the suggestion does not seem too paradoxical in the context of prag-matism, a decisive discrepancy between the theory and the prac-tice. It cannot be denied that the course of technological develop-ment in America has revealed an overwhelming emphasis on means at the expense of ends. A recent history of technology has the apt, but alarming, title, *From Know-How to Nowhere,* and many observers, among them numerous scientists, have admitted that the larger, vaguer and more difficult questions about ends have either been postponed or ignored altogether in favor of "soluble" technical questions that place more means or instruments at our disposal. The paradox just mentioned has to do with the double-barrelled character of pragmatism, and leads us to consider whether its representatives in fact espoused a purely technical conception of reason. On the one hand, the proposal that ideas are operative and should be put to work does offer a basic rationale for a technological order, and there can be no question that the pragmatic outlook fostered the development of applied science. On the other hand, it is quite illegitimate to overlook the fact that Dewey, especially, regarded the "means-end continuum" as a major philosophical problem and he specifically rejected the widely held view that ends are intuitively grounded beyond ratio-nal scrutiny and that rational discussion must be confined exclu-sively to the selection of means. Whatever view we may take of the validity of his arguments for this position in *The Theory of Valuation,* we cannot reasonably ignore his insistence that not only are ends *not* "beyond disputing", but that they are what it is most important to argue about. Dewey repeatedly criticized the legitimacy of immediate desires and ends unconnected with knowledge of what would be required to achieve them, in favor of ends that are "approved by reflection". This approach to the appraisal of ends does indeed depend heavily on the relative merits of different means, but the fact remains that Dewey did not seek to avoid the basic problem.

Peirce, moreover, in his account of the "normative sciences"—esthetics, ethics and logic—argued for an ideal of "concrete reasonableness" in human affairs, and opposed the "greed philosophy" fostered by American individualism and social Darwinism with his theory of evolutionary love according to which the values of cooperation, community and the mutual enhancement of human capabilities are to prevail. It is difficult to see how, in the face of these ideas, it can be maintained that pragmatism excludes rationality from the determination of ends. James' "Meliorism" provides another example to the contrary. He had a firm belief in the power of the energetic will of each individual to help make the world a "better place" than it was before. The ideals of freedom, personal integrity and self-realization are dominant in his basically humanistic philosophy. One may indeed argue that, as regards the socioeconomic pattern of American society, the power of technology and of technical reason had become so great in this century that no counterforce could prevail against them. But it is manifestly incorrect to argue, as Horkheimer does, that the pragmatists did no more than contribute to the subjectivizing of reason. The truth is that no one of them accepted a formalized reason as the pattern of rationality. Dewey's concept of *intelligence* is shot through with norms; Peirce, though he had great faith in the resources of formal logic, nevertheless argued for rational self-control both in thought and action under the guidance of the "normative", and James frequently asserted that where life conflicts with logic, so much the worse for logic.

It is interesting to note that Horkheimer never asks to what extent freedom, equality and justice actually prevailed in those historical epochs when the ontological reason whose eclipse he laments was the dominant mode of thought. In fairness to him, however, I do not believe that he is proposing to turn back the clock, as it were, and if one considers the instructive comparison made at the end of *The Eclipse of Reason* (p. 183), it appears that Horkheimer is in fact closer to the pragmatists than he realizes. In a critique of positivism and skepticism on one side, and objective idealism and rationalism on the other, he claims that each side falls into error. The former positions are said to find no meaning in general concepts worth salvaging, while the latter hold to the eternal meaning of concepts and norms but overlook their historical relativity. These judgments express precisely what the classical pragmatists said about these philosophical positions!

We must turn now to the second charge, made especially by Kołakowski and Habermas, that pragmatism is essentially a form of positivism. I shall not deal with this claim at great length because it is quite clearly mistaken, but the reason for the misunderstanding is not difficult to find. If one reads Peirce's original paper, 'How to Make Our Ideas Clear', and ignores the critical notes he added later (esp. to 5.402), one will suppose that, for Peirce, the diamond is "hard" only when actually put to the singular test and that the meaning of the predicate is exhausted in the one transaction.[6] But, as Peirce pointed out, the meaning of a general concept is never identical with any singular fact (or act), but rather with the conditional behavior (what *would* X do under Y circumstances?) of an object over stretches of time. His rejection of nominalism, his defense of the reality of what he called "generals" (*not,* as is often thought, the "existence" of universals), tendencies and potentialities, and his insistence on the "independent reals" as a necessary presupposition of science must all be cited as evidence that Peirce's pragmatism at any rate is no positivism.[7] Dewey's rejection, moreover, of the classical conception of experience underlying modern positivism and his attack on reductionism make it quite impossible to classify him as a positivist. While James did stand closer to traditional empiricism than the others, his religious humanism, theory of freedom and the self, and his "piecemeal" supernaturalism put him at odds with any form of positivism known to me.[8]

The best source for the Marxist critique of the pragmatists' theory of truth is Kołakowski's essay, 'Karl Marx and the Classical Definition of Truth'.[9] He begins correctly with the historical fact of the introduction at the end of the last century of *practical activity* into the theory of knowing, and he distinguishes two forms of this

6. In his account of "Peirce's positivism", Kołakowski takes note of the development in Peirce's thought (*The Alienation of Reason,* p. 153), but claims that it was his "earliest writings" that made him important in the history of "positivism"!

7. Anyone still entertaining doubts on this head should study Peirce's critical review of Karl Pearson's *The Grammar of Science,* in *Collected Papers of Charles Sanders Peirce,* vol. 8, ed. Arthur W. Burks, Cambridge, Mass., 1958, Sec. 132–43. There Peirce defends "the majesty of truth" and "reasonableness itself" as the only proper motivating force for scientists, as opposed to "the stability of society" or other utilitarian and Darwinian motives.

8. It is both instructive and ironic that in his chapter, 'The Pragmatist Account of Truth and its Misunderstanders', in *The Meaning of Truth,* James cites as the first misunderstanding the thesis that "Pragmatism is only a re-editing of positivism".

9. L. Kołakowski, *Marxism and Beyond,* London: Pall Mall Press, 1968. It is important to notice that this discussion is based exclusively on James' views and does not reflect anything of James' responses to criticism contained in *The Meaning of Truth.*

view represented respectively by Marx and James. As soon becomes evident, this initial distinction is interpreted as an *opposition* between the two conceptions. According to Kołakowski, Marx appealed to the *effectiveness* of human action as a criterion enabling us to *verify* the knowledge we need in order to undertake any sort of activity. James, on the other hand, is said to have introduced practical *usefulness* as a factor in the *definition* of truth, and he takes this factor not as a tool for establishing the truth of our knowledge independently of ourselves, but as something that *creates* the truth. The opposition previously mentioned is now clear: Marx adheres to the "classical" conception of truth where the relation between the judgment and the reality is independent of man's knowledge, whereas on James' theory it is man's practical activity that "creates" the truth or knowledge.

Whatever may be the case as regards Marx's view, Kołakowski is mistaken in his interpretation of James. Although he cites no specific passages from James, it seems quite evident that Kołakowski is relying on those admittedly (by James himself) loose and unguarded statements that "truths are made", that the true idea is the one that "works", that truth has something essential to do with the "satisfaction" of the knower, and that the true is the "expedient" in the way of thinking—statements that made it necessary for James to restate his position in *The Meaning of Truth* and attempt to overcome misunderstanding. In support of my contention that Kołakowski misrepresents James' view, I shall advance three considerations, beginning with an ambiguity in the concept of "practical activity" that often goes unnoticed, passing on to the authority James accorded actual fact in his correspondence theory of truth, and ending with the role of critical testing in the process of discovering truths. Insofar as all the pragmatists regarded knowledge as issuing from a critical process, they paid attention to what an enquirer *does* in the way of intervening and manipulating subject matter for the purpose of testing hypotheses and possible answers to theoretical questions, but they manifestly did not maintain that this "activity" *creates* truth, but only that it is necessary for *discovery*. This activity on the part of the enquirer in the acquisition of knowledge, must not be confused with the "practical activity" involved in the subsequent *use* of the knowledge in a technological or engineering context. To obtain the gas laws, Boyle had to devise experiments and carry them out in practice; a knowledge of such laws might be essential for the "practical activity" of inventing a refrigerating unit, but there is nothing in James that permits us to regard our success or failure to produce such a unit as having anything to do with the truth or falsity of judgments, hypotheses, ideas being tested in theoretical inquiry and its "practical activity". We shall not, to be sure, succeed in producing such a unit if our ideas are false or our information incorrect. But for James at any rate the activity entering into the acquisition of knowledge is not to be confused with whatever activity goes into its use once it has been obtained. Kołakowski would have been on sounder ground in his interpretation of James and especially the emphasis he places on what James called "satisfaction", if he had shifted the focus to the properly "practical" sphere—the moral, religious and metaphysical—where theoretical verification, on James' view, is not possible and where we have to appeal to the consequences that would follow if we acted on a belief which we believe but do not *know* to be true. I cannot follow this line further, because I am chiefly concerned to set the record straight as regards James' theory of truth.

James repeatedly maintained that truth is correspondence between ideas and reality (not a "copy," as Kołakowski well understands) and he described his epistemology as "realistic". A most telling example of such a view is to be found at the beginning of his essay, 'The Will to Believe'. A person in bed with a high fever may *say* that he is perfectly healthy, but, says James, he is *powerless to believe* that in the face of the manifest fact. James, in short, sided with Hume and against Descartes; belief is totally bound down by the datum and will is in abeyance. Citing the complementary character of matters of fact and abstract ideas in the knowing situation, James wrote:

> Between the coercions of the sensible order and those of the ideal order, our mind is thus wedged tightly. Our ideas must agree with realities, be such realities concrete or abstract; be they facts or be they principles, under penalty of endless inconsistency and frustration.[10]

I fail to see, in the face of such statements, how it is possible to maintain that, on James' theory, truth is being "created" by some sort of practical activity. It is most likely that this confusion stems from James' next step, which is to ask what "agreement" concretely means. James was quite right in seeing that to define truth in terms of some such universal relationship as that of agreement or correspondence is not the same as indicating how one would go about

10. William James, *Pragmatism,* New York and London: Longmans, Green & Co., 1907, p. 211. "The Hundredth decimal of π, the ratio of the circumference to its diameter, is pre-determined ideally now, tho no one may have computed it."

determining in individual instances what this relation means and when it obtains. Simple cases where an idea can be said to "copy" its object—we see the "2" on a watch dial and do not confuse it with the "5", and we distinguish the "long" hand from the "short" one—present no problems, but the vast majority of ideas, judgments, hypotheses do not copy their objects in that sense. To deal with agreement when it does not mean copy, James, like Peirce and Dewey, called for the *interpolation* of a controlled, critical process to be carried out by an enquirer seeking to determine whether some idea being tested *is* in agreement with its object. Here is where the possibly confusing ideas of "working", "leading", "fitting" enter the picture; they represent the structure of the process of *testing* or an order of operations intended to disclose whether in fact the idea being tested is true or false. If I want to test the simple proposition, "This car has front-wheel drive", the constituent ideas must direct me to the appropriate object and indicate what I am to expect to find if the proposition is true. When I make the inspection under this guidance and find that the driveshaft is in fact connected to the rear wheels, I conclude that the proposition does not "agree" with its object and is therefore false. But none of this activity "creates" any truth or falsity, and in fact James was more sanguine in his appeal to the authority of present fact than either Peirce or Dewey. "In the end and eventually," he writes, "all true processes must lead to the face of directly verifying sensible experiences *somewhere* which somebody's ideas have copied."[11]

Had James been less concerned to shock his rationalist opponents and less inclined to a nominalism or particularism, he would not have obscured the quite realistic cast of his theory by going on to say that truth is only a collective name for verification processes and that truth is "made". The latter assertion does all the damage, even if it does not and could not consistently mean on James' view what it appears to mean, especially when connected with James' emphasis on "using" truths in contexts other than the purely theoretical. Facts, he says, simply are: they are not by themselves "true". "Truths emerge from facts" in the form of *beliefs* about them; and in calling Truth a "function" of beliefs that start and terminate among the facts, he is saying no more than that the *true* belief is the one that, should one wish to verify it, is seen to be in accord with its object. That none of this is meant to support the thesis that we "manufacture" truth in the course of discovering it, can be seen from what James said about knowledge and the past: "When new experiences lead to retrospective judgments, using the

11. Ibid., p. 215.

past tense, what these judgments utter was true, even though no past thinker had been led there."[12]

I return at this point to my previous claim that "practical activity" is ambiguous and that we must seek its meaning in accord with the context in question. The activity that figures in the context of knowledge is controlled by the purpose of theoretical inquiry and even if we were to follow James in his references to "satisfaction" and "usefulness" in this connection,[13] both would still have to be understood as describing ideas and beliefs that meet the test of verification. If, however, we move into contexts other than that of theoretical knowing, the picture changes and the focus shifts from truth to the *relevance* and the *appropriateness* of some belief or of some item of knowledge for realizing a desired goal. If we wish, as amateur botanists, to be able to identify plants as we come upon them in the field, we shall need just that information, selected from a great deal more, which we can use *under field, not laboratory, conditions*, for achieving our goal. Usefulness here concerns relevance and not truth, since we are assuming that all the information is "true". Kołakowski misses this and seems to think (p. 60) that the truth of a judgment for James is simply a function of the "usefulness" or advantage to the individual of accepting or rejecting it. As I have already pointed out, however, considerations of this kind enter only when we are not concerned with theoretical knowledge itself, but are guided instead by the purposes defining the moral, religious and metaphysical contexts. In those contexts our aim is not the determination and explanation of facts, in James' phrase, "already in the bag", but rather to act, transform the world and interpret it in accordance with ideas that, in the nature of the case, cannot be a matter of prior knowledge, if of knowledge at all. We act on these convictions with faith and risk, and here, according to James, we do appeal to the consequences of such belief and action and to their "satisfactoriness" in enabling us to realize ourselves in the world. But even in these precarious contexts, it is *not* James' view that we can believe anything we wish, even what is manifestly contrary to all we know, if somehow such belief contributes to our success in life *á la* Henry Ford (p. 62)!

Kołakowski restates the original opposition between pragmatism and the classical conception of truth in the claim that the former is concerned primarily with an organic adaptation to the

12. Ibid., p. 233. Italics in original. This view is reinforced in *The Meaning of Truth* and it is difficult to see how it conflicts with Kołakowski's conception of the classical theory of truth, as he claims James' theory does (p. 61).
13. I agree here with Peirce in not wanting to use this terminology since "satisfaction" is not normally understood to mean "satisfaction of the theoretical impulse".

world, while the latter aims at an objective reflection of the world. This opposition, however, cannot stand as it is, and what Kołakowski himself says shows why this is so. He points out (p. 75) that both Marxism and pragmatism are alike opposed to the view that consciousness (knowledge?) is an ever more perfect imitation of an external world acting on the mind to produce a copy. And he notes that both positions conceive of consciousness as functional, a tool with which to master circumstances and not merely to mirror them. The crucial difference, however, between the two positions is once again said to be the difference between Marx's adherence to an "objective" conception of truth and James' criterion of subjective satisfaction, also described as "biological correspondence". The reason this simple opposition cannot stand (quite apart from the misrepresentation of James) is that Marx was not content to "reflect" the world in knowledge, but demanded that the world be transformed just as the pragmatists did. On the other hand, as I have pointed out, James was no less concerned than Marx to discover what is objectively true about the world and if this be described as "adaptation" to it, that can only mean being in *accord* with the facts and having a *knowledge* of the patterns or laws according to which things behave. In short, for James, an understanding of "what's what" about the world is a necessary condition for changing it. Moreover, as James argued in his critique of Herbert Spencer's theory of the mind,[14] a one-way "adaptation" of the mind to the world tells only half the story; the other half is the creative power of the mind to transform the environment in accordance with human needs and purposes.

Simple contrasts between the "objective" approach of Marx, and the "subjective" approach of the pragmatists will not "work", because both Peirce and James defended a form of *correspondence* in their theory of truth, and even Dewey's *transform* conception of truth which represents a more radical break with the tradition than the thought of the other two, has a *conform* element in it at the stage of inquiry he called the "determination of the facts of the case". A more profound and fruitful exchange between Marxism and pragmatism can take place when there is a deeper understanding of pragmatism and one which is not derived primarily from the loose phrases and slogans of James which he himself came to acknowledge as such and sought to correct in his replies to critics.

14. See 'Remarks on Spencer's Definition of Mind as Correspondence', *Journal of Speculative Philosophy* (1878), pp. 1–18; reprinted in *Collected Essays and Reviews*, ed. Ralph Barton Perry, New York and London, Longmans, Green & Co., 1920.

3

Two Defenses of Freedom:
Peirce and James

"Two Defenses of Freedom: Peirce and James" was presented at a conference on themes in classical American philosophy sponsored by the Department of Philosophy at Tulane University in 1987. James' "The Dilemma of Determinism" and Peirce's "The Doctrine of Necessity Examined" are noteworthy in that they represent a striking contrast in approach while essentially arguing for the same conclusion. Both thinkers are defending real possibilities, spontaneity and chance in the scheme of things, but whereas James uses the dilemma to force the determinist to confront two undesirable consequences of the view, Peirce proceeds directly to examine and ultimately reject six reasons that have been advanced in support of determinism. The approach in each case is characteristic of their mode of thinking, something that James would have put down to "temperament." The essay appeared in Tulane Studies in Philosophy, *vol. 35 (1987), pp. 51–64 and is reprinted with the permission of the Department of Philosophy of Tulane University, New Orleans, Louisiana.*

It is difficult to imagine a better or a more illuminating occasion for an excursion into what we may call comparative philosophy than that provided by the two essays I propose to consider, Peirce's "The Doctrine of Necessity Examined," and James' "The Dilemma of Determinism." The interesting.fact is that, while these essays differ widely in their approach, something to be expected from the diverse orientation of their authors, both thinkers are arguing for virtually the same thesis. Each is attacking mechanical determinism and attempting to establish an element of chance, spontaneity and real possibility in the order of things. How each goes about the task at hand, however, is a vivid study in contrasts, one that is most revealing as regards their conceptions of philosophy, of logic and of

All references in the text to Peirce's "Doctrine of Necessity Examined" are to the *Collected Papers of Charles Sanders Peirce*, Edited by Hartshorne and Weiss, Cambridge (Mass.): Harvard University Press, 1935, Vol. 6. References are to sections, *not* pages. All references in the text to James' "The Dilemma of Determinism" are to *Essays in Pragmatism*, edited by Alburey Castell, New York: Hafner Press, 1949.

the nature of belief, especially where metaphysical issues are involved. I shall return at the end to some comparisons that I believe throw some light on the respective merits, and perhaps limitations, of each approach.

James' essay was published originally in 1884, in the *Unitarian Review;* Peirce's appeared in *The Monist* in 1892. Peirce makes no reference to James' paper, but James, in a later reprinting of the "Dilemma," added a note calling attention to Peirce's article and citing it as further evidence that, as he says, the juice has not yet been pressed out of the "free-will controversy." In what follows, I shall reverse the historical order and consider Peirce's paper first since it is more concise and nicely focuses the main issues. James' discussion is more diffuse, largely because of his concern for the psychology of belief, the need to prepare the ground before a consideration of metaphysical issues, and finally by his use of the dilemma in setting forth his argument. Peirce, by contrast, goes straight to the problem of determinism as he envisaged it and he shows little concern for the mind-set of his readers.

The doctrine Peirce proposed to examine is, as he says, "the common belief that every single fact in the universe is precisely determined by law" (6.36). As we shall see, for a special purpose further on, Peirce had recourse to an alternative formulation of necessitarianism, but the above statement remains central, even though he gave a more precise reading of this belief when he began to consider the arguments that have been offered in its defense. After noting that Aristotle rejected determinism as set forth by Democritus, but also that the doctrine of necessity, due to the successes of mechanics and physics, had great vogue in the later 19th century, Peirce goes on to state more specifically the position he is to argue against. "The proposition in question," he writes, "is that the state of things existing at any time, together with certain immutable laws, completely determine the state of things at every other time" (6.37). If, Peirce continues, we expand this general thesis to include all acts of will and ideas of the mind and are thus led to include minds as parts of the physical world determined entirely by the laws of mechanics, we have what he called the mechanical philosophy, "the usual and most logical form of necessitarianism" (6.37). The remainder of the essay is a critical examination of each of several reasons that have been offered in defense of this view plus Peirce's proposal of what is true about the universe if the necessitarian thesis is false.

The first and most frequently cited reason in support of this thesis, says Peirce, is that it is a presupposition or postulate of

scientific reasoning. This view, I would add, was by no means confined to Peirce's time; B. F. Skinner, for example, has been appealing to it for decades as a necessary assumption if the study of
human behavior is to be scientific. Peirce, however, regards the
postulate approach as worthless, since postulating a proposition
not only fails to make it true, but, as he says, does not give any
motive for believing it at all. For him, to postulate a proposition is
to express the *hope* that it is true and nothing more. This summary
dismissal, however, is followed by a more elaborate argument intended to show that "the whole notion of a postulate being involved
in reasoning appertains to a by-gone and false conception of logic"
(6.40). Here Peirce is, of course, referring to non-deductive inference, chiefly induction, but we know from his paper, "The Grounds
of the Validity of the Laws of Logic," that he had an analogous
argument against axioms being at the foundation of deductive
logic. In both cases his appeal is to what takes place in the actual
process of reasoning itself, or what he refers to in the case of induction as inferring *experientially* and *provisionally.* The issue joined
here is one that goes far beyond our present purposes, but I shall
attempt to summarize the argument with an eye on the main point
which is that no postulate of the necessitarian sort is actually required in scientific reasoning. The nub of his argument is this and
it nicely shows how Peirce could appeal to actual scientific thought
and not only to logical "reconstructions" of it: all inductive or am-
pliative inference is based on *sampling,* including, of course, whatever devices may be needed to ensure a set of representative samples; all inferences from the samples are made *experientially* and
provisionally; by "experientially" Peirce meant that the conclusion
does not go beyond possible experience of the subject matter under
consideration, and by "provisionally" he meant that we do not claim
to have actually reached any assigned degree of approximation, but
only that if our experience is indefinitely extended we shall be able
to *correct* any previously inferred ratios and, in the long run, determine within what limits experience fluctuates. Peirce's claim is that
inductive inferences made in the course of actual inquiry are experiential and provisional and require no postulate concerning
what *must be* the case. In summary he says that a postulate is the
statement of a material fact which, precisely because it is postulated,
we are not entitled to use as a premise, even if its truth is necessary for
validating an inference. Any such postulated fact must be such as
either to present itself in experience or not. If it will present itself,
we need not postulate it in provisional inference since, when it does
appear, we can use it as a premise. If it would never present itself,

our conclusion remains valid as far as possible experience goes, and that is all that Peirce claims. Postulates, he concludes, are cut off either by the experiential or provisional character of inductive inference. An interesting feature of this analysis is that it shows Peirce's concern, if not obsession, to nail everything down, as it were, in securing his point. For, curiously enough, in the preceding paragraph he had made his point in a clearer and less circuitous way in the claim that the conclusions of science are never more than probable and never assert "that anything is precisely true without exception throughout the universe" (6.39). If this is so, then the necessitarian postulate is not in fact required for scientific reasoning. So much, then, for the postulate defense; the next question is whether necessitarianism can be defended by observation.

At this point Peirce introduces a second characterization of the necessitarian position, one he regarded as especially appropriate for the matter of measurement, namely, the claim "that certain continuous quantities have certain exact values" (6.44). The argument here can be telescoped without loss of anything essential. Drawing on his oft-repeated claim that increase in precision of measurement also increases the possibility of errors—bank accounts, he was fond of saying, are more accurate than refined comparisons of masses and lengths—so that in the end one must appeal to the method of least squares for estimating the probable magnitudes of errors in physics, for example, hence, Peirce concludes that any claim that a continuous quantity has an exact value must be based on *something other than observation*. This was the point he wanted to establish.

It is of the utmost importance to notice that Peirce is not arguing in his consideration of observation and measurement that departures from precise accordance with laws of nature are merely a matter of error in observation. His is a stronger position that has to do with the structure of the natural order itself. The central point is this and Peirce will amplify it in the course of the discussion: the observations generally offered as evidence for mechanical causation do show that there is regularity in nature, but they have no bearing on the question of whether the regularity is exact and universal. And here Peirce repeats for emphasis his previous point that the more precise the observations, the more certain there is to be "irregular departures from the law" (6.46). Peirce, in short, is going to argue for an element of chance in the universe. At this juncture, however, his main conclusion is that the doctrine of necessity cannot be established by observation.

Peirce's next target is the attempt to defend any proposition on the ground that we cannot help believing it, or that its not being so is inconceivable. In keeping with his earlier discussion of this approach in "The Fixation of Belief," Peirce called it the *a priori* position. He gives it little credence even when, as he says, an attempt is made to bolster up the position with empirical arguments, the chief of which is that the exact regularity of the world is a natural belief and natural beliefs have often been confirmed by experience. Peirce's response shows how much he is depending upon a distinction between regularity and exactitude. Natural beliefs, he claims, even if they have some foundation in truth, always require correction as is shown by the fact that the earliest formulations of the principles of mechanics were "exceedingly erroneous" (6.50). Claiming that the general approximation to truth in natural beliefs is a case of the general adaptation of genetic products to ends, Peirce points out that the adaptations of nature, marvelous as they often are, are not perfect and hence no natural belief, including the principle of causation, can be *exact*.[1] Care must be exercised here if Peirce is not to be misunderstood; he is not denying what he calls approximate regularity but this, he claims, does not account for diversification, specificity and irregularity—the same laws operate when the die comes up two or six—and hence there must be objective chance in the universe.

The positive view for which Peirce is arguing becomes clearest when he turns to the discussion of sciences that deal with the course of time and there undoubtedly the theory of evolution is uppermost in his mind. His main thesis is that the operation of mechanical law is by itself insufficient to account for the actual diversity to be found in natural systems. Rejecting the idea that whatever arbitrary specifications there are in the universe were introduced "in one dose" at the outset, so that the amount of variety remains constant, Peirce declares, ". . . I . . . think that the diversification, the specification, has been continually taking place" (6.57). He offers five basic reasons for his view. First, he asks us to consider the life of plants, animals and minds, the history of states, institutions and ideas plus the succession of forms described in paleontology,

---

1. It is difficult to believe that this feature of Peirce's argument was uninfluenced by James' long footnote (p. 39, n. 3) about the "whole history of popular beliefs about nature." In this note James maintained that if the ordinary procedure of inferring from the known to the unknown were applied to the "phenomenal materials that spontaneously offer themselves," no one would be led to believe in a general uniformity, but only to the view that law and lawlessness "rule the world in motley alternation."

geology and astronomy, and his conclusion is that "everywhere the main fact is growth and increasing complexity" (6.58). Hence, he claims that there must be an agency in nature that interferes with the reign of mechanical necessity if we are to account for increase in complexity and diversity.

Secondly, Peirce holds that only by admitting pure spontaneity or life as a character of the universe, restrained by law but producing infinitesimal departures from law and, rarely, great departures, can we account for the variety and diversity manifest in it. ". . . mechanical law," he says, "cannot account for this in the least" (6.59). As we know, Peirce was not always consistent in the way he presented his arguments; at times he all but inundates us with illustrations and at others, like the present case, he offers none. But his claim is easily illustrated; suppose we consider as the model of a mechanical system, a machine that produces nails of a specific size from a supply of drawn wire. The operation is such that the system *exactly repeats* itself so that, in principle (I omit the facts of metal fatigue and worn edges which mean that even in such a system exact repetition will not be achieved), the thousandth nail is no different in form from the first. Peirce's point is that if this were an accurate model for the universe, diversity and complexity would be, if not impossible, quite unintelligible; there can be no novelty in exact repetition. The point is even more obvious if we consider that an essential feature of Darwin's theory was the fact of *variation* within the same species, and, without becoming involved in either the matter of these variations being "accidental" or the species problem itself, it is clear that a system of exact repetition under any circumstances can have no place for the novelty signalled by diversification.

Peirce's third reason is something of a melange. First he says that the necessitarian regards irregularity as something we must not attempt to explain, while at the same time he takes laws of nature to be ultimate facts requiring no explanation. Peirce then insists that the hypothesis of spontaneity explains irregularity in general and that, moreover, once necessity has been limited, there is a place for another sort of agency that is operative in the mind in the formation of associations that provide a clue to understanding how the uniformity of nature could have developed. In short, although he does not develop the idea of regularity as the result of the tendency to form habits at this point, Peirce is claiming that his view is capable of explaining the regularity as well as the irregularity in the universe and that, in taking the former as a brute fact, the necessitarian is blocking the road of inquiry. Peirce's mention of another kind of causality in this connection is, of course, reminiscent of Kant's view, but there is a very considerable difference between them. Kant left the universe of mechanical necessity standing and then sought to introduce the dimension of freedom or self-determination as equally real, except that he was unable to connect these two externally related domains in a satisfactory way. Kant was, of course, understandably under the sway of Newton and Darwin was not yet in sight, hence he did not have the advantage enjoyed by Peirce of seeing the development of the life sciences to the point where the inadequacy of the old mechanical necessity was revealed. Like James, Peirce saw that the "block universe" must be shown to be false as a cosmic theory, if freedom and the efficacy of human decisions are to be made intelligible in the actual world.

Peirce's fourth reason is based upon his estimate of the major consequence of the necessitarian view, namely, that, in taking the universe to be a closed system, necessitarianism must regard "the whole action of the mind" (6.61) as one more part of that system. This conception, says Peirce, "enters consciousness under the head of sundries, as a forgotten trifle" (6.61), whereas if the rigid exactitude of causality is overcome by even the least amount, "we gain room to insert mind into our scheme, and to put it into the place where it is needed, into the position which, as the sole self-intelligible thing, it is entitled to occupy, that of the fountain of existence . . ." (6.61).

The fifth reason shows forth Peirce's ironic streak; he tells us that it is the "chief of my reasons" (6.62), but that he can only hint at it, and that it must remain "private" because he is not sure that other mathematicians will find his deductions satisfactory. The hint he gives is that his chance-spontaneity hypothesis has consequences that can be developed in detail with mathematical precision, and that in fact he has already done so with a remarkable amount of agreement with observed facts.

The paper concludes with a few points that help to make his position as a whole more clear. To the charge that chance is unintelligible, Peirce replies that all the unintelligibility is on the necessitarian side because that view remains content with two brute facts—inexplicable, immutable law on the one hand, and equally inexplicable specification and diversity on the other, with no account of their connections. In order to avoid misunderstanding, Peirce points out that he does not propose to account for any phenomenon by adducing chance, but rather, in his own words, "I make use of chance chiefly to make room for a principle of generalization, or tendency to form habits, which I hold has produced all regularities" (6.63). That Peirce had no intention of helping himself to a blank check, as it were, with the idea of chance can be seen in his reference to "chance in the form of a spontaneity which is to some degree regular" (6.63), which in turn suggests that spontaneity may develop itself in a certain and "not in a chance way." Of great interest at present in the midst of the Hegel revival now taking place is that the idea of the development taking place "in a certain way" is said to be represented by the objective logic of Hegel. Peirce leaves the matter open, but he does assert that Hegel's position is as much opposed to the necessitarian view as his own. This is, of course, true because Hegel's "necessity" is certainly no mechanical affair.

Peirce's final statement of what he has done in the essay is important and will figure in the later comparison with James' approach to which we are about to turn. Peirce claims that he has fairly examined "all the important reasons" (6.65) for holding to universal necessity, and that he has "shown their nullity" (6.65). His challenge is, either show me my errors, or give up the doctrine.

In approaching James' essay, I would like first to propose a parallel that I find illuminating and one that, to the best of my knowledge, has not been suggested before. Consider, first, James' principal aim which is to make "two of the necessarily implied corollaries of determinism" (p. 37) clearer than ever before so that the reader can decide for or against that doctrine with a better understanding. Consider, further, his disclaimer at the outset that he has any intention of *proving* that the freedom of the will is true; he hopes only to persuade some in the audience to follow his example of assuming it to be true and acting as if it were. This disclaimer is followed by the further explanation that the truth of the doctrine ought not to be "forced willy nilly down our indifferent throats" (p. 37), something, presumably, that a coercive demonstration would accomplish, but should instead be "freely espoused" by anyone who could also reject it. James, in short, is introducing an element of choice or decision with respect to the theory of freedom itself or, in his well-known words, "our first act of freedom, if we are free, ought in all inward propriety be to affirm that we are free" (pp. 37–8). Thus coercive demonstration is excluded.

James, it appears, regards the issue in question as one that cannot be resolved in purely theoretical or, as he was fond of saying, intellectual, terms, and this brings me to the parallel mentioned above. In the *Critique of Pure Reason*, Kant, after presenting the antinomies, one of which, of course, involves the question of freedom, and declaring that their objective resolution is beyond our theoretical powers, dramatically introduced the idea that reason has an "interest" in the conflicts. Consequently, he proposed to consider "upon which side we should prefer to fight, should we be compelled to make choice between the opposing parties" (A465-B493), all with the understanding that the appeal to our interest is without bearing on the theoretical validity of any arguments. Kant, as is well-known, saw the theses among which is the claim that freedom is a reality, as representing the interest of morals and religion, while the antitheses are all on the side of science. James' writings are filled with this sort of division of interest and he repeatedly called attention, as in the notorious case of his argument against Clifford, for example, to the force of Clifford's antecedent commitment to science in determining his view of what can conscientiously be believed about religious and moral matters.

James' position is very close to Kant's in at least two respects; neither believes that the freedom question can be settled on purely theoretical grounds, and both relocate the issue in another court of appeal that is ruled by interest—James' "passional nature." Kant changes the *venue* to the domain of practical reason and James locates the discussion in the individual consciousness, hence the use of the dilemma, more a rhetorical than a logical device appealing to what the opponent will admit (or maintains) and to his/her subsequent response to the equally undesirable consequences said to follow from the position being maintained. The difference between them, however, must not be overlooked. James, even allowing for the subjectivity implied in the dilemmatic approach, does join the issue for, despite his disclaimer about "coercive demonstration," he has definite arguments to offer, the best being the anomaly manifested in the judgment of regret. Kant, by contrast, does not believe that an "objective" resolution is possible and concentrates on the problems of reconciling reason with itself, so that in the end the question of freedom is consigned to the sphere of practical reason. What strikes me most in this parallel is the streak of skepticism exhibited by both thinkers. Where metaphysical issues are involved, they agree that *knowing* the truth of the matter is beyond our power, and hence that we must be content, in the case of James, with a volitional judgment that makes appeal to our interests and needs,[2] or, in the case of Kant, with a postulate necessary for the practical use of reason.

To return to James' argument, we must note the two suppositions upon which he tells us that his discussion is based; the first is

2. "Now, evidence of an external kind to decide between determinism and indeterminism is, as I intimated a while back, strictly impossible to find" (p. 40).

that in proposing and discussing theories about the world, we do so in order to gain a conception of things that gives us "subjective satisfaction" (p. 38), and the second is that, given two conceptions, the one that appears to us the more rational may legitimately be regarded as the truer one. These suppositions are both heavily dependent on James' earlier essay, "The Sentiment of Rationality," in which he characterized rationality, with respect to both theoretical and practical conceptions of the world, as a sense of fluency of thought and of peace and ease that comes when we move from a state of perplexity to one of rational comprehension. This is what is meant by the "subjective satisfaction" referred to above. His idea is not unlike Peirce's notion of the irritation and hesitation occasioned by doubt being overcome by the attainment of belief. James, as we know, was always concerned to relate belief to the total personality of the believer which is the reason he paid so much attention to the features a belief must have in order to get itself believed. I cannot go into the details, but two examples will help to make his meaning more clear. On the theoretic side, he claims that a conception of the world that fails to do justice to both the fact of singular and discrete things, on the one hand, and of uniformities, unities and continuities, on the other, will not provoke the sentiment of rationality. A sand-heap world like that of Hume fails in this respect no less than the "block universe" James attributed to Royce. On the practical side, he claims that, since the most important feature of a thing is its relations to future consequences, a philosophy must define expectancy with respect to the future and not leave us with the uneasiness that comes from the sense that anything you please may happen next. Again, the appeal is to the capacity of a philosophical view to meet these human demands, and when they are met, that view will be "peacefully accepted by the mind" (p. 15). It should now be obvious how important these and similar considerations[3] will be in James' argument for freedom.

In opening his positive argument, James calls attention to "all the usual arguments on the subject" (p. 39) and claims that they have been encumbered by two highly charged words, "freedom" and "chance." The first, he says, has invariably been used in a eulogistic sense and the second as a term of opprobrium. He proposes to retain *chance* and to dispense with *freedom;* his reason for the choice is quite clear. He believes that old fashioned determinism

3. How seriously James took these human demands into account can be seen from another example. A philosophy, he claims, that does not provide something for the will to struggle against or to strive for, will never get itself believed.

was "hard" and was often identified with fatalism, whereas he takes note of the appearance of a "soft" determinism by which he means some version of the idea that "true" freedom is simply necessity understood. James' target here is no mystery; he is attacking all attempts to interpret freedom as self-determination, largely because he saw that position as not critical enough of determinism and not sympathetic enough to indeterminism. We need not join the issue; it is clear that James wants to defend indeterminism and to attack determinism directly without becoming involved in the intricacies surrounding the long discussion of the nature of freedom. And he was confirmed in his approach by his belief, correct in my view, that it is possible to state the one central issue that sets the two views in direct opposition to each other and thus rules out the possibility of both being true—that issue turns on whether or not there are real possibilities in the order of things, and James draws it by a brief account of what each position claims to be the case.

Determinism, he maintains, is the view that the parts of the universe already laid down absolutely determine what the other parts must be; in his language, "the future has no ambiguous possibilities hidden in its womb" (p. 40), so that the only possible future is the one that has already been fixed for all time. Indeterminism, he says, holds that there is an amount of "loose play" in the parts so that no one of them necessarily determines what the others shall be; there are possibilities in excess of actualities which means that of two alternative, conceivable futures, both may "now be really possible." It is important to notice here that, in support of his claim, James, like Peirce, Whitehead, Bergson and others, appeals to the ultimacy of the actual process of becoming when he says, "the one (alternative) *becomes* impossible when the other excludes it by *becoming* real itself" (p. 41; italics added). Indeterminism, in short, insists on the reality of possibility as a constituent mode of being. Determinism denies this and claims that necessity and impossibility are the only modes of reality, which is to say that a "possibility" not realized was never a possibility at all. Or to put the matter in its more familiar form, what actually happens, on the determinist view, is the only state of affairs that could have happened.[4]

4. James was less circumspect than Peirce and spoke of possibilities "existing" somewhere, while Peirce objected to that way of speaking on the ground that the Nominalist tradition beginning with Ockham eroded the older idea of modes of being and ended with but one mode—existence. The point is that, if possibility is a real mode then possibilities have their own being and there is no need to say that they "exist."

Having quite clearly captured the central issue between the two parties, James goes on to remind us of what he had previously said about the conditions governing the way the matter will actually be decided by thinking individuals. It will not be decided on the basis of facts or any objective, external evidence; what makes us into "possibility" or "anti-possibility" advocates is different conceptions—faiths, he calls them—of what constitutes rationality, and hence we are back to the sentiment of rationality again. But, as before, this arena of discussion is determined by skepticism and an appeal to our lack of knowledge. James envisions a total divorce between fact and possibility—"If we have no other evidence than the evidence of existing facts, the possibility-question must remain a mystery never to be cleared up" (p. 42). This, however, is evidence of James' metaphysical naivete and his captivity to fact despite all his polemics against positivism. Possibility as a mode of reality is a mystery only for those who have but one real mode—existence—understood as present, actual brute fact. The point is, again, that James' appeal to the sentiment of rationality, while not without its own rationality, is a response to a too skeptical estimate on his part of what the nature of the real order of things—and not what conception of that order will give satisfaction to human beings—would tell us about the question we are trying to resolve.

James' essay is a venture in endurance; we are into a third of it before we are told that we are "within sight of our subject" (p. 47) and that largely because he has had to spend so much time defending the sentiment of rationality and exorcizing the very concept of chance he so boldly wanted to maintain. The main point of that excursion is that "chance" is said to mean no more than the claim that whatever happened could have turned out otherwise. This conclusion is by no means nominal, since it is based on the sound claim that, as illustrated by the example of James' return home after his lecture through either Oxford Street or Divinity Avenue, either alternative, *after the fact* would appear just as rational as the other. Suppose, says James, I go through Divinity Avenue, what must the determinists say? That I could not have gone through Oxford Street because that would constitute the "chance" alternative—a terrible gap in nature. Before the choice, however, either street seems an equal possibility, so that if he had happened to take the other route—Oxford Street—the one he actually chose, Divinity Avenue, would then become the "chance" alternative. James' contention is that, so viewed, the "necessary" alternative and its "chance" counterpart would be indistinguishable. Chance is thus admitted and defused of its negative rhetorical force.

After all this preparation of the ground aimed at fostering a positive reception for his views in the minds of the audience, and a repetition of his contention that "from any strictly theoretical point of view, the question is insoluble" (p. 47), James goes on to show what is really the genius of his imagination. When he talked, as he so often did, about the consequences of ideas, he left himself open to misunderstanding. For him, this was no matter of logical implications alone or even of behavior consequent on believing in the ideas involved, but rather of a portrayal in the most concrete terms of what sort of universe one would be living in if this or that conception of it were true. This construal was not primarily dependent on the matter of the actual truth of any conception, but simply on bringing home to the potential believer what it would mean to him or to her to be living in the universe described by the belief in question if it were true. It was in this way that James attempted to show the "consequences" of believing in some general conception of the nature of things. And, for his present argument, that meant presenting the *difference* between what would characterize a world of chance and a deterministic world in the most vivid practical terms.

I trust that it will now be clear how important James thought it was to prepare the soil before he attempted to sow any seeds. He is now ready to present his chief consideration—the judgment of regret—and to ask what are the implications of such judgments if the world of determinism is the true one. The "dilemma" of determinism (more aptly called the dilemma of the *determinist* since the argument must, in the nature of the case, be *ad hominem* in the sense that it appeals to what the opponent holds and to his or her response to the consequences of that belief) has to do with the dialectic resulting from the appearance in a deterministic world of judgments to the effect that it would have been better if something other than what happened had taken place. The dilemma, as you know, has generally been regarded as more of a rhetorical than a logical device, but it suits James' purposes admirably since it enables him to make the determinist *feel* the implications of his position in the form of the two undesirable or unpleasant consequences that James claims follow from the meaning of the judgment of regret. Taking as an example the Brockton murder in which a man brutally did away with his wife because she bored him, James says that the occurrence "is a field for a crop of regrets" and that it represents a "bad moral fit" (p. 48) because we deeply feel that something else would have been better in its place. From the determinist standpoint, however, nothing else could have taken its place from which James concludes that determinism means pessimism and the defining of the universe as a system in which what ought to be is impossible. In the end, he says, we should regret not only the murder, but the entire order that determines it to happen. To avoid this horn of the dilemma, the determinist must totally abandon the judgment of regret, and James is even willing to show how this might be done, namely, by claiming that a universe with a principle of evil in it is better than one without it, so that even cruelty and treachery may in time prove their worth, as long as we do not give way to regret and remorse. James calls this view deterministic optimism.

He is not, however, willing to let the determinist off the hook. What, he asks, are we to say about the status of the judgments of regret as existing facts? If these judgments are to be declared wrong because they lead to the pessimistic universe, then other judgments, say those of approval, ought to take their place, but this is impossible and hence James contends that we are back where we started—the universe is such that what ought to be is impossible. He summarizes this part of the argument as follows:

> Murder and treachery cannot be good without regret being bad;
> regret cannot be good without treachery and murder being bad.
> Both, however, are supposed to have been foredoomed; so something must be fatally unreasonable, absurd, and wrong in the world. It must be a place where either sin or error forms a necessary part. (p. 50)

Here of course, James is assuming that this consequence will be totally unwelcome to the determinist because his world must be one of uncompromising rational necessity. James, always leading his opponents on, asks the question as to whether there is a way of escape from the dilemma. There is such a way, he says, and that is to adopt the viewpoint of subjectivism. I shall not undertake a recounting of the entire discussion; it is too long, in any case, and I have always thought that the argument would have benefited from a less circuitous and repetitive development. Each time I read the paper, I cannot avoid the sense that it ends at least three times! The main points, nevertheless, can be brought out, together with James' conception of the major difficulty facing the three forms of subjectivism he distinguishes and the reason why this inadequacy turns the alternative into an unpleasant choice. The subjectivist thesis is this: what happens in the universe is not as important as what we think or feel about it. Thus the inevitable acts we regret may be good and our error in judging them regretful may also be good if it is the case that the world system has no goal or function other than being a contrivance for "deepening the theoretic consciousness of what goodness and evil in their intrinsic natures are" (p. 51). What counts, to use James' favorite expression, in nature's book, is not the doing but the knowing, and this goal is beyond pessimism and optimism. On this view, evil serves mainly to awaken our understanding of evil, and the error of believing that what happened might have been otherwise serves to make us more acutely aware of what it means for something to be lost without recovery. In making this appeal to the education of consciousness, determinism, according to James, ceases to regard the goods and evils of life in a totally objective way and sees them instead as a means of producing various forms of consciousness in us. This move to subjectivism is said to be the only way in which the determinist can avoid the pessimism that James has already found to be the stumbling block of the necessitarian view.

Since this line of thought was far more relevant in James' time—it was in fact his response to the views of Herbert Spencer, Sir James Stephen and others—than it is in our own as far as the straight argument goes, I shall telescope the discussion in order to bring out James' main point even if there may be at present few determinists still opting for the subjectivism he offers them as a nostrum. His claim is that if we take up subjectivism in a practical way, we find ourselves going down-hill. If there are no duties, James says, good in themselves and to be done regardless of our feeling about them, and if the deepening of our subjective knowledge and feeling is the chief purpose of life, we must in the end find ourselves in the land of the Lotus eaters—a land of sentimentality and sensual enjoyment. This is the other horn of the dilemma and it is supposed to be no less welcome to the determinist than the pessimistic one. Before proceeding to the comparisons between the approaches of Peirce and James promised earlier on, I would like to make but one critical comment on the preceding argument. The argument from the judgment of regret seems to me the strongest part of James' essay, and it is not altogether clear that he needed to burden it so much with the pessimism theme, since it is certainly a serious objection against determinism that an actual fact—in this case judgments of regret of the sort we make all the time—implies something that makes no sense whatever on the determinist view, namely, a reference to what might have been otherwise, together with the claim that something else would have been better than what actually happened. This logico-metaphysical point holds quite independently of pessimism, optimism and all the other isms that may be used to designate general outlooks. James, however, was never satisfied with these "intellectual" arguments; he had to invade and overcome the inner citadel of the opponent's mind, feeling, predilection and temperament by something more than logical considerations. In so doing, he often underestimated the cogency of logical factors, even when put forth by himself. And yet it seems clear that he was quite confident of the "rational" superiority of his defense of indeterminism *vis a vis* the claims of the determinist, even if his avowed intent was to do no more than make the advocate of determinism fully aware of the difficulties inherent in the position so that no easy acceptance of it would be possible.

I would like to add here a word of my own concerning the issue underlying both essays. The key, in my view, to the freedom/determinism problem is found in the matter of possibility as a real, and not merely logical, mode. Ever since Kant's peculiar treatment of the modal categories, there has been a tendency, especially among so-called empiricists, to attempt to get along with but one real mode, namely, existence, while relegating others, possibility, necessity, to a merely logical status. The point is nicely illustrated by Carnap who correlates existence alone with *factual* truth and describes the other modes as L-true, that is, as a function of language. This elevation of existence plays naturally into the hand of the determinist for whom every process can have but one outcome, since there are no real possibilities beyond the necessitated one. The exposure of this dogma, as Peirce and James both saw, is essential for any doctrine of freedom. And, I should add, the recovery of possibility as a real mode frees us from the need to talk about the "existence" of possibilities since existing is not the only mode of the real. Possibilities are just that, possibilities, and to assert their reality is to deny that in any process it is the case that only one thing can happen and also that anything you please can happen. Real possibility excludes both necessitarianism and chaos.

Since comparison requires the specification of the *respects* in which the items are to be compared, let me propose two; the first is the nature of the approach and the form of argument, and the second is the conclusions reached. As we have seen, Peirce tackles the issue head on, so to speak, through a critical examination of the reasons that have been given in support of the doctrine of necessity. He simply takes for granted an intelligent reader who understands the problem and the meaning of the terms in which it is discussed, and expects that the reader will either see and accept the cogency of his arguments, or point out where he has gone astray. Unlike James, Peirce does not involve himself in considering the mind-set of the reader or his or her particular interests and concerns; the argument is meant to carry itself and does not have to awaken any "sentiment of rationality." There is, moreover, no hint in Peirce's treatment of a volitional element in fixing belief such as is evident in James' idea that one must freely espouse the indeterminist position if one accepts it at all. James specifically denies the possibility of a coercive demonstration, the main reason for his use of the dilemma, but this should not lead us to suppose that Peirce was claiming to be offering such a demonstration. Peirce was well aware that, strictly speaking, it is inappropriate to speak of proof except in mathematics and, perhaps, logic, and that with regard to metaphysical issues we can do no more than attend to facts, including relations, laws, ideas, etc., and assess critically the arguments intended to account for them. He was far more sanguine than James in the belief that we have the capacity to proceed in this direct way. James, as we saw, was more skeptical about the "intellectualistic" approach and its power to convince the reader, and I am sure that this attitude was fostered by his uncertainty in the face of metaphysical questions. One has the lingering sense that James believes that we "really" do not know which of any of the philosophical alternatives involved in discussions of freedom or God is true. Hence, the approach through options, volitional judgments and dilemmas whereby the meaning of the alternatives is expressed in terms of the sort of world we would experience and would be living in, if this or that alternative were true. I noted this point earlier in connection with the parallel with Kant. Santayana detected something of this skepticism on James' part and called it "agnosticism"; I would not go that far, but I do believe that James underestimated the force of reason and was too psychologistic in his many declarations that reason comes on the scene only after the decisions based on our "passional nature" have been made. We must not, however, be unfair to James especially in view of the fact that the essay contains much more than the presentation of the dilemma; there are numerous acute analyses and his focusing of the issue between determinism and indeterminism on the reality of possibilities causes the problems to stand out even more clearly than it does in Peirce's paper. I suppose that in the end the contrast in the approach of these two thinkers should not be at all surprising. Peirce made a considerable investment in logic, while James was repeatedly affirming the belief that where logic and life collide, it is so much the worse for logic. Their orientations, moreover, are decisively different; Peirce's is cosmological and ontological, while James' is clearly anthropological. Peirce thinks from a theoretical distance and addresses himself to the rational public; James speaks from within and to the total experience of the individual person. Peirce attempts to dislodge faulty reasoning and errors about the nature of things; James aims at overturning mountains of personal temperament, predilection and prejudice by a curious combination of logical reasoning and psychological strategies. I see no reason, especially in connection with problems like that of freedom, why both approaches may not be legitimate, even if I am inclined to find Peirce's more objective approach the better way of dealing with such issues. James' followers should, of course, say that my use of the term "inclined" here simply exhibits his thesis and indicates my own "sentiment of rationality."

As regards the conclusions reached in the two essays, one must say that they are, while not identical, highly similar. Both reject the deterministic position and both argue for the presence of chance and spontaneity in the universe. James quite obviously spells out the human and experiential meaning of the alternatives far more concretely than Peirce does, or could ever do. Like Kant, at least in the first *Critique,* Peirce is content with claiming that once the necessitarian thesis is overturned, there is room for the restoration of the mind, its ideas and decisions, to their proper place in the scheme of things. While this is no doubt true, it gives little indication of what freedom means in concrete terms or anything to compare with the richness of James' vivid portrayal of the human situation, or, more specifically, the situation of the individual who is trying to decide for or against the deterministic universe. Why not have both approaches? Each, in my view, is philosophically sound while embodying different virtues. Moreover, when two philosophers with such divergent backgrounds agree on a very important issue, is that not some sign of the presence of truth? I believe it is, flying in the face of our present skeptical and distrustful tendency to believe that if any two philosophers agree, they must both be wrong!

4

Radical Empiricism

"Radical Empiricism" was read at a Meeting of the Aristotelian Society in London in March of 1965. That is indeed a long time ago, but I am retaining the paper for two reasons. First, this important part of James's thought has not been given the attention it deserves, possibly because of some conflicting statements James made about its relation to his Pragmatism. Secondly, the occasion presented a unique opportunity to discuss James's thought with British philosophers most of whom were acquainted with James only through the criticism of Russell who dubbed James's position "Transatlantic Truth." They were much surprised to learn that James said he was following Hume, except that Hume had not gone far enough in his empiricism; Hume, James says, should have gone on to discover that connections and transitions are as much a part of experience as terms. That is, of course, what makes experience "radical" for James. "Radical Empiricism" appeared in the Proceedings of the Aristotelian Society, *vol. 65 (1965), pp. 205–18. The Aristotelian Society, 1965. Reprinted by courtesy of the Editor.*

The appeal to experience in philosophical thought is obviously not a novelty. From Aristotle's recognition of the claims of *empeiria*, through Hume's rejection of every thesis that sense experience supposedly cannot support, to the demands of modern logical empiricism no less than those of recent phenomenology and philosophies of pure experience, the appeal to experience has been consistently invoked as a criterion by which to estimate the validity of our rational constructions. The ubiquity of this appeal may lead one to suppose that experience represents a clear, readily available and inexhaustible mass of *data* held in common by all men and universally acknowledged as a touchstone for judging all claims to truth. Unhappily, this is not so. The many different philosophical outlooks in which the appeal to experience has figured suggest at once that experience has not been understood by all of them in the same fashion. The fact is, as the tradition of modern critical philosophy has shown, that the appeal to experience, though it always involves some invitation to return to a consideration of what actually happens in everyone's experience, has invariably been an appeal to experience *interpreted* in accordance with a principle or with some differential way of approaching what we find or encounter. And by experience interpreted we do not mean merely that there are different ways of describing or taking one and the same item encountered such as, for example, where I say that a certain figure looks like a rabbit and you say that it appears to be a duck. The interpretation involved is both wider and deeper; it embraces a theory of experience *überhaupt,* that is to say, the specification of a principle or principles (whether quite explicitly expressed or left in implicit form) in accordance with which a decision can be made as to what is to count as an experience. Aristotle, Russell, James and Dewey, for example, incorporated in their respective philosophical schemes an appeal to experience as a criterion, but it is clear from their views that the general nature of experience, how much and what it can contain, differs from one position to another. Even if the four schemes mentioned were to be lumped together as empirical philosophies standing opposed to an absolute rationalism such as that of Leibniz, the fact would still remain, despite the common denominator, that these empirical philosophies do not permit us to understand experience in the same way. From this fact it is reasonable to conclude that the appeal to experience is never naïve and that the theory of experience involved in every such appeal already contains within itself the answer to many philosophical questions.

The purpose of this chapter is to direct attention to one of these empirical philosophies, that of radical empiricism as proposed by William James. In view of the importance at present of several different philosophical approaches that share the aim of having us confront experience afresh, of asking us to take, as it were, a second look at the facts, it will prove helpful to consider several theses advanced by James in the elaboration of what he called radical empiricism. James's attempt has been much misunderstood in large measure because of the widespread failure to grasp the double-barreled character of the critiques made against the classical empiricism of Hume and John Stuart Mill. From one side we must take note of the stream of rationalistic idealism stemming from Kant and Hegel according to which the empiricism of atomic fact and psychological principles of association was deemed inadequate and must be supplemented by an *a priori* reason standing beyond experience. On this view necessary principles of reason replace habit and custom as embodied in the principles of association, while the atomic *data* are replaced by a coherent system of more or less necessary truth. Less well known than the foregoing criticism is the attack launched by James in his radical empiricism; according to this view the account of experience advanced by Hume and Mill is also found to be inadequate, but not because experience needs to be supplemented by a transcendent reason; on the contrary, James's charge is that classical empiricism was not empirical enough and failed to note all that experience contains.

For James, experience is far richer than the many conceptual substitutes that were supposed to be its ultimate constituents, and, when sufficiently analysed, experience is seen to be the source of all the conjunctive relations that were excluded from experience by classical empiricism and then had to be introduced from various extra-experiential sources. Radical empiricism in its simplest formulation is the thesis that experience contains conjunctive relations of various grades of intimacy and externality and not only terms disjoined and separated. Experience, in short, contains transitions and tendencies; it is not exhausted by atomic elements. Nouns and adjectives are not the only names for the contents of experience; prepositions, copulas and conjunctions are also required if we are to have a faithful analysis of all that experience delivers. This second line of criticism, embracing the claim that the inadequacies of classical empiricism can be corrected by a more subtle empiricism, by a fresh analysis of experience as it actually comes to us, has been unduly neglected. I propose to consider briefly two claims of radical empiricism advanced by James—the theory of pure experience and the theory of experience as containing conjunctive relations— together with one critical question: Can *all* relations be developed from pure experience or do some retain an *a priori* status?

Before proceeding, a self-critical word is in order. It may seem strange to introduce a position that proposes to begin with experience rather than with language. James, of course, developed his thought before the "linguistic turn" came to dominate philosophy and before it came to be believed that the analysis of language is the only valid avenue of approach to philosophical problems. Moreover, it is clear that, were he writing to-day, James would have been on the side of those of us who believe that language is too abstract to be *the* starting-point for philosophy. Radical empiricism, despite its non-linguistic orientation, has a peculiar relevance for the current philosophical situation. That relevance can be made clear by citing two facts about contemporary philosophy.

First, whereas the analytic philosophy of the 1930s and 1940s was rooted in an uncritical acceptance of the empiricism of Hume and Mill, current analytic philosophy appears to be informed by a broader conception of experience evidenced in the concern for many uses of language as expressive of the plural nature of experience. Radical empiricism likewise insists on that plurality within experience. Second, and more important, is the fact that contemporary analysis, in some of its forms at least, requires us to take a fresh look at experience in order to discover what our terms mean, whether some detail has been overlooked, whether we have succeeded in expressing accurately all that we find or encounter. As I interpret some of the statements of Wittgenstein, I find an undeniable appeal to experience in the sense advocated by radical empiricism. We are asked by him to return to actual situations—involving both saying and doing—in order to locate what James called the "cash value" of our concepts and verbal expressions. When, for example, Wittgenstein says: "Ask yourself: What does it mean to *believe* Goldbach's theorem? What does this belief consist in . . .?" and then goes on to consider whether it is a "particular colouring of our thoughts," *etc.,* he is illustrating the same return to experience as a court of appeal that James recommended. He even arrives, I may add, at James's conclusion, namely, that the answer to the question of the nature of the belief will be found in its consequences. But that is not the point of the present discussion. Or again, the account Wittgenstein gives of "familiarity" and of the "naturalness" ingredient in certain experiences, furnishes a second example.[1] The answer lies in the analysis of experiences had, of situations encountered, of expressions uttered on these occasions. Although Wittgenstein approached the topic with more emphasis upon what is *said* in the appropriate cases than James might have done, the point in common between them remains—each demands that we start with the actual trait, feeling, idea, belief in question and base our analysis entirely on what is encountered.

It might be said that James and Wittgenstein differ in that the latter stressed "doing philosophy" or the carrying out of singular analyses, whereas James was more interested in developing a general theory of experience. It is true that James did develop a general theory, but this did not prevent him from making many detailed analyses of particular experiences. Wittgenstein, on the other hand, did not confine himself to particular analyses; his writings are filled with statements expressing a general theory of the enterprise in which he was engaged. We can readily distinguish between Wittgenstein's singular philosophical analyses of, for example, what we are to understand by the difference between *saying* words and *meaning* them,[2] and his general statements about philosophy and

1. *Philosophical Investigations,* trans. G. E. M. Anscombe, Oxford, 1953, 596
2. Ibid., 507

the nature of the philosophical enterprise, such as "In philosophy we do not draw conclusions".[3]

I

The central thesis of the theory of pure experience is that experience as it comes directly has no clear duality in it such as that traditionally described by the distinction between consciousness and content, thought, and thing. After identifying "pure experience" with the "instant field of the present" (*Essays in Radical Empiricism*, 23, New York, 1912; hereafter, *ERE*), James goes on to say that such experience is only virtually either subject or object. Pure experience has no general nature of its own. It is a pure *that*, a virtual somewhat, to be sure, but unknown as this specific *what* until it is "taken", talked about, analysed, identified, classified and categorised. The duality of subjects and objects is not found in experience as pure; these and other categories come into play when we attend to what it is that we have experienced. James expresses the point in his demand that we take the experience of change at face value:

> to take it at face value means first of all to take it just as we feel it, and not to confuse ourselves with abstract talk *about* it, involving words that drive us to invent secondary conceptions in order to neutralize their suggestions and to make our actual experience again seem rationally possible. (*ERE*, 48–9.)

Pure experience is prior to distinction of types and levels. The separation, says James, "into consciousness and content comes . . . by way of addition" (*ERE*, 9) and is not primitive. The separation is a result of analysis; since the duality is not guaranteed from within direct experience, the way is open for more than one interpretation of what the duality signifies. James's proposal is not, as has sometimes been thought, to eliminate the distinction between thought and thing by returning to an undifferentiated experience or feeling, but to reinterpret the traditional subject/object distinction in terms of contexts and functions. If, for example, I sit in a room reading a book it is allowable to regard the book as a complex physical thing cut out from, but sustaining many relations with, other things in the surrounding world, at the same time that I perceive the self-same book as a series of experiences in my own

3. Ibid., 599

personal history. James's proposal is to regard this perceptual situation as the intersection of two processes in which an identical item figures twice over, just as in the case of two intersecting lines in a plane where there is an identical point that is on each line. On the one hand, there is the long and complex series of operations that terminates in the book being in my hand in that room at a given time; this series comprises the histories of the house, the room, the book and myself as a person in the world. On the other hand, there is the shorter series of events that go to make up my conscious history terminating in my perception of the book on just that occasion. Because of the intersection or conjunction of the two series, the book figures in two contexts at once and functions differently in each without ceasing to be the same book. In one context it is "my field of consciousness" and in the other it is "the room in which I sit reading the book". These contexts are identifiable; we have but to indicate the relation in which the items within them stand to each other. It is possible to consider the book either from the standpoint of its perception or its physical presence in my hand.

My perception of the book is an event which had as predecessors in the series my interest in and desire to pursue the topic forming the subject matter of the book and the perception is succeeded by recollections, deductions, criticisms, *etc.*, that do not figure in the series of events making up the other context, that of the house and the room in which I was sitting. In the latter case, the presence of the book in the room was preceded by its having been delivered in a parcel, and it may be succeeded in time by its sale to a second-hand book dealer. These related items in turn do not figure in the field of consciousness context.

Experience, to use a favourite expression of James's, is "double-barrelled"; it can legitimately be taken as functioning in more than one context depending on the items with which it is found together and the relations obtaining. In one context, experience is taken as states of mind and we come to know this context through the types of relation appropriate to the items in the process. In the example, the relations holding between the book and the room will all be more external than those obtaining between the states of mind that arise as I read the book. In another context, experience is taken as content, exhibiting the appropriate space, time and causal relationships. The important point is that direct experience does not possess the duality of consciousness and content; the distinction results from the ways in which experience can be taken.

II

It is evident that radical empiricism depends heavily on the reality of relations; without them experience remains a bare *that* not "taken" at all but left merely as an undifferentiated whole of feeling. "Taking" means relating an item of pure experience to its associates and describing it in terms of "whats" or contents, the meaning or "cash-value" of which is furnished by future experiences that are consequences or termini of a process of analysis and inquiry. The idea of taking as relating introduces an idea that is at the heart of the radical empiricist conception. James maintained that conjunctive relations are found in experience and that consequently they do not need to be imposed by the knower on an otherwise atomic collection of empirical *data*. Here James both follows and departs from Hume. James says of his own position that "it is essentially a mosaic philosophy, a philosophy of plural facts, like that of Hume and his descendants" (*ERE*, 42). On the other hand, James could not accept Hume's main thesis that "all our distinct perceptions are distinct existences . . . the mind never perceives any real connexion among distinct existences".[4] According to James this principle is at fault because, while it appears to be no more than a transcript of what experience warrants, it actually means a selective or differential treatment of experience in which some items are given priority over others. The principle as stated provides for disjunctions but not for conjunctive relations and, as such, it omits items directly experienced. The blue colour of the book is found *with* the cover of the book and the cover *with* the pages and the total conjunction of the items in the physical context is found *with* the room at that time and place and *with* the reader as well. Items of experience are found *with* other items and not only as disjoined.[5] To emphasize only the disjunctions—"distinct existences"—is to reduce experience to terms such as nouns and adjectives while neglecting the connections and transitions expressed in other parts of speech. In response to this reduction, James invites us to return to experience as directly had; he finds no ground in experience for excluding conjunctive relations; on the

---

4. Hume, *A Treatise of Human Nature*, Selby-Bigge ed., Oxford, 1896, Appendix 636.
5. This does not mean that James regarded all conjunctive relations as internal; his main concern was for the recognition of the presence of relations of the conjunctive sort in experience. Many of these relations he regarded as quite external.

contrary, no item of experience is ever found absolutely distinct and separate, but always with various associates. In a most ambitious statement of his thesis, James writes:

> Prepositions, copulas, and conjunctions, "is," "isn't," "then," "before," "in," "on," "beside," "between," "next," "like," "unlike," "as," "but," flower out of the stream of pure experience, the stream of concretes or the sensational stream, as naturally as nouns and adjectives do, and they melt into it again as fluidly when we apply them to a new portion of the stream. (*ERE*, 95.)

Whether, of course, *all* relations do actually "flower" from pure experience, is a question that remains to be decided.

James was not always careful in the formulation of his position and there is some ambiguity in the term "conjunctive relation." Sometimes this expression means "continuity" and the direct experience of transition from state to state; at other times it means "being with" without further qualification. Direct experience contains both the plurality of distinct items—disjunctions—and the unity and continuity of items—conjunctions. Radical empiricism concentrates on the latter because of their previous neglect, but it acknowledges both features as equally present. James expresses the basic sense of conjunctive relation by the term "with," but it is well to note that this term is *not* coextensive in meaning with the term "and". "With" means an actual conjunction (or possible conjunction based on past experience and reasonable expectation), whereas "and" is taken to mean a purely logical connective—the most external of all connectives, since in the schema "*A* and *B*" the connective does not prevent any term from replacing the variables. "And" creates a universe of discourse and nothing more. "With", on the other hand, expresses the fact of actual associates in experience and implies a denial that atomic items of experience are ever found.

The final test of James's thesis would involve carrying out his programme for all relations, but, since such an undertaking is obviously out of the question, we must concentrate attention on one relation—continuity or continuous transition. For it is by means of this relation that James proposes to interpret the cognitive relation and at the same time avoid the bifurcation of things into two distinct worlds of knower and known.

The model for the experience of continuity is found in the passage of one experience into another within the serial history of the same self. When, for example, we set a goal for ourselves, map out the particular steps through which it is to be achieved, and contemplate the satisfaction of the result, we are aware of a series of ideas and feelings that are at once distinguished from each other and pass into each other in a well ordered way. Two different selves may row together in a boat and thus have numerous items of experience in common in the physical context and yet each is aware (or is capable of becoming aware by attending to the matter) that his own experiences pass into each other with a continuity not found when either attempts to pass from one of his own experiences to an experience had by the other. It is not that the transition is impossible; on the contrary, we all have some knowledge of each other's experiences (which is sometimes more reliable than supposed knowledge of our own experience), but we must gain this indirectly through a conceptual process, involving language, symbols and signs and in doing so we are aware of a discontinuity. My experiences are not directly felt to pass into yours as my own are felt to pass into each other. For James the felt continuity and the sense of passing from one of my experiences to another of my experiences without encountering the sense of a gap such as I find when I seek to pass from one of my experiences to one of yours, represents the "original" of continuity and of sameness. Neither relation is grasped as a static state or simple content; its cash value in experience is just the awareness of the *passing*. Participles play a major role in the analysis of experience.

James's attempt to construe the cognitive relation in terms of the conjunctive relation is at once bold and instructive. On the theory of radical empiricism, the relation between knower and known is understood, not in terms of some ready made theory of knowledge, but rather by returning to what we actually find when we entertain the idea of something and regard that idea as furnishing us with knowledge of the thing in question. Knowledge is a relation that holds between two experiences at the point where it is legitimate to speak of one experience knowing the other. We must see how the conjunctive relation or the experience of continuity makes cognition intelligible.

Let us begin with an idea that purports to refer to or be about an item of experience. The idea may be an image that is more or less adequate in the sense of resembling its object or it may be no more than a word directing interest and attention to an identifiable region of experience. Whatever the form assumed by the sign or token, it must serve to tell us what object we "had in mind" at the outset and in what way the object is qualified. It is James's contention that the knowing function of the idea, image, *etc.*, is *not* intrinsic to its own constitution, depending on its vividness or high degree of resemblance to the object, but rather that the knowing function is external to the bit of experience that serves as the sign and consists instead in certain relations that hold between it and another bit of experience that is the aim or goal of the knowing process. It is impossible to determine by any insight or immediate intuition that any initial bit of experience taken as a sign knows or cognizes anything; therefore, we must pass beyond the immediate character of the sign and look for some indication of where it may lead. In short, the idea or sign with which the cognitive process begins must have consequences in the sense that it can function as an indicator or map leading us to the object that it means. If, moreover, the sign in question expresses what is true, it will lead us through a series of experiences to its intended object. The veridical idea passes by a series of experienced transitions from an intention to an intention fulfilled. When the process is completed and the experience intended becomes an actual experience, we may speak of the sign or token as an experience that knows another experience.

According to James, we have no insight into any cognitive relation other than the one in which we successfully pass, without discontinuity or disappointment, from the intended object to the bit of experience that is the object intended. The strength of James's account lies in its criticism of the view that an idea or proposition can be known to be true merely by intuitive inspection. If such inspection ever fails, as it obviously does, then we must resort to a critical process that takes us beyond the sign or bit of experience that is to serve as a token. Such a critical process is one in which we seek the consequences of the original sign. A knowledge claim must always have a warrant to the effect that the original sign intends and expresses something about the intended object that can be found in the object if we follow where the sign leads. The process taking us beyond the initial idea is the process of critical testing; from the outcome of this process only can we learn whether the intention was fulfilled or disappointed. The cognitive move is always from intention to outcome; truth means intention fulfilled and error is intention disappointed.

Such is the generally pragmatic fashion in which radical empiricism deals with the cognitive relation. But the question that remains is this: even if we allow that James has correctly expressed the general shape of the cognitive situation, is it the case that all relations involved in the knowledge process and in experience generally can be derived from pure experience without appeal to a synthetic or constructive activity on the part of the one who knows? For it may be the case that *some* relations—space, time and continuity—were illegitimately excluded from experience by classical empiricism without it also being the case that *every* relation can be found to be present in some direct or felt experience. In short, may it not be that radical empiricism is correct in its criticism of Humean empiricism without also being correct in the claim that all relations can be accounted for by the appeal to direct experience?

III

The fact is, and James was himself aware of the difficulty in the discussion of the *a priori* found in the final chapter of his *Principles of Psychology*, radical empiricism is unable to account for triadic relations on the basis of pure experience. These are relations in which two distinct terms *A* and *B* are related to each other in virtue of the fact that each is in turn related to the same third term *C*. Schematically this relation is expressed in conditional form, if *A* R *C* and *B* R *C,* then *A* R *B*. Now it is one of the merits of James's approach that he never sought to avoid or gloss over difficulties in his position. Despite his sanguine confidence in the philosophy of pure experience and in the view that the stream of thought contains within itself all the relations that were excluded by classical empiricism, he still did not overlook the problem of how to obtain the relations ingredient in what he called the pure sciences—logic and mathematics—from experience as an order of items presented to the mind from without. James was troubled by the logical operation of comparison and the expression of comparative judgments. Borrowing a figure from Plato's *Meno,* James began to consider the possibility that our mental apparatus might contain, in addition to the contents derived from pure experience, certain other elements, "born within the house," and thus not read off from an examination of the stream of thought. James had his own physiological and psychological way of explaining the presence of elements that are somehow ingredient in experience and yet are not directly to be found in the stream of thought, as the conjunctive relations were taken to be. I propose to offer a brief but different line of argument to support the conclusion that an analytic act of comparison—whether of an elementary or more complex sort—requires a synthetic or constructive activity involving three-termed relations that are not "given" or felt as such in the stream of experience.

The first point is that when we have to compare two items we are unable to do so directly without the introduction of a mediating item or term. We do not compare two items merely by giving an exhaustive description of each.[6] This point is readily seen if we

6. Comparison is treated at greater length in chapter 9.

consider the usual response to an examination question in which the task is to compare, for example, the poetic art of Wordsworth with that of Keats. The untrained mind almost invariably lists the information it contains about one poet along with the information it contains about the other, hoping that somehow a comparison will result. But it is clear that no comparison takes place until there have been introduced relevant and specifiable *respects* or third terms to which each of the extreme terms can be intelligibly related. In the example, the poetic art of the two poets can be significantly compared only in so far as we delineate precise respects—treatment of emotional tone, vividness of imagery, attention to detail, *etc.*, that function as common third terms. The success of our final statement about the two poets depends upon the skill with which we are able to relate each in turn, not immediately to each other, but to the relevant respects or third terms.

If we attend to the nature of these third terms we can see that they do not present themselves as a part of the felt stream of thought after the fashion of the conjunctive relations such as "with," "next" and "between" which James finds in his pure experience. It is difficult to know what item in the stream of experience would be the "original" for a relevant third term establishing a triadic relation required for comparison. Such a term could not be merely one item besides others in a stream of singular terms. On the contrary, a significant third term required for comparison is an abstract term, capable of generalization and its *relevant* introduction into an act of comparison requires some ingenuity. That is to say that before we can make significant comparisons, we must ourselves find relevant third terms that will prove both fruitful and illuminating. From a logical standpoint this remains true even if we take simpler examples involving no more than colour or shape. It might be thought that when we perceive a brown object and a blue one in close proximity and say that they differ, we are merely *seeing* a fact that is expressed in a comparative judgment. But this is not the case; the relevant respect of colour has already been selected and applied and the fact that we make such judgments without being aware of a complex set of logical apparatus does not alter the need for the third term. If we could not abstract and attend to such third terms no comparisons would be possible. The respect in question in a given case may be more or less clearly in mind, and we may make some comparisons so easily or habitually that they appear to be an immediate reading off of the result. Logically, however, the third term is always presupposed and to find and apply it requires, especially in the case of complex and subtle comparisons, a constructive act amounting in many cases to ingenuity. It is difficult to see how such third terms functioning in triadic relations can be said to be contained in the stream of pure experience.

The upshot of the foregoing discussion may be stated as follows: the radical empiricist approach is a needed corrective both for an empiricism that would reduce experience to terms and qualities devoid of all connexions and transitions, and for a rationalism that refuses to return to experience again once it has established a conceptual system. But the position is inadequate because the stream of experience does not contain all of the concepts and relations in terms of which it is to be understood and interpreted. Without the so-called "house born" concepts and logical operations involving abstract and generalizable terms there could be no systematic interpretation or explanation of experience. The stream of experience is neither self-organizing nor self-interpreting. A world of pure experience consistently adhered to as a philosophical doctrine would lead, if not to a world of pure nonsense, at least to one of unreason.

James seems to have overlooked the possibility that the view according to which there is, in the stream of direct experience, an "original" for every term in discourse, is mistaken. Although his empiricism is richer, and therefore more faithful in reporting the full range of what we actually find, James never seems to have broken away from some sort of copy-correspondence theory. Despite his own official attacks on the copy theory of knowing, he seems to have assumed something like it himself. Hence he is forced to find counterparts in the stream of experience for every term. The main difficulty is that not every concept employed in the description, interpretation or explanation of the stream of experience is related to the stream in precisely the same way. Some concepts are, as has been suggested, at the "edge" of a system and confront the stream more directly; other concepts—philosophical concepts, value concepts, scientific concepts—are at what might be called "logical distance" from the stream and, while their interpretative value may show that they are ingredient in or relevant for the interpretation of experience, we cannot find counterparts for them as we can for the concepts at the "edge".

Try as we will, we do not escape the problem of the *a priori*, the problem, in Kant's language, of the concepts that begin with experience, *i.e.*, have empirical meaning, but do not arise out of experience in the sense that we can find obvious "originals" for them in the stream of direct experience. This problem remains, but it has been obscured often enough by the confusion of the *a priori* with the "analytic" or the so-called logically true or significant based on logical considerations alone. The problem of the *a priori* is the problem of concepts that have empirical meaning and are thus not subject to treatment on the basis of logical considerations alone, and yet these concepts are not "empirical" in the sense that the stream of experience has them as "given" or there to be read off. That the problem is an important one can be seen from the fact that the concepts in question form the majority of those required in both science and philosophy. The position known as radical empiricism acknowledged the importance of these concepts, but was unable to give a convincing account of their status.

5

The Reflexive Turn, the Linguistic Turn, and the Pragmatic Outcome

"The Reflexive Turn, the Linguistic Turn, and the Pragmatic Outcome" is essentially a critique of critical philosophy or the idea that before we involve ourselves with philosophical questions and issues we must first make an examination of our intellectual equipment in order to determine whether it is adequate to the task. In short, critical philosophy—what Hegel called knowing before you know—whether in the initial concern for the nature of knowledge to be found in Locke and Kant or in the later interest in setting our logic and language in order represented by Quine and others, is really asking whether a certain kind of philosophy is possible at all. *The underlying concern is the problem of* disagreement *among philosophers—we should not forget that it was the failure of Locke and his friends to come to an agreement about a philosophical issue that led him to set about examining our understanding to see if it is capable of dealing with the sort of issue they were discussing—and one way of coping with that was to reduce philosophy to what it was thought could be agreed upon, namely logic and certain prescriptions about the use of language. One result was the* postponement *of discussion of first-order philosophical questions on the supposition that these could be taken up again after we had set the houses of logic and language in order. Unfortunately, as I point out, disagreements broke out once again at the meta level and we were back at the beginning. Dewey attacked the entire enterprise of what he called the "epistemology industry" and pointed the way to new beginnings. It is this development I have in mind when I use the expression "the Pragmatic outcome." "The Reflexive Turn, the Linguistic Turn, and the Pragmatic Outcome" appeared in* The Monist *53, no. 4 (1969), pp 588– 605. Copyright © 1969,* The Monist, *La Salle, Illinois 61301. Reprinted with permission.*

One of the important philosophical advantages stemming from study of the historical development of philosophical movements and traditions is the insight that comes from observing the logical out-working of a set of ideas over a period of time that far exceeds the lifetime of any individual thinker. An Aristotle or a Hegel may develop a philosophical mode of thought in an almost unbelievably comprehensive way, but no individual can grasp all the implications and ramifications of his philosophical vision, no matter how monumental his powers may be. Many individuals, however, working over many years within the same framework of ideas can accomplish what no one of them alone could achieve. It is often said that philosophy is not an experimental science, and, in an obvious sense, this is true. But it is not entirely true. We can view the history of a tradition like Platonism, for example, or Augustinianism, as a vast experiment made by many thinkers with a set of ideas in which each thinker, building on what has gone before, seeks to develop further the basic premises of the position, proposing new logical alternatives, correcting errors, meeting objections, discovering further implications, and consolidating the results. In the case of a profound tradition, nothing less than this extended historical dialectic of ideas suffices to make plain what the basic position implies. Moreover, since climates of opinion change, the proponents of a given view will find that, in the course of time, new opponents appear, raising questions and posing problems that could not easily have been envisaged by the thinker who started the tradition. Sometimes these objections prove fatal and the tradition comes to an end; sometimes the objections are successfully overcome and the position finds new life and a more viable form of expression. The history of a tradition, therefore, is an indispensable resource for philosophical understanding.

The development of modern critical philosophy in its many forms furnishes an excellent illustration of what is to be learned from tracing the internal logical pattern of a mode of thought over an extended period of time. The attempt to deal with the problem of disagreement among philosophers and to determine what questions can or cannot be answered in a way that will command general assent, has been one of the persistent philosophical enterprises of the past two centuries. At present we are in a position to survey the record of this attempt and it is invaluable; in understanding the logical development it represents, we can better comprehend the nature of critical philosophy, the issues it raises, the assumptions it makes, and the further problems occasioned by the reappearance of disagreement within the enterprise of critical philosophy itself.

Whatever position one may hold philosophically, either with regard to its method, purpose, or substantive conclusions, no one attempting to think philosophically at the present time can ignore the fact that for some decades now a considerable portion of the energy of philosophers has been devoted to the discussion of philosophy itself, its method, its tasks, its utility (or lack thereof), and especially its relation to, or distinction from, natural science. This development is, of course, not without some foundation in the character of the philosophical enterprise itself. The fact is that philosophy as a reflective activity is always double-barreled in the sense that what philosophy is, and purports to do, are questions that constantly accompany direct inquiry into substantive philosophical issues. Moreover, there is implicit in every attempt to raise, and resolve first-order questions such as the problem of human freedom, the correct account to be given of causation, or the theory of the self, some conception of the nature and proper business of philosophy. For a variety of reasons, however, the self-reflexive question about philosophy has for a long time had the upper hand; fruitful discussion of issues, hitherto regarded as first-order questions, has often been thwarted or at least postponed by consideration of the reflexive question. The situation, moreover, has been further complicated by the fact that disagreement concerning the proper answer to the reflexive question itself has led once again to the formation of different and opposed schools of thought which tend to become so completely self-contained that communication is greatly curtailed and is, in some cases, almost entirely at an end.

At the outset, I admit to having what might be called a practical concern about this state of affairs, largely because I believe in the importance of philosophy and the contribution which it can make to the understanding of all aspects of contemporary life and culture, and to the resolution of current perplexities. While it is *not* the aim of this essay to dwell primarily on the consequences for the present and future of philosophy which follow from its continued uncertain condition, I want nevertheless to focus my practical concern briefly by pointing out several of these consequences in the hope that their detrimental aspect will furnish some incentive for attempting to improve the situation.

There are at least three consequences, most evident in the contemporary academic picture, which result from our continued uncertainty concerning the nature of philosophy and what it can do. *First,* there is the *internalized tendency* which shows itself at two points: (1) the repeated discussion among philosophers about what they are supposed to do as philosophers, and the consequent sense of needing some form of justification; and (2) the discussion by philosophers almost exclusively of what other philosophers have said or written, as if philosophical issues were never raised by reflection on or analysis of the features and traits of actual situations and events, but depended entirely for their being on the occasion when some philosophers actually had the temerity to advance some specifically philosophical theses so as to provide their colleagues with legitimate subject matter! *Second,* the preoccupation of many philosophers with their own occupational therapy has frequently led to a loss of both community and communication with those working in other fields of inquiry both within the academic community and elsewhere. This loss greatly reduces the chances of learning from these inquiries and of influencing, in philosophical directions, the thinking going on in these fields. *Third,* the failure of philosophers to deal more *directly* with philosophical questions and especially with critical appraisal of alternative solutions, or to communicate their results more effectively to nonphilosophers when they do deal with these questions, has helped to produce on the contemporary scene a battery of "amateur" philosophers who take up essentially philosophical questions without possessing the requisite knowledge or the discipline to deal with them properly. A few illustrations well known to all of us will help to clarify the point. The field of English literature today contains a great many "literary critics" who are essentially disguised philosophers attempting to answer some of the questions trained philosophers often are inclined to ignore; many history departments are overflowing with "intellectual historians" who are struggling with philosophical topics usually without the necessary equipment to interpret them properly. And most striking of all, while many philosophers continue to look with suspicion on so-called traditional philosophical problems in an attempt to find a way for philosophy which will bring it more in accord with science, a considerable number of scientists and others properly tarred with scientific connections, have taken on the role of speculative philosophers and are telling all of us the truth about life, about personal knowledge, and about the place of values in a world of science. I can only suppose that such a paradoxical development is in part as least an outcome of the failure of philosophers to deal effectively with the issues to which these amateurs are addressing themselves.

On the assumption that the foregoing brief description of the present situation reveals a state of affairs for philosophy which is very far indeed from ideal, I set for myself the task of seeking to understand, *first,* how philosophy managed to get into its present state, and *second,* what hopeful signs there may be on the current scene which will point the way to a more salutary future for the philosophical enterprise. In order to keep the course of this discussion as clear as possible, let me first signal the two turns in the development of modern philosophy which I regard as having been decisive in determining our present situation, and second, let me anticipate the conclusion at which I arrive in interpreting certain trends in current philosophical discussion. The first of the two turns, I call by the name, "reflexive turn" marking the start of critical philosophy, and it is illustrated jointly, although in quite different ways, by Locke and by Kant; this turn is characterized first by the delineation of certain questions to which philosophers were said to be incapable of giving answers that commanded agreement, and secondly by a consequent shift from the discussion of these questions as such to a different sort of discussion, one, namely, in which the inquiry concerns the nature, competence, and scope of our human apparatus for treating questions of the logical type that occasioned the initial disagreement. Implicit in the critical or reflexive attempts by Locke and Kant to carry out the analysis and evaluation of our cognitive capacities, were several assumptions, one of which at least proved absolutely fundamental. It seems paradoxical when stated, although many philosophers since have continued to make that assumption and only recently has it come to be questioned by those who would profit most from questioning it. That assumption is that critical philosophy takes place on a special level of its own and that it can be carried out in a "neutral" or nondifferential way that keeps it from taking sides with regard to substantive philosophical theses. Although the philosophers of the reflexive turn concluded that there are strict limits to the competent and legitimate employment of understanding in reason, and to the scope of human cognition, they did not apply these strictures to the course of critical reflection itself, but believed instead that we can attain a neutral critical standpoint, so that when we are discussing our competence to answer certain questions, we somehow stand beyond the limitations that this very same discussion claims are in force when we seek to answer directly the questions which set off the inquiry in the first instance.

The second turn in modern philosophy, now identified as the "linguistic turn," though by no means identical with its predecessor in aim or method, nevertheless has continued the enterprise of critical philosophy by addressing itself to the problem of philosophical disagreement with the basic proposal that we resolve that problem by analyzing not objects or events, but language and its use. Many philosophers of the linguistic turn have continued to hold the view that critical philosophy can be carried out in a "neutral" way and that it is possible to conduct analyses which do no more than clarify, explicate, or elucidate the sense of statements, and therefore do not interpret the expressions to be analyzed in an essentially differential way. The internal development of analytic philosophy, however, has gradually led to an acknowledgment of the fact that disagreement is possible on the critical or metaphilosophical level itself, and consequently that the claim of neutrality needs to be reexamined. For some, at least, this means that if we have no final insight into the "nature" of man or Being, we have no such insight into the nature of philosophy. Some analytic philosophers have suggested that philosophy take a more pragmatic turn, which means, on the one hand, an acceptance of the fact that disagreement, first met on the level of explicit metaphysics, now reappears on the critical or analytic level, and, on the other, that the neutrality claim, or the quest for certainty in critical philosophy, must be given up and an appeal made instead to the purposes of our inquiries and uses of language rather than to an absolute criterion of meaning or verifiability.

The conclusion which I anticipate at this point is that philosophy can be reoriented and that more fruitful discussion of all philosophical issues will once again become possible if philosophers will abandon the quest for certainty in metaphilosophy, as was done long ago for noncritical philosophy, and acknowledge the impossibility of carrying out programs of critical philosophy in a nondifferential way. Insofar as determining the nature of philosophy is an independent enterprise, the point to be seen is that the task must be carried on in the same fashion as any other philosophical discussion, namely as a dialectical or critical comparison and competition between views advanced or proposed, with the aim always that of finding the account most comprehensive and internally and externally consistent for a given philosophical function. In short, instead of looking, in Cartesian fashion, *back* to first principles and criteria for the purpose of seeing what a proposed approach to philosophy is capable of, *before* it is expressed and tested, let us look in pragmatic fashion *forward* to what a proposed approach actually does accomplish in scope, adequacy, and consistency when we consider the actual interpretations advanced from that perspective.

Having marked out the general outline and direction of the path to be trodden, let me now go over the ground with attention to the relevant detail. To begin with, the reflexive turn in philosophy represented by the philosophies of Locke and Kant especially, came about as a result of reflection on the fact of disagreement among philosophers in their attempts to resolve a certain type of question. Kant, as is well known, contrasted the universal import of the knowledge represented by science with the existence of different schools of thought in the domain of metaphysics; there can be no doubt that one of the fundamental motives behind the writing of the first *Critique* was Kant's desire to determine in a systematic and definitive way the sort of subject matter or the type of question with which human reason is capable of dealing. Locke, in a well known passage in "The Epistle to the Reader" at the beginning of his *Essay,* described the reflexive turn in the clearest possible terms. The passage bears further analysis.

> . . . I should tell thee, that five or six friends meeting at my chamber, and discoursing on a subject very remote from this, found themselves quickly at a stand, by the difficulties that rose on every side. After we had awhile puzzled ourselves, without coming any nearer a resolution of those doubts which perplexed us, *it came into my thoughts that we took a wrong course;* and that *before* we set ourselves upon inquiries of that nature, it was necessary to examine our own abilities, and see what *objects* our understandings were, or were not, fitted to deal with.[1]

According to Fraser, the question which caused the initial difficulty had to do with the relations between religion and morality, and it is clear that the topic in question was regarded by Locke as typical of questions which resist resolution in a way that leads to any clear agreement on the part of the disputants. As a means of resolving the underlying problem, Locke proposed the reflexive turn, according to which, *prior* to inquiring into the initial question, it is necessary to inquire into the nature of our understanding for the purpose of ascertaining exactly what objects it is competent to deal with. I am not concerned here primarily with the particular analyses through which Locke carried out his program, but instead with the character of the reflexive turn itself and the assumptions on which it was first made. It appears, first, that critical inquiry is *not* to be an inquiry into the original question concerning the relation between religion and morality; it is presumed that the latter is the sort of question with which we are unable to deal in a definitive way that leads to agreement. Instead, we are to inquire into the nature of our understanding in a manner which in no way involves discussion of the first-order question, although the results of our critical account are supposed to enable us to understand why we are unable to arrive at a definitive answer to the proposed question, and indeed to all questions of the same logical type. Notice, however, that there is no suggestion that the critical turn should itself be self-reflexive; no critical questions, that is, were raised concerning our ability to carry out the critical inquiry; it was assumed that,

1. A. C. Fraser, ed., *Locke's Essay Concerning Human Understanding* (Oxford: Oxford University Press, 1894), vol. 1, 9. Italics not in original, except for "objects."

whatever human limitations stand in the way of our resolving the sort of question that called for the critical turn in the first instance, these difficulties are vacuous or inoperative when it comes to executing the critical analysis itself. The crucial assumption of the existence of different levels of thought or discourse was readily made and it was taken for granted by many that it is possible to proceed confidently with the critical analysis as if it were in a privileged position vis-à-vis inquiries into disputed questions and that, being in such a position, critical analysis is *ipso facto* free of the limitations or difficulties attached to discussion of the initially perplexing issues which we are supposedly unable to resolve.

I suspect that at least two further assumptions lay at the root of this confidence in critical philosophy with respect to the carrying out of analyses under the aegis of the reflexive turn. First, there was the lingering doctrine of intuitive clarity (which, incidentally, reappeared later in the concept of analysis), according to which, to quote the frequently used expression of the seventeenth- and eighteenth-century philosophers, "the mind is more readily known than the body." This assumption prompted the belief that questions concerning the operations of the mind, the reception and compounding of ideas, the use of reason and the making of judgments, can be treated from an "inside" perspective which presumably is not itself infected by those limitations that attach to reason or understanding when they address themselves to metaphysical questions. Even Kant, who rejected intellectual intuition, sometimes wrote as though the successful carrying out of his critical or transcendental analysis required, as Paton has expressed it, "a special and direct insight into the necessary activity of a rational being as such."[2] Second, and closely related, was the assumption of a critical standpoint that is beyond the reach of differences of opinion that result in schools of thought so that, from that standpoint, it is possible to formulate the conditions surrounding the raising of a certain type of question without in any way being involved in actually raising the question itself. Thus Kant could oppose criticism to both skepticism and dogmatism on the ground that both extremes make assertions of a substantive and differential kind in answer to disputed philosophical questions, whereas criticism, or the critical standpoint, is taken to be free from involvement in philosophical questions that occasion a dispute. Consider the following two statements made by Kant in the first *Critique:*

2. H. J. Paton, *The Categorical Imperative: A Study in Kant's Moral Philosophy* (Chicago: University of Chicago Press, 1948), p. 246; he cites Kant, *Critique of Practical Reason* (Prussian Academy Edition), vol. 5, 30.

1. In discussing the grounds on which a critical solution for the problems raised by the antinomies could be achieved, Kant writes:

> The critical solution, *which allows of complete certainty, does not consider the question objectively,* but in relation to the foundation of the knowledge upon which the question is based. (A 484 = B 512; italics not in original.)

2. In commending the critical philosophy in general, Kant says,

> The critique of pure reason can be regarded as the true tribunal for all disputes of pure reason; *for it is not involved in these disputes*—disputes that are immediately concerned with objects—but is directed to the determining and estimating of the rights of reason in general, in accordance with the principles of their first institution. (A 751 = B 779; italics not in original.)

These passages express with admirable clarity and candor the claims made in behalf of the critical standpoint established by the reflexive turn. That standpoint is declared at once neutral and capable of attaining certainty. It is neutral in the sense that from it we can consider the conditions in accordance with which a certain type of question arises, and we can conclude that such questions cannot be substantively answered, all without raising the question itself in the sense that someone seriously proposing an answer to the question could legitimately be said to have raised it. Moreover, it is said that, from the critical standpoint, we can specify the relevant conditions and determine the unanswerable character of the sort of question with which the antinomy, for example, deals in a manner which is itself certain and presumably without a significant alternative. The critical standpoint is, in short, a detachable one, so that one who adopts it is not involved in making assertions about objects, but only about certain aspects of the relation between ideas or concepts and their objects or putative objects. According to Kant, none of the limitations standing in the way of reason's attaining complete satisfaction in its theoretical employment, infects or affects reason in its critical employment. In the latter case, reason moves with neutrality and certainty.

Without in the least intending to identify what has come to be called the linguistic turn with the reflexive turn as I have described it, one can, nevertheless, note some striking similarities between the two. To begin with, there is the similarity in the problems that led to each turn. The origin and development of linguistic philosophy has been conditioned at every point by the awareness of disagreement among philosophers and the attempt to find some clear way of eliminating such disagreement and of reaching conclusions that command universal assent, at least in principle, after the fashion of the natural sciences. The move to language itself, what has been called "semantic ascent," was prompted by the belief that discussion carried forward on the object level holds out less promise of agreement in results than discussion directed to the structure and use of language. The approach to philosophical problems through the analysis of language is the contemporary counterpart of the epistemological or reflexive analyses of the former turn. The basic similarity is not seriously affected by the claim that analysis is a logical affair and is thus independent of considerations having to do with the "mind" or the supposedly psychological investigations of Locke and Kant, because the distinction between the "logical" (so-called) and the "psychological" is to my mind more unclear than any other distinction I know of in current discussion. The fact is that the modern analytic enterprise has proceeded along precisely the same lines as those marked out by Kant: in both cases, philosophical theses antecedently identified as metaphysical have been evaluated solely in terms of certain critical or "formal" features—*syntax, logic, semantics*—said to govern either the form of our understanding or the proper use of our language. Like its predecessor, the linguistic turn means the marking off of a form of critical or second-order thinking or use of language—metalanguage—aimed at the analysis of the languages in use in science, philosophy, and whatever other intellectual enterprises there may be.

As is well known, various principles or criteria were proposed that were aimed at eliminating insignificant discourse and at establishing a firm basis for reaching agreement in philosophical discussion. The original positivist meaning criterion, proposals for the construction of an ideal language, and the appeal to ordinary language as a canon for analysis were the most important proposals advanced to meet the desired need. The important question that arises at this point is: To what extent have the proposers of these criteria continued to believe in the essential neutrality of their critical rules or principles for the pursuit of metalinguistic philosophy? An examination of all the proposals is out of the question, but it is clear that the neutrality thesis was maintained at least at two crucial points, *first,* in Ayer's original presentation of the verifiability theory of meaning, and *second,* in Carnap's early conception of logical analysis. Let us briefly consider each in turn.

Ayer regarded his original verification position as neutral in the sense implied by his rejection of Bradley's claim that anyone proposing to show the impossibility of metaphysics is providing a rival metaphysics of his own. In order to secure his position and at the same time to distinguish it from Kant's (which he erroneously regarded as a "psychological hypothesis"), Ayer appealed to a "rule" for determining the "literal significance of language," and it is clear that he regarded that rule as one which *all* philosophers would have to accept on pain of talking nonsense. Ayer, that is, did not think of his meaning criterion as the specification of a differential philosophical principle which might have legitimate alternatives. Subsequent discussion, however, has made it clear that the "rule" in question cannot be stated in a way which is entirely independent of differential philosophical theses. As Rorty's recent discussion makes plain, at the very least the rule in question presupposes that nominalism is valid, and, I would add, it also presupposes that experience is exhaustively made up of identifiable atomic sense data. In view of these considerations, it is difficult to see how the neutrality thesis, at least in Ayer's case, can be maintained.

Carnap's conception of logical analysis as the successor of Kant's critical tribunal of reason furnishes an even clearer example of belief in the neutrality of the analytic standpoint. In 1935, in his discussion of "Verifiability" in *Philosophy and Logical Syntax,* Carnap characterized logical analysis as the enterprise of making clear the sense of each assertion of science and of everyday life, and of stating exactly the relations between the members of any set of such assertions. Moreover, he maintained that "one of the principal tasks of logical analysis of a given proposition is to find out the method of verification for that proposition."[3] In the space of a seven-paragraph development and exhibition of logical analysis at work, Carnap asserts, among others, the following theses in what purports to be an exercise of clarification:

(1) Epistemology is nothing other than a special part of logical analysis plus the raising of some psychological questions concerning the actual knowing process.
(2) A statement about a present perception is directly verified by having that perception at the time specified.
(3) The statement, "This key is made of iron" is an hypothesis.
(4) Every assertion in science is a statement about present perceptions or other experiences.
(5) A so-called "natural law" in science is an hypothesis.

And in summing up the brief analysis contained in the preceding paragraphs, Carnap says, "What we have been doing so far is *logical*

---

3. Rudolf Carnap, *Philosophy and Logical Syntax* (London: Kegan Paul, Trench, Trübner & Co., 1955), p. 10.

analysis,"[4] and he goes on to indicate that the next part of his program involves applying the foregoing considerations derived from "logical analysis" to certain traditional philosophical statements.

My concern is not primarily with the particular theses Carnap advanced, but rather with the basic assumption they imply, namely, that somehow by a process called "logical analysis" which is supposed to represent no more than a clarification presumably of certain assertions of a scientific or ordinary sort, one can arrive at the special theses I have just indicated and expressed in shorthand form. The fact is that each one of these theses has been, and legitimately can be, subject to extended discussion and argument, and, moreover, no one of them, with the exception of (3) has been arrived at by any identifiable analysis of the initial statements. The further fact is that they represent a formulation of Carnap's philosophical position, and a set of proposed *interpretations* of the nature of knowledge, verification, natural laws, etc. And even if it were in fact the case that, as some philosophers have tried to do, Carnap was merely analyzing or clarifying initial statements, it is difficult to see how anyone could have arrived at such a list of differential philosophical theses merely as a result of attempting to pursue a program of logical analysis. The point is, that quite apart from their validity or invalidity or the supporting reasons that might be given for them, the particular theses in question represent explicit philosophical interpretations defining a differential philosophical position or point of view; they cannot as such be launched under the auspices of a neutral analysis or clarification program. When the correct status of such analyses is more clearly understood, it will be seen that they always do more than express in a supposedly clearer way what has already been asserted by some initial statements. No one analysis of the sentences said to occur in science, for example, even an analysis restricted to language and logic in import, can legitimately be said to be dictated by science itself. Different analyses are always possible and the differences among them will reflect more ultimate philosophical differences. Thus Peirce, who was certainly as well acquainted with the methods, the techniques, and the logic of science as any contemporary philosopher of science, understood the statements of science to mean or to imply (1) that there are "objective reals," as he expressed it, and (2) that there are "generals" in existence which provide a ground for continuity and which help explain why it is that no object is exhausted in any one of its occurrences or interactions.

4. Ibid., p. 15; italics in original.

Carnap's account, on the other hand, though it purports to be the result of "logical analysis," conflicts with that of Peirce; and the conflict must be traced back to differences in their philosophical positions. These differences can be circumvented, in principle, only by legislating a standard or criterion which, because it is supposed to be neutral, is to be binding on all who wish to discuss the issues in a clear way. But the difficulty reappears when we discover that every formulation of a binding criterion reintroduces differential philosophical theses. The only possible conclusion, and it appears that contemporary philosophers are becoming increasingly aware of the need to draw it, is that since disagreement among philosophers appears again at the critical or metalinguistic level, there can be neither a neutral legislative formula for determining the meaning or the proper use of language, nor a neutral type of analysis that can serve to guarantee agreement on that level.

A fruitful way out of the difficulty, in my view, is to take a third turn—the pragmatic turn—or what I have called the pragmatic outcome. This turn involves abandoning the quest for the neutral criterion and recognizing that there can be no guarantee of either certainty or neutrality at the critical level. Two papers to be found among the literature of analytic philosophy signal this turn and some attention to them will repay our efforts.

The first is Quine's paper, "Two Dogmas of Empiricism" (1951), and the other is Carnap's, "Empiricism, Semantics and Ontology" (1950). The most important aspect of Quine's discussion, apart that is, from the central attack on the "two dogmas," is his questioning of the extent to which it is possible to give clear and "absolute" formulations of the content of such indispensable concepts as "analytic," "synonymous," "semantic rule," "postulate," etc., apart from an appeal to some context of inquiry with a specified purpose. The understanding of these concepts, he claims, must be admitted to be relative to "an act of inquiry," or to some operations "to which we have seen fit to direct our attention."[5] And if we direct attention to the context of empirical inquiry, we are led to ask, not merely how two languages are related to each other, but what relation or relations obtain between a statement or a formulated claim on the one hand and the experiences relevant to its critical appraisal on the other. Following this line of thought, Quine was led to ask some basic questions about the "size" of a significant unit of expression and thus to challenge the program requiring a term-by-term process

5. W. V. O. Quine, *From a Logical Point of View* (Cambridge: Harvard University Press, 1953), p. 35.

of empirical reduction based on the assumption that the term is the simplest unit of meaning. Moreover, still attending to the course of inquiry, he was led to question whether, in every body of purported knowledge, it is not necessary to distinguish different types of statement and different types of concept. Not every statement, as he correctly saw, confronts direct experience nor are all statements tested by the subject matter in the same way; it is necessary to distinguish the *edge* of a body of knowledge from its *interior*, so that it is not always evident from the discovery that a statement at the edge is confirmed or disconfirmed, what the implications are for the interior statements and concepts in the system. Quine concludes that the distinction between the factual and linguistic components in knowledge, previously enshrined neatly in the analytic-synthetic distinction taken as an absolute disjunction, must be interpreted as one of degree, so that in confronting recalcitrant experience, we have to decide what to adjust in our body of knowledge on the basis of pragmatic considerations, by which he means, considerations set by the purpose of the inquiry at hand. No one, I believe, is in a position to claim that this pragmatic appeal resolves all the problems involved, but what it does do it to direct attention again to the concrete context of inquiry and helps us to remind ourselves of the basically rationalist character that has pervaded much modern empiricism in its search for absolute criteria on the critical level. Armed with logical and linguistic criteria, the modern empiricist has often confronted experience, not to follow its guide, but to force it into a predetermined pattern dictated by the assumptions of some differential philosophical scheme.

The second paper I wish to cite contains several sentences that further underline the pragmatic turn. In discussing the validity of introducing particular linguistic forms into a language system, Carnap writes:

> (A) For those who want to develop or use semantical methods, the decisive question is not the alleged ontological question of the existence of abstract entities but rather the question whether the *use* of abstract linguistic forms, or in technical terms, the use of variables beyond those for things (or phenomenal data), *is expedient and fruitful for the purposes for which semantical analyses are made,* viz., the analysis, interpretation, clarification, or construction of languages, of communication, especially languages of science.[6]

6. Rudolf Carnap, "Empiricism, Semantics, and Ontology," *Revue Internationale de Philosophie,* 4 (1950), p. 39; Italics not in original. (Reprinted in Carnap, *Meaning and Necessity: A Study in Semantics and Modal Logic* [2nd ed.; Chicago: University of Chicago Press, 1956.])

(B) The acceptance or rejection of abstract or, again, linguistic forms, just as the acceptance or rejection of any other linguistic forms in any branch of science, will finally be decided *by their efficiency as instruments,* the ratio of the results achieved to the amount and complexity of the efforts required. To decree dogmatic prohibitions of certain linguistic forms *instead of testing them by their success or failure in practical use,* is worse than futile; it is positively harmful because it may obstruct scientific progress.[7]

My point in citing these passages is obviously not to raise the question of abstract entities, nor again to commend the pragmatic appeal expressed in them as the final solution to all the issues raised by modern philosophers, analytic or otherwise, *but rather to call attention to the appearance of the pragmatic turn within the internal development of linguistic philosophy itself.* The above statements represent a definite shift from an a priori approach which specifies absolute criteria for linguistic forms in advance of inquiry, and then applies these criteria in an essentially programmatic way to whatever issue is under discussion. The appeal to the *outcome* or result is a truly empirical appeal to what actually happens when an analysis is made with the use of certain expressions rather than others. That result cannot be entirely determined in advance in accordance with absolute criteria.

In the end, I take the appearance of the pragmatic turn among critical philosophers as an acknowledgment of the fact that, although the critical or linguistic approach was devised in the first instance to deal with the problem of disagreement among philosophers when they tried to answer traditional questions alleged to be unanswerable, disagreement has proved unavoidable on the critical level itself. That is to say, the attempt to eliminate disagreement at the metaphilosophical level has proved to be a failure and there is now frank recognition among some analytic philosophers at least, of the need to find a new court of appeal within which to consider philosophical issues. Whether many analytic philosophers would follow me in my explanation of why the various proposals that have been made to eliminate disagreement have failed, is perhaps doubtful. My thesis, which I can only sketch briefly, is that belief in a secure, critical level of thinking, whether represented by the idea of a transcendental critique, a neutral form of analysis, or an absolute criterion of significance, is a mistake. There is no such level of thought which is incorrigible in itself and superior to some lower level which forms its object.

7. Ibid., p. 40; italics added.

It is now time to assume a more critical stance in the face of critical standpoints themselves. There still exists a tendency to suppose that the critical standpoint represents a "privileged position" such that when we make assertions purporting to refer to events, to experience, to reality, or even to Being we are supposed to be on perilous ground; but when we make assertions about the relation between a concept and an object or between an object language and some other language, we are supposed either to be carrying out merely neutral analyses, or to be abstracting so completely from lower order considerations that what we are saying on the critical level is incorrigible.

Since, however, knowing, despite features peculiar to itself, is known as a process among other processes taking place in the world, there is no reason why philosophical treatment of that process, including its method, logic, and language, should constitute a special sort of inquiry absolutely different in kind from, let us say, philosophical inquiry into the nature of causation, the self, history, art, or morality. The belief that the analysis of knowledge constitutes a case apart is a carry-over from a time when it was believed that knowledge is a special nonnatural occurrence into which we have peculiar insight because of its intimate relation to our mind or understanding. But if the doctrine that we have special insight or "privileged access" to the knowledge of our own selves is suspect, as indeed it is, why is the claim of a privileged status for critical standpoints not equally suspect?

Every critical or "meta" standpoint has to face the question of its own status vis-à-vis the objects, languages, or types of thought which constitute its subject matter or domain of inquiry. The conclusions attained from a critical standpoint—the specification of meaning criteria, and the like—are meant to have some normative force, and if this force does not derive from the claim that they are true or in some sense well-founded, we are under no obligation to accept them. My reading of the history of modern critical and analytic philosophy suggests that this question has finally come to be faced, and that there is now a recognition that the normative force in question must fall somewhere between two boundaries. These boundaries are, at one end of the spectrum, stipulation of meaning, and, at the other, empirical hypothesis. If, for example, we were to consider a version of the positivist criterion for cognitive significance from the standpoint of its normative force—i.e., the claim it is supposed to have on us to accept it—we might commend it simply as a stipulation of what the term "meaningful" is to mean, adding perhaps that the demand of "clarity" requires such a meaning. Or, we might take the criterion to be an empirical hypothesis to the effect that it formulates what "meaningful" means in science. The difficulties attached to each alternative are well known; stipulations either have "reasons" behind them which are in effect pragmatic in the sense that some aim is accomplished through them that could not otherwise be accomplished, or they are "mere" stipulations to be countered with other and opposite stipulations. Thus stipulation is too weak a status for a meaning criterion. On the other hand, to construe a meaning criterion as an empirical hypothesis would seem to provide it with greater force, but, unfortunately, the self-reference involved leads to some contradictions. Thus neither alternative is satisfactory.

It seems to me that the predicament has been seen, and that the appearance of the pragmatic turn I have mentioned above constitutes both a recognition of the difficulty and an attempt to deal with it by asking that we estimate analytical results in terms of the purposes of inquiry and in terms of the adequacy with which a given set of linguistic forms or a given set of concepts and rules actually elucidate and explain the subject matter into which we inquire.

Critical philosophy should return to a dialectical arena. The quest for certainty at the meta level must be given up. The attempt to eliminate disagreement in advance must also be abandoned. Like all philosophical inquiry, critical philosophy must ultimately appeal to a critical comparison among proposed alternatives where the emphasis falls not so much on the fulfillment of antecedent criteria as upon what a given set of concepts or linguistic forms can actually *do* in the fulfillment of philosophical purposes.

6

The Critique of Abstractions
and the Scope of Reason

"The Critique of Abstractions and the Scope of Reason" was my contribution to a Festschrift *for Chargles Hartshorne entitled,* Process and Divinity. *I was concerned in this essay to focus on two themes—the obvious indispensability of abstractions coupled with the need to show their connection with the world we experience, and the scope of reason, especially whether it can have a synoptic and synthesizing function as a counterbalance to its analytic role. These themes were at the center of Hegel's thought and they occupied the attention of the Pragmatists along with such thinkers as Whitehead and Bergson. As Hegel saw, most of the adverse criticism leveled against reason and "intellectualism" was rooted in the belief that thought has only an analytic function which dismembers without being able to unite and thus restore the integrity of experience. Hegel also saw that no knowledge is possible without abstractions, but that they must be kept under control so that they will not come to replace the world of concrete things and events which they are meant to illuminate and interpret. I wish to clear up a confusion I caused by linking Dewey and Whitehead through their common concern for the "criticism of abstractions." Both were clearly concerned with the issue, but I erroneously identified Dewey's program for philosophy (as distinct from metaphysics) as a criticism of abstractions instead of a "criticism of criticisms" by which he meant to introduce the dimension of valuation.*

I take note of two ways of criticizing abstractions; one I call the "dialectical recovery of the whole" illustrated by Hegel and, on a lesser scale, Whitehead, whereby abstractions reveal and, so to speak, criticize themselves by being brought into relation to the wholes from which they were abstracted. The second way I call the way of functioning or instrumentalism, whereby abstractions are set to work in the course of experience and are judged in accordance with their consequent success in describing, explaining and interpreting the subject matter. The upshot of the discussion is the need for a concept of reason that is broader than its analytic function thus allowing for synthesis and a return to concrete experience. The essay is reprinted from The Hartshorne Festschrift: Process and Divinity, *William L. Reese and Eugene Freeman, eds., by permission of the Open Court Publishing Company, La Salle, Illinois.*

The story of modern philosophy is largely the story of the criticism of reason undertaken from many points of view and prompted by diverse motives. Thinkers as different in outlook as Kant, Hume, Kierkegaard, Freud and James have had a hand in criticizing the nature and status of reason in relation to our cognitive experience of the world and to the realization of our purposes and aims as active beings. Reason has been subject to internal criticism aimed at the disclosure of its structure and capacities and it has been judged in accordance with its success or failure in contributing to the self-realization of the individual self. Although other ways than his have been discovered for carrying on the reflective critique of reason associated with the name of Kant, critical scrutiny of reason continues and the question of the scope of reason is in the center of discussion at the present time.

Philosophical thought since the Enlightenment has focused numerous problems about reason and its relation to our life and world. In the various forms of the Romantic movement, for example, the distinctions and arguments of reason were set over against the integrity of living experience and direct participation by the individual in the concrete situation. Wordsworth's identification of "murder" and the "dissecting" thought is typical of the Romanticist reaction to analysis; thought fragments and dismembers things, it kills and does not revivify. For others the issue was posed as that of the opposition between the partial character of thought and the wholeness and integrity of concrete situations. Or again, reason has been charged with dwelling in the sphere of the possible as opposed to the actual and of providing man with a means of avoiding decision and action in historical life. So understood, reason is able to weaken the will and spoil the "native hue of resolution." More recently with some of the philosophers of existence, reason has been described as a wholly "theoretical" power which by its very nature puts the individual at a distance from both himself and the world. The complaint is that reason can express only what is universal or, as Bradley put it, what is so true in general that it must be false in particular.

In addition the growth of modern science has had much to do with the evaluation placed upon reason in our current situation. The thought processes exemplified by mathematical physics have been regarded by many as the essence of reason so that it has come to be thought that reason is capable of dealing with nothing but high level abstractions. The identification, moreover, of reason with natural science leads to the belief that reason is confined to theoretical knowledge and that it must exclude from its domain the "practical" concerns of life—art, religion and ethics. If we are to recover a broader conception of reason in the modern world we shall have to reconsider it with particular attention to the meaning and status of abstractions. We must ask whether it is true that reason is confined to analysis alone and whether it is necessarily in conflict with immediate concrete life and experience. For much of the criticism leveled against reason has been based on the assumption that it is incapable of synthesis or constructive activity and that it is unable to provide us with safeguards against the confusion of its own abstractions with the larger concrete situation from which they have been drawn. This latter problem is most clearly evident in the modern educational situation where we are confronted with a multitude of bodies of abstract and specialized knowledge without very clear ideas of their relations to each other or their relative importance to the immediate situation we face.

Calling attention to the above plurality of problems centering in a common theme serves at the same time to point up the complexity of the topic. It is neither possible nor profitable to attempt to deal with all of the issues involved; we shall make more progress by singling out one basic problem. I propose to concentrate on abstractions, what they are, why they are necessary and what strategy is required for relating them to each other and to that concrete life and experience which is the ultimate referent of all serious philosophy. We may make a preliminary statement of our problem as follows: since the comprehension of ourselves and the surrounding environment requires analytic thought and this in turn means discrimination, selective focus and abstraction, what safeguards shall we devise in order to avoid confusing abstractions with the concrete reality from which they have been drawn and to which they ultimately refer? This question is not to be confused with the question of the verification of theories or the justification of statements containing abstract concepts. It goes much deeper. The issue turns on the status of abstractions in relation to each other and to concrete experience even when there is no question about the well-founded nature of these abstractions. The basic importance of the problem is signalized by the fact that Dewey and Whitehead, though their philosophies are based on different motives and have diverse orientations, each described philosophy as the enterprise whose proper business is the "criticism of abstractions" or the reflective inquiry which identifies abstractions and their kinds in order to show their relations to each other and to direct experience. For both thinkers philosophical vision is required to accomplish the result.

We scarcely need to be reminded that although the terms "abstraction" and "abstract" are often used as though their meaning were perfectly clear in contrast to the concrete, philosophers at least have not always understood these terms in a single sense. In order to clarify our problem, we must commence with some indication of the meaning of an abstraction. We shall not claim to give a definition: Kant was right on this point when he held that mathematics alone can begin with definitions and that philosophy, just because it has to cope with a concrete world, must postpone definitions until the very end of inquiry. We can, however, begin with a notion of abstraction sufficiently clear for our purposes.

Abstraction is both a rational process and a result fixed in a concept and expressed through language. Neither aspect can be neglected; one draws attention to the power of human reason and its intervention in an ongoing process, while the other focuses upon the outcome of the intervention, the final embodiment of knowledge. The abstraction in the sense of a result must not be disconnected from the process through which it arises because, as we shall see, no abstraction is intelligible entirely apart from the purpose of the thinker standing behind it. Abstraction in its generic character means discrimination and selection for emphasis involving both the inclusion or concentration upon an aspect or feature of a thing or collection of things, and the exclusion as not relevant of what is other than the selected feature. If, for example, our aim is to determine the number of items in a collection, we shall, in the first instance at least, concentrate on the counting and the identification of each item as one and only one, while paying no attention whatever to the colors and shapes of the things in question. The concentration upon each item as one and the neglect of the features of color and shape illustrate the inclusion and exclusion features of abstraction.

It is important to notice that there is no way of describing an abstraction which does not involve the notion of a purpose or a principle of selection; an abstraction expresses or includes what is relevant to a purpose in thought and excludes what is irrelevant to that purpose. Thus, for example, the determination of the value of a given national currency on the international exchange might largely exclude the esthetic value of many commodities, whereas an international art exhibit might succeed in its main objectives without any reference whatever to the economic value in exchange assigned to the works exhibited. In each case the features of things considered relevant and those irrelevant are determined by taking purpose into account.

In addition to the generic meaning of abstraction as inclusion and exclusion, there have been at least three ways in which this generic meaning has been interpreted. The differences are more than a matter of emphasis; they point ultimately to different ways of understanding the nature of things. First, an abstraction has been understood as the selection of a *part* of some whole—whether the whole of reality as with some idealists or some finite whole— such that the abstraction includes the part and excludes all of the other features that would go to make up the whole. In this sense, to be abstract is to be partial and thus incomplete. Secondly, an abstraction has been taken to mean a fixed or static element with clear and enduring boundaries carved out of a passing or flowing reality. In this sense to be abstract is to include a "frozen" excerpt or feature and to exclude the continuous process or flow of things which is in itself without convenient stopping places. Thirdly, an abstraction has been taken to mean a universal or generic feature which transcends the immediate situation or what is present for perception. In this sense to be abstract is to be an essence comprehensible in itself without regard to this or that occasion upon which it may be exemplified. All three senses involve the generic meaning of abstraction as selection but it is important to note that whereas the first and third senses stress the partial or incomplete character of abstractions, the second sense implies that abstractions are inherently *distortions* of a reality which can be apprehended only in an immediate way as an undifferentiated continuum. It follows that in accordance with the second sense abstractions are illegitimate and must finally be dispensed with whereas in the other two cases they are not only allowable but indispensable and the way is then open to show how they are related to each other and to the concrete reality from which they have been derived.

Underlying the special senses of abstraction we have noted is the generic description; abstraction means selection or inclusion and exclusion in accordance with some purpose in view. In every case the meaning of an abstraction is not independent of the purpose for which it was selected. Relevance or irrelevance of a given factor or aspect of a situation is always to be determined by reference to the purpose involved. Thus, for example, if we are interested in coming to understand the *temporal* character of our world and experience we must first identify that feature by abstracting. Now if our purpose is, as it undoubtedly would be in science, to understand temporality as a bare fact for a system of causal explanation, we would have to regard as irrelevant to that purpose our individual and personal sense of duration, the so-called psychological time, as well as the qualitative character of temporal position which in historical reality is described as the "right" time or the time that is "providential." The excluded elements are excluded on purpose at the same time that the relevant factors are selected on purpose. The difficult problem at this point is to guard against our tendency to think and act as if what we have disregarded as irrelevant for one purpose may safely be disregarded absolutely; this would be, from a philosophical viewpoint, the most disastrous justification of the proverb—"out of sight, out of mind."

The dual character of abstraction as both including and excluding needs further attention. Let us consider a piece of furniture, for example, and set as our purpose the determination of its fair market price. I take this to be attending to what can be called the economic aspect of the thing. To carry out our purpose we must select for attention and analysis certain aspects of that piece of furniture and also certain factors in the social and economic system in which it exists. What we select or abstract has its positive character in the fact that it is genuinely relevant to the accomplishment of our original purpose. And as such the abstracted elements have a legitimate status and function, since whatever else we may say about them they were selected for their relevance and because they enable us to achieve our stated aim. This I call the positive aspect of abstractions, that they include a portion of reality and that, when well founded, they enable us to understand, to describe and to manage things. Failure to take seriously enough this positive aspect has often led philosophers to think of abstractions only as "mere abstractions."

But there is the other side of the coin. To direct attention or select is to exclude as well as include and this fact is more problematic. In our illustration, the concentration upon the economic aspect of the piece of furniture means the exclusion from consideration of any aspect of the object which cannot be shown to be relevant to the determination of its fair market price. The object is being considered *only* in regard to its economic aspect and this aspect does not exhaust its being. This is what is meant by saying that an abstraction is partial and leaves something out of account.

Some decades of discussion about reductionism have taught us to be wary of our ineluctable tendency to identify anything with "nothing but" one of its aspects or features; we are less prone than we once were to identify the concrete and whole object or situation with an abstraction. And there is, I believe, considerable agreement as to the illegitimacy of such identification. We cannot correctly say, to use an old and well worn illustration, that the playing of a violin by a master is nothing but the production of sound waves from the friction between a horse's tail and a cat's gut. But in denying the identification, we must go on to consider what is implied by the denial. First, it is not false to describe certain features of a situation in terms of abstractions appropriate to, let us say, physics. For the fact is that the violin in the illustration has a physical constitution and when it is played, even when it expresses the most sublime music, certain purely physical conditions are being fulfilled. What is open to objection is the identification of an aspect with the whole, or a claim made in behalf of the abstraction to cover more ground than is stated and implied in the purpose for which it was made. We can, nevertheless, distinguish between well and ill founded abstractions made for a certain purpose and this fact precludes our saying that an abstraction is false merely because it is partial and does not express the whole. An abstraction is seen as partial, *not from within* the purpose which controls it since it was made precisely to fulfill that purpose, but only in relation to some wider purpose which takes more into account. But the fact that an abstraction does not fulfill some other purpose does not preclude its being well founded within its own intent and under the control of its own purpose. There are, however, more serious cases where an abstraction becomes materially altered when excluded elements are later brought into the picture. And here the genuine but thorny philosophical problem of internal relations presents itself, for when the omitted elements in a situation have the retroactive effect of altering a previous abstraction the concrete situation is not left standing where it was before. We are led at once to ask how the omitted elements, the exclusion of which make abstraction possible, are related to what we have already selected and clearly grasped. If philosophy is not to forfeit its claim to speak about and be relevant to concrete life and experience, it cannot avoid this problem.

The underlying issue is an essential one and is not posed merely as the outcome of this or that particular way of viewing the world. Precise and disciplined thinking in any domain requires clear concepts expressive of analytic distinctions and as soon as we attempt to carry out such thinking we are landed at once in abstractions. We are then faced with the problem not only of guarding against taking the partial for the whole, but of preserving the unity and integrity of experience at the same time. For analysis always breaks the unity of things directly experienced into a plurality of aspects and parts and we have continually to ask: How is the unity of experience and our own unity to be preserved? We are asking, in short, *whether reason has any synthetic function in construing the world or whether its activity is exhausted in analysis,* the dismemberment of what initially comes to us with integrity and wholeness.

It will be helpful to begin by calling attention to three responses which our basic problem has elicited from philosophers in the recent past. First, there is the refusal to acknowledge any problem here, either by claiming that it is "speculative" and beyond our reach, or by insisting that empirical inquiry is possible without our becoming involved in any such problem; thought, so this view runs, is thought and it is under no obligation to reproduce or duplicate reality. Here the identification of thought with analysis is accepted and there is no further problem; abstractions do not call for philosophical interpretation and they occasion no difficulty. In the second place we must recognize the position that does see a genuine problem here but poses it as an absolute antithesis between life, immediate experience or intuition on the one side and conceptual thinking on the other. This response not only acknowledges a problem, but does so enthusiastically and delights in finding every possible opposition and paradox between the abstractions of analytic thinking and the nature of things as disclosed in direct experience. Abstractions are then condemned as abstractions, reason in the form of analysis is limited to producing partial and distorted views of the world, and the proposed solution is that it is necessary to find a channel other than reason for grasping the nature of things. There is no attempt to reinterpret reason; it is left to its own self-destruction, a victim of its own abstractions. This approach acquiesces in the view that reason is no more than analysis; the only difference between this view and the first response is that while the first takes analysis as ultimate and legitimate, this view rejects analysis as distorting reality and seeks instead for some other form of insight. Acceptance of the claim that reason finds its whole being in analysis means avoidance of the hard problem of showing how abstractions may be related so as to reconstitute the wholes of direct experience. Intuition-type positions may have their heart in the right place as regards the criticism of abstractions but their failure consists in an over-readiness to surrender reason to the atomist while at the same time trying to make up the deficiency by appeal to an immediate apprehension which remains unconnected with analytic thought. Or if not completely unconnected, immediate apprehension remains so completely a matter of first person participation that general concepts expressive of general structures can be no more than distortions of the reality so disclosed.

The third response is by far the most complex; it is also the most rewarding. Like the second and unlike the first, it acknowledges a problem of major proportions in relation to abstractions and seeks to resolve it directly. It sets for itself the task of criticizing abstractions not in the sense of condemning them out of hand, but in the sense of exposing their partiality and then trying to find a strategy for relating them to each other so as to preserve the integrity of experience. This response, understood in its main aim, seeks to save reason from its own abstractions. It is the only approach that correctly grasps the problem and it alone can hope to deal effectively with the task of keeping concrete reality from being dissolved into abstractions and of saving reason from the just criticisms leveled against it when it relies uncritically upon its own abstract products.

I want to consider two solutions that have emerged in modern thought, each of which exhibits the general pattern of this third response. The first is the *way of dialectical recovery of the whole,* and the second may be called the *way of functioning or instrumentalism.* Each has its own truth, even if both have to be supplemented further.

1. The Way of Dialectical Recovery of the Whole

This solution finds its supreme illustration in Hegel and the key to understanding it is found in the thorough-going identification of the abstract with the partial and of the concrete with the whole. Isolated, atomic or self-enclosed existence is denied and the underlying strategy of this position is to show that abstraction can never be the same as complete separation. Discrimination does not mean the loss of all connection between the item or aspect discriminated and its environing context. Contrary to what has been said, this solution does not mean the denial of analysis, for Hegel always defended mediation and analysis, but it does mean that the results of analysis cannot stand as self-contained and independent results. From the other side, Hegel's approach means the ultimate justification of thought, but it is a very rich type of thought which includes showing how the abstractions produced by analysis are related to each other so as to re-establish the concrete whole which seems to be left behind by the understanding that distinguishes but does not unite. Hegel's way, in other words, means the removal of partiality through organic and systematic recovery of the whole as a system of intelligibly related aspects or parts. His doctrine that mediation or abstraction is "immediacy becoming" or the self-specification of the subject matter denies at the outset any difference in kind between an immediate and integral given experience on the one side and the conceptual

111

distinctions demanded by reason on the other. His formula is: *First distinguish and then unite;* synthesis can be achieved because all intelligible aspects or parts are related to each other in the whole. We are invited by this strategy to complete the process of mediation and thus to reconstruct the concrete reality.

The truth in this approach is that the partiality of abstractions is revealed only when they are set against the wholes to which they refer or of which they are aspects. Partiality is never disclosed for what it is as long as we remain wholly within the specific or limited purpose that produces it. Physicists, for example, will never see the partiality of their abstract descriptions as long as they confine their vision to those features of things with which they can successfully deal. But the disclosure of partiality shows the inescapability of appealing to the concrete world and at the same time raises the question as to whether the criticism of abstractions can ever be carried through from a standpoint which regards all abstractions as on the same level. To this we must return.

If Hegel's strategy contains an element of truth it also involves a fatal error. To say that the concrete is the whole is to identify it with a non-differential concept; it is to identify it with what cannot be apprehended as such. For human reason, at any rate, the whole must always be grasped in some differential way, in one aspect or part; as soon as this is done, however, we no longer have the whole. Hegel saw this problem and it is precisely why the whole is left by him implicit until the process reaches its culmination in fully self-conscious spirit. But as later outworking of the position has shown, the recovery of the whole must then become a *program* for a process that is never completed. The concrete problem is this: How can we estimate the status and especially the importance of an abstraction when all we have to guide us is the concept of an ultimate totality? The answer is that we cannot do so; unless the whole is given some differential character such as being an organism, or a self, we have no way of saying how the various partial purposes behind all abstractions are related to each other. For every abstraction is, as such, equally abstract and the only way in which an abstraction can get to be "more or less" abstract is by reference not simply to the whole, but to the whole as characterized in some differential way. Hegel, of course, knew this and he sought to meet the difficulty by the differential conception of the whole as self or spirit. When it was necessary for him to place the emphasis on the wholeness or completeness of the concrete he put forward the Absolute as totality, but in order to keep the Absolute from falling into a bare or empty totality he brought forward the idea that the nature of the whole is spirit. It is in relation to this differential idea that he was able to judge that, for example, the category of quantity is less concrete than that of measure and all the categories of being are less concrete than those of essence. Put in this way, however, the criticism of abstractions is not merely an affair of discovering partiality and of relating it to the whole, but rather of determining the *relevance* of a given abstraction for expressing the whole taken as having some differential character. The difficulty here, and almost every critic of Hegel has made this point in one way or another, is that of establishing the importance of an abstraction in a finite and specific situation. To see the whole from the standpoint of God may be to relate everything to everything else so successfully that finite distinctions of importance simply disappear.

Dewey, above all other thinkers of the past 50 years, perceived the difficulty attaching to every attempt to criticize abstractions merely by confronting them with the concrete taken as the whole. He was uneasy in the absence of a differential concept or specific situation such as might provide special criteria for judging abstractions. Dewey went even further and began to doubt the legitimacy of a general *theory* of abstractions or what might be called a speculative resolution of the problem. In meeting the issue he brought forth his own alternative, the second way of approach to the criticism of abstractions, the way of functioning or instrumentalism.

2. The Way of Functioning or Instrumentalism

Without involving ourselves primarily in tracing historical influences, we can clearly see that Dewey was close to Hegel at several important points. Like Hegel, he rejected isolated or atomic existence and even defined philosophy as criticism aimed at the removal of "rigid non-communicating compartments"; isolation he regarded as unnatural and at the opposite extreme from that thoroughgoing interaction of all things which is of the essence of his metaphysic. Unlike Hegel, however, Dewey had no inclusive category save Nature and Nature was conceived by him in a thoroughly pluralistic way except for the unity it may receive from its being disclosed through a single method. He did not, moreover, conceive the process of criticizing abstractions as a purely logical one based on the interrelation of categorical structures alone. In criticizing the primacy and ubiquity of the knowledge relationship, Dewey had also to reject the exclusive emphasis placed by Hegel on knowing as the supreme expression of all reality. By contrast, Dewey's thought is thoroughly anthropological; in emphasizing the human situation or predicament he claimed that the generic traits of existence take on their proper importance when they become related to human concerns and figure in the success or failure of human plans and purposes. In place of Hegel's more exclusively logical interpretation of incongruity or conflict as contradiction in a dialectical scheme, Dewey focused on the active and progressive sense in which situations are incongruous or break down rather than on their static and structural aspect. He was led consequently to concrete, practical problems of a social and moral nature where the resolution of conflict so understood requires active and overt transformations of things. The bearing of these features peculiar to Dewey's approach upon our basic theme is not far to seek.

Abstractions or selective emphases, in Dewey's language, are inevitable wherever reflection occurs, but is seemed to him that their one-sidedness might be rendered harmless if only the fact and act of selection were taken into account along with the facts selected. Abstraction is regarded by him as one act of choice beside others and abstractions are set to work in a stream of activities so that the conditions and consequences of such selection will become manifest. In place of a general theory aimed at the logical relating of partial aspects to each other, we are to rely upon a public method of operation available to all who care to trace out the conditions and follow the consequences attendant upon a given act of abstraction. Everyone is invited to set the abstraction to work in the continuum of experience in order to see where it leads and what transformations it can effect. Thus, for example, in order to estimate the meaning and legitimacy of such selective biases—these are Dewey's favorite examples—as that the real is the simple, or that atomic sense data are experientially primitive, or that the knowledge relationship is omnipresent, we must trace out the results or consequences of assuming these selections to be true. In this way they are brought back into relation to concrete experience and we have an opportunity to decide whether experience is thereby rendered more intelligible or opaque or whether it becomes more or less subject to control. By taking abstractions neither as finalities nor as absolute starting points but rather as instruments or ways of handling things in order to achieve some purpose, practical or theoretical, Dewey was able to avoid some of the problems that have vexed other thinkers attempting to define, for example, the relations between the precise concepts of physics and the objects and situations disclosed in direct experience. This is more obvious in regard to the abstract concepts and theories of natural science than with respect to the selective emphases of philosophy and the distinctions of interest and purpose that so obviously confront us in the course of actual life. To interpret theory in science as instrumental is to focus upon its function in guiding inquiry and in enabling us to control nature, rather than upon its status as disclosing in descriptive terms the ultimate nature of things. Because of this functional approach, Dewey could never see the point of a theory such as Whitehead's method of extensive abstraction designed for the purpose of building a bridge between well founded abstractions and the presentational situation. Such criticism of abstractions seemed to him unnecessary because he viewed the problem of relating them to the concrete as a functional and dynamic affair having a specific focus in each case rather than as a theoretical affair to be resolved by formulating a conceptual relationship *überhaupt* between abstractions and concrete nature.

That the functional approach has made its own contribution to the task of criticizing abstractions cannot be denied, but it is not clear that a naturalism of Dewey's type has sufficient resources in itself for showing the relative *importance* of the various aspects of life to each other. The problem raised by the breaking up of integral experience into features which, when taken by themselves, are abstract, is not to be resolved merely by admitting that abstraction does occur and making the fact public property. Abstractions require criticism not only in the sense that we sometimes make errors and abstract badly, but in the broader and more urgent sense that we need to know the relative *importance* of the various partial aspects of life under which we live—the economic, political, religious, moral, etc. If it is true as we have said that every abstraction or selective emphasis is based upon and expresses some purpose in thought (cf. Whitehead: "Thought is one form of emphasis"), then the relating of various systems or sets of abstractions to each other in order to fix their relative importance will require critical comparison of basic purposes and cannot be done with a working pluralism harboring no values beyond the social. If Hegel was inclined to lose finite or differential distinctions of importance through an overweening emphasis upon the whole, the radical pluralism of Dewey's functionalism goes to the other extreme, thus avoiding the problem of a final context.

Nature and man's success or failure in controlling it provide us with as much of a final focus or standard as Dewey's pluralism can allow. But the lack of unity in his vision of human life begins to make itself felt; the only unity we find is that of method and this is in itself too abstract to provide the guidance that we need. Setting abstractions to work in order to exhibit their consequences does indeed make room for criticism in the sense that we are then able to see the fruits they produce. Moreover, exhibiting our principles of selection as a matter of public knowledge does enable each of us (at least in principle) to retrace for himself the functional meaning which the abstraction has. But an abstraction unmasked, so to speak, is not *ipso facto* made less of an abstraction, unless indeed it is held that self-consciousness all by itself effects a remedy and this is a thesis which I believe Dewey would scarcely want to advance. We still face the problem of having some unified view of things based on a concept of *ultimate* importance by which the *relative* importance of abstractions can be judged. For if we are to accomplish the criticism of abstractions by confronting them with concrete life, we shall not be able to avoid saying what we take the concrete to be.

I am unable here to develop a full solution to the problem of criticizing abstractions, especially since I believe it is more important to draw some implications from the foregoing discussion for current views of the status and scope of reason. I am able, however, to indicate the line I believe the solution should follow. We need to start with the contention that abstractions are inevitable; without them no understanding of anything is possible and this means that it is sheer folly to condemn them in any wholesale fashion. Secondly, abstractions are always made for a purpose and from this condition there is no escaping. We may, for example, consider one and the same individual man from an esthetic standpoint and express our apprehension in a portrait; we may consider him as a physical organism and express the results of investigation through an x-ray plate or an anatomical diagram; we may consider him as a moral being and describe him as untrustworthy or as not to be depended upon. In each case the context of consideration is dependent upon a purpose; concentration upon this feature or that of one and the same concrete individual is focused by an interest or an end in view. This interest or purpose controls the meaning and scope of the abstraction. Thirdly, we have the need in philosophy for a recovery of a sense of *importance,* for without a doctrine of the ultimately important there can be no treatment of the relative importance of abstractions to each other. No philosopher of recent years has seen this point more clearly than Whitehead.

But I wish to suggest that if we are to recover this sense we shall have to understand the ingredient of valuation and importance in concrete experience; it will be necessary to reverse a pattern of long standing. Ever since Kant, and perhaps earlier, the tendency has been to begin reflective inquiry with science, i.e., with our most precise and therefore most abstract type of thinking. We have set out from natural science as the archetype of safe, certain or near certain knowledge and have then entertained the hope that in some way an advance can be made to the good, or morality, or value which will enable us to estimate the importance or relevance of that knowledge and the ends to which the power it bestows should be directed. When we start with our most abstract and therefore our most precise thought we encounter great difficulty in moving to the concrete and to a sense of importance by a process of construction; the result is an indefinite postponement of all the urgent concerns and in fact they are often never allowed to enter at all. But surely this is to proceed in the wrong way. It is not true that we can reach concrete moral values by first beginning with the method or conclusions of science and attempting to extend it to the sphere of importance; on the contrary, scientific inquiry is itself incapable of being initiated and sustained without antecedent commitment to norms and values that are by no stretch of the imagination derivative from science. Without the commitment to the reality of a truth that no man has constructed and which is not the exclusive property of any nation or class, and a loyalty to the strict prosecution of a method for disclosing it, science is impossible. Science is a hard achievement just because it requires self-discipline, but this is a moral and, in many cases, a religious virtue; it is not a product of science but the life that sustains it.

We must start our philosophizing with the concrete human situation—man is the only being for whom the problem of abstractions and importance becomes explicit—we must start, that is, with man as the religious, moral, social, political being and then move from there to the abstractions of specialized knowledge which are directed to the realization of specific ends within these various aspects of the most concrete human situation. The real situation for man, in short, the concrete, is the moral, religious, political situation; all else is abstraction in relation to that and cannot be allowed to stand by itself. There is no way to the concrete concerns defining man's life and situation in the world if we first begin with the abstractions of theoretical knowledge any more than it is possible to reach the individual if we first begin with universals and then attempt some process of specification. To start with the abstractions of our most precise knowledge means that we shall be condemned to end with them as well and thus fail to reach the concrete. But if we start with the most important aspects of our experience and our life in the world we shall have a vantage point from which to view, criticize and evaluate the abstractions required by all reliable knowl-

edge. If there are no abstractions apart from purposes, then purposes, valuation and importance are all present at the start; in the
beginning was the purpose and Royce was right when he argued
that there is no pure intellect but that all thought and knowledge
stand essentially related to the will.

To return to the bearing of the earlier discussion upon the scope
of reason, there is one central point to be made. To deny that there
is any problem with regard to abstractions and to identify reason
solely with analysis or, what amounts to the same thing, to hold that
reality is basically atomistic in character, is most emphatically *not* to
be a friend of reason at all, but to make a large contribution to its
eventual dissolution. Contrary to what has been believed by most
defenders of the sufficiency of analysis, it is the narrow view of
reason that produces obscurantism, primitivism and explicit irra-
tionalism. The more we abandon responsibility for the criticism of
abstractions while at the same time acquiescing in the view which
identifies the scope of reason with that of analysis, the more we
invite those dealing with the most concrete human concerns to be
done with rational criticism altogether. For those whose main concern centers in the problems of morality, religion, and politics see at
once that if reason is exhausted in formal logic and the production
of analytic distinctions without regard for either their relative importance or the integrity of experience, it becomes futile to think of
rational criticism in these areas of thought. It is no pure accident
that on the current scene the philosophy of existence appears side
by side with highly formalized conceptions of reason and at a time
when the dominant trend in philosophy identifies reason with analysis alone. Difficult and vague but highly important human questions do not remain in exile merely because they are banished by
formalistic reason. But under such circumstances discussion of
them is bound to fall beyond the scope of rational criticism if we
confine it to the horizon of analysis and assume no responsibility
for those abstractions to which analytic thought inevitably leads. At
present, therefore, nothing is more important than the recovery of
reason in a sense broad enough to embrace both analysis and a
doctrine of importance that will enable us to criticize abstractions in
the light of our most concrete life and experience.

II
Community and the Self

7

Royce: The Absolute and the Beloved Community Revisited

"Royce: The Absolute and the Beloved Community Revisited" was presented at the Boston University Colloquium on Philosophy and Religion and was published in a volume entitled, Meaning, Truth and God, *ed. Leroy S. Rouner, vol. 3,* Boston University Studies in Philosophy and Religion, Notre Dame *& London, 1982. Royce's philosophy, embracing both individual and community, represents an important part of the vision concerning nature, man and God which, unfortunately, until very recently was allowed to disappear from the scene. Royce went out of fashion largely because he was going against the oncoming stream of the Pragmatists and new forms of Anglo-American empiricism. His name meant just about all that was coming under attack—he demanded a speculative system, he held firm to the outlook of idealism and he insisted on the need for an "Absolute Knower," or simply the Absolute.*

Royce's belief in the inescapability of the Absolute was based upon his ingenious argument set forth in a chapter entitled, "The Possibility of Error" in The Religious Aspect of Philosophy. *Royce clearly had Kant's transcendental approach in mind, except that he changed the focus. On the supposition that starting with knowledge, as Kant did, could be countered by the skeptical claim, Royce proposed instead to start with the fact of error—"real" error, that is, not its mere appearance—as something that has to be admitted. The problem then becomes, what conditions must obtain in the case of a real error? The general shape of what are now called "transcendental arguments" is simply that, if one can give a plausible account of what these conditions* are, *and what they are conditions* for *is actual, then the conditions themselves cannot be merely possible. In the particular case, Royce was arguing that a real error must be about an object that* transcends *both the erroneous judgment and the individual knower, otherwise the object would be defined exclusively by that judgment and that knower and could not be in error. Underlying this quest for such an object is Royce's idea that, following Peirce and Kant, an idea is to be judged only in accordance with "its" object and no particular judgment can refer to or "pick out" its object without recourse to a system of knowledge—what the Absolute knows—whereby one can individuate an object as the one referred to and "no other." Whatever one may think of the validity of this argument, it cannot be sent packing merely by insisting as James repeatedly did that the knowledge possessed by the Absolute is not available to us and hence it does no good. But, of course, that is not the point; Royce was claiming that* reference *to such a whole of knowledge is necessary*

*if any particular judgment is to have its object about which it could be in error.
What Royce did not see is that arguments to the conditions do not "prove"
anything in a deductive way, but rather call attention to what needs to be
assumed in order to account for something taken to be actual, whether knowledge or error.*

*What needs to be underlined, however, is that the later Royce, after pub-
lication of* The World and the Individual, *dropped the Absolute and replaced it with the idea of the community of interpretation in which there is an
assured place for the individual, for the reality of time and change, but no place
for the* totum simul, *the all-at-once apprehension possessed by the former
Absolute. Royce offered a masterful and exact analysis of the structure of the
community, of how the community is related to its members and how the members
are related to each other. Individual and community are brought together in
ways that show the reality of both and their mutual interdependence. Royce's
application of the theory to the religious community resulted in one of the finest
works in the philosophy of religion ever to appear on the American scene. In
this paper I set out to show how the later Royce developed novel ideas that go
beyond the Royce that so many have found uncongenial. The chapter is from
the* Boston University Studies in Philosophy and Religion, *edited by
Leroy S. Rouner, © 1982 by University of Notre Dame Press. Reprinted by
permission of the publisher.*

Anyone who like myself has studied Royce's philosophy over a long
period of time—my *Royce's Social Infinite* was published in 1950 —
must keep coming back to a problem posed not only by the development of his thought, but even more pointedly by his own interpretation of that development set forth in the course of remarks he
made at a dinner given in his honor not long before his death. Ever
responsive to criticism, Royce was keenly aware of the objections
leveled against his doctrine of the Absolute by Howison, James, and
others; and he also took note of questions being raised about the
continuity of his thought. In the philosophy of what has come to be
called the later Royce, expressed in writings subsequent to *The
World and the Individual*, the Absolute disappears, as it were, and
attention is focused on the doctrines of loyalty, community, and
interpretation. In the remarks mentioned above Royce was at pains
to insure the continuity of his philosophy, maintaining that the
notion of the community was present in his thought from the beginning.[1] Earlier on I disagreed with this interpretation in the be-

1. Speaking of his career and intellectual development, Royce said, "When I
review this whole process, I strongly feel that my deepest motives and problems have
centered about the Idea of the Community, although this ideal has only come
gradually to my clear consciousness" ("Words of Professor Royce at the Walton Hotel
at Philadelphia, December 29, 1915," *Philosophical Review* 25:3 [May 1916]: 510).

lief that it had an ad hoc character suited to the occasion and that Royce was misreading his earlier statements in order to prove his consistency. I have changed my mind on this at least. The community idea is indeed to be found in earlier works, notably in his book on California and in *The Spirit of Modern Philosophy*, where it figures largely in his conception of the higher or more inclusive self and in his conception of objectivity as dependent on permanence and a community of ideas. This much continuity, however, does not resolve the more difficult problem of what happened to the Absolute. I shall suggest further on that Royce was, sometimes quite imperceptibly, responding to criticism of the Absolute focusing on the reality of time, development, novelty, and individuality and that he came ultimately to believe that the doctrine of community provided a better solution to the problem on the One and the Many than the Absolute with its *totum simul* consciousness apprehending all individuals as "drops in this ocean of absolute truth."[2]

I shall approach the problem of the fate of the Absolute, if that expression is not too paradoxical, in three steps: first, an account of the conception itself in terms of what I shall call Royce's fundamental conviction; second, an interpretation of the ingenious argument offered for the reality of the Absolute Knower in the chapter from *The Religious Aspect*, "The Possibility of Error"; and third, a brief consideration of difficulties encountered by his absolute idealism and an indication of how his last philosophy was intended to meet them. I trust that the reader will understand that Royce laid great store by his technical skill in philosophical discussion and that the ground to be traversed is quite intricate; I obviously cannot cover it all and I shall hope not to make it more confusing.

Royce's Fundamental Conviction

It has been said that a comprehensive and systematic thinker, like the hedgehog in the fable, knows one big thing or has one grand idea which he or she articulates, shapes, and reshapes, in an effort to give it the fullest possible expression. In Royce's case, that idea is the reality of a time-spanning consciousness, an Absolute Self to whom all truth, and indeed error too, is known. Royce saw this idea as consonant with the biblical hope of being able to know as we are known, and he saw it as the cornerstone of the thought of Augustine. This commanding idea—that the meaning, truth, and pur-

2. Josiah Royce, *The Religious Aspect of Philosophy* (1895; reprint ed., New York: Harper & Brothers, Harper Torchbooks, 1958), p. 441; cf. Josiah Royce, *The Philosophy of Loyalty* (New York: Macmillan, 1908), p. 395.

pose of any fragment, whether it be a momentary thought, a physical object, an event in one's history, are to be found only by appeal to a whole which is, for a finite knower, out of sight—figured in every context of Royce's philosophy. In the sphere of knowledge, no isolated judgment taken by itself and apart from a whole of experience can be deemed true or false; in self-development and the unfolding of consciousness we are always in the situation of having to be more than we are at any moment in order to understand what we are at that moment;[3] in the ethical dimension, the full understanding of the worth of a deed depends on its relation to the whole life of which it is a part; and in religion the significance of any event for our individual destiny can be fully grasped only from the perspective of a Self capable of apprehending a person's life as a whole.

Later on, in *The Problem of Christianity*, this idea was to receive a most forceful application in Royce's interpretation of Jesus' preaching about the Kingdom of God. Since each member of that company is viewed by God who has a conspectus of the totality, each of us is to regard our neighbors and act toward them not only in accordance with our limited view of their welfare but with an imaginative grasp of the way they would appear if we could know their lives as God does. Royce reiterated this fundamental conviction ever and again, and it was the copingstone of his idealism. To know the present context of experience, a particular object, an event in one's life, necessarily requires the appeal to an other, and that, in turn, to an other; if the entire process is to have unity, coherence, and permanence, there must ultimately be an Absolute Self whose experience is of the totality. Royce was indeed captivated by this vision of an Absolute Experience wherein what is apprehended by finite individuals only fragmentarily and discursively is grasped all at once, *totum simul,* with nothing omitted. As we shall see, however, the doctrine that what is, is always all there—not a new doctrine, but one to which Royce gave a novel voluntaristic twist—was to give rise to its own difficulties, not the least of which centered on reconciling this *totum simul* Absolute with Royce's very perceptive theory of the individual self as a purpose to be realized and a task to be performed.

3. "In order to realize what I am I must . . . become more than I am or than I know myself to be. I must enlarge myself, . . . go beyond my private self, presuppose the social life . . ." (Josiah Royce, *The Spirit of Modern Philosophy* [New York: Houghton Mifflin and Company; and Cambridge, Mass.: The Riverside Press, 1892], p. 215).

In noting Royce's captivation with the idea of an Absolute Experience, I do not mean to say that he regarded it as sufficient merely to wax enthusiastic about the notion. On the contrary, despite the not-inconsiderable rhetoric and even unction to be found in his writings, Royce had an overweening confidence in the power of logic, and he spoke unabashedly of the need for proof in philosophy. And in fact he was convinced that in his famous argument from "the possibility of error," to which we shall shortly turn, he had established beyond all wish, hope, and even postulate, the existence of the Absolute Knower. I do not regard it as an expression of any lack of faith in rationality to say that I do not follow Royce in his belief in proof in philosophy. Proof, if such there be anywhere, is to be found only in axiomatic systems which are *ipso facto* abstract, and, despite the dream of Descartes, no comprehensive account of what there is can be cast in such a mold. Clarity of analysis, the adducing of consistent reasons, and the meeting of objections are all we can do in philosophical thought, and, in my view, that is enough. Royce clearly wanted more, and he was spurred on by his unlimited trust in versions of the self-referential argument; on more than one occasion he claimed that he could start with the premises of those who proposed to refute him and show that even they had to appeal to his truth! With regard to the particular argument from error, as distinct from the matter of proof in general, I shall say at this point no more than that I believe Royce validly showed something there, although exactly what that something is is more difficult to say than you may imagine. If my interpretation is correct, his argument is of a transcendental sort, and that is no matter of linear proof.

The Argument from the Possibility of Error

How seriously Royce regarded his account of error can be seen in his later reference to it in *The Spirit of Modern Philosophy*. There he described the chapter from *The Religious Aspect of Philosophy* as "containing a metaphysical discussion of the proof of the main thesis of Objective Idealism."[4]

No part of Royce's philosophy can be understood apart from the fundamental assumption which has been in one way or another the cornerstone of all modern idealisms, especially those derived from that development running from Kant to Hegel. I am referring to the thesis that the key to the understanding of being is through

---

4. Ibid., p. vi.

being known. The assumption is that a proper understanding of the relation between an idea (judgment) and its object holds the key to the nature of reality. In that relationship we have something of the nature of a privileged position or unique access to reality; we lay hold of the real when we understand what it would have to be like and what conditions it would be called upon to satisfy if it were to be known and apprehended in its truth. We would never get on to our task were I to stop to consider the problems raised by this assumption; we must allow it for the argument's sake and then point out that in Royce's version of idealism the knowing involved is deeper and richer than that envisaged by more rationalistic systems. Royce introduced a voluntaristic dimension into the position, declaring that there is no "pure intellect," all logic being that of the will. The upshot is that all intellectual endeavor is oriented by purpose and intention so that the truth of any set of representations depends on what and how you are attempting to represent.

Since I have categorized Royce's argument for the Absolute Knower as a "transcendental" one, it will be necessary to clarify that notion for a start. The introduction of this way of thinking must be credited to Kant, and it represents something quite novel in the history of Western thought. Kant proposed to begin with knowledge as a fact, that is, with the assumption that Newton's mechanics and the mathematics ingredient in it are forms of objective knowledge about an existent world. Having made this assumption, he then went on to ask how this knowledge is possible, by which he did not mean how do we arrive at it from the standpoint of method, but rather what conditions must be fulfilled if we are to understand the rationality and thus the reliability of a knowledge already regarded as actual. The quest for the conditions which make the actual possible is the task of transcendental philosophy. This reflective enterprise is novel in that it cannot be carried out on the basis of either of the two classical forms of thought: deduction, and induction or probable inference. This position in the hands of Kant, and in my view of Royce too, assumes the form of an idealism because of what Kant called his "Copernican Revolution," which for our purposes will be taken to mean the reversal of the long-standing belief that in knowledge thought must conform to things. For Kant things must be understood as conforming to thought if knowledge is to be possible, and that is why what he called the a priori conditions for knowledge are to be found in human faculties of sensibility, understanding, and reason. All intellectual endeavor, in short, is dependent on synthetic activities of the subject.

Royce followed this pattern of thinking in his argument for the Absolute Knower, but he did so with a characteristic Roycean twist. Seeing that beginning with the fact of knowledge is vulnerable because the skeptic can claim that we have no knowledge, Royce began instead with the fact of error, that we make real mistakes, a claim he thought could not be doubted. Royce, then, was asking, How is error possible? and he aimed to show that it is not possible unless there really is an Absolute Knower to whom is present the whole of experience. The upshot, in Royce's view, is that anyone rejecting his conclusion is forced to hold that error is impossible, and this contradicts the facts. As I have pointed out, the argument is long and intricate, and, moreover, it is not always clear; I shall attempt to elucidate the crucial points.

The first consideration is to determine what it is for an idea (judgment) to be a "real" error. Harking back to a point made by Kant and much emphasized by Peirce, although often overlooked by many, Royce claimed that an erroneous judgment is not in error with respect to any object you please, but only in relation to *its* object, that is, the unique object the judgment aims to characterize. One can see the force of this point from a simple illustration. If I look at a blackboard on which are drawn diagrams of the conic sections and say, "That one is elliptical in shape," and someone says, "You are wrong; it is circular," my judgment would be in error only if in fact I had intended the circular figure—which I did not. Under such circumstances, one would say, "The circular figure is not the one I meant, not the proper object of my judgment, and hence I made no mistake." If I do make an error about an object, the error must be about the intended object; and if it is a real error, that object must have a tenure beyond my individual thought and intention. If this were not so, it would be impossible for anyone to make a mistake, because the judgment that the blue object I mean is blue cannot fail to be correct since that and no other object is the intended one. On this basis no error is possible. The price of this infallibility, however, is that nothing is being said about an objective world going beyond the individual mind. Royce insists that a real error must be about a real object which is at the same time the object intended by the judgment. How are these conditions to be fulfilled?

The principle behind Royce's answer to this question we have already noted; no finite thought, content of experience, or judgment can be known, thought, understood without going beyond it. In this case what we are seeking to understand is an error, that is, a judgment about a judgment. It is Royce's contention that when we say to ourselves, "This color now before me is red, and to say that it is blue would be to make a blunder," we represent what he calls "an including consciousness" which is far more complex than that of the initial judgment. Three distinct elements are included within the unity of this expanded consciousness: "first, the perception of red; secondly, the reflected judgment whose object is this perception, and whose agreement with this object constitutes its own truth; and, thirdly, the erroneous reflection, *this is blue,* which is in the same thought compared with the perception and rejected as error."[5] The inclusive thought is necessary because in a real error the object intended must be the same object intended by the true judgment in comparison with which the error is exposed, and, on his view, this comparison can be made only within the unity of a thought to which the error, the truth, and the same intended object are present. Royce concludes that this complex must be present for one inclusive thought, so that error is possible as a moment in this higher thought or consciousness which makes the error a part of itself while knowing that it is an error.

But, one may ask, Why must there be an Absolute Knower? Why cannot each individual self-conscious being realize the complex unity just described? Royce's answer, although one must work through his many restatements of the argument to find it, has two features. The first is that no single judgment taken by itself can be an error. Error is possible only as actually included in a higher thought which provides the judgment with a completed object; for example, the object in its whole truth, by comparison with which the error is judged to be error. The idea is that if error is a fragment or an incomplete thought, that fact can be discovered by comparing it not with other fragments but only with the completed object. No finite knower possesses that object; we can intend it and find error about it, but we do not have that object available to us for comparison with our isolated judgment. Only an Absolute Knower could do that. Secondly, Royce argues, there is an infinite mass of error possible, and since the possibilities of error are infinite, there must be an infinite thought to expose them through comparison with the truth about these objects. That task is beyond the power of finite knowers or any finite collection of them.

I must leave the exposition here with apologies for not having made it all clearer. I shall, however, make three brief comments about Royce's claim. First, much of the difficulty in following the argument stems from two features in Royce's presentation. One is

5. Royce, *The Religious Aspect of Philosophy,* p. 423.

his having restated the case several times but with some novel feature on each occasion. The second has to do with differences in the kinds of objects he considered and the bearing these differences have on what it means to say that the infinite thought furnishes the real object of our judgment. The physical objects, things of the world, are available to us as such, even if we don't have the whole truth about them. The situation is somewhat different when we consider the knowledge of selves. In a discussion I have omitted, Royce availed himself of a humorous remark made by Mark Twain that in every conversation between two people, there are six participants—the real John and the real Thomas, and their respective ideas of each other and of themselves. His point is that a real error on John's part about Thomas must be about the real Thomas. While John can *intend* that Thomas, the complex unity of thought, feeling, and the like, constituting the real Thomas is not directly available to John, but only to a Knower who possesses the whole and completed truth about Thomas. The point is ever the same; a real error requires that it be about a real object, but its meaning as an error consists in its being compared with the corresponding true judgment about the same object present to the same inclusive thought. What Royce is assuming here, but not admitting as clearly as he might have, is that a singular erroneous judgment can be exposed as such not by comparison with a fragment, but only from the standpoint of a Knower who possesses the whole truth about a complete object.

This brings me to my second point: for Royce, everything depends on the knowing purpose involved. It is not the object as such that we seek, but the truth about it; and this is the reason Royce needs a completed object or the whole truth about that object and no other to counter all the error that is possible. Only an Absolute Knower has that truth, and that is why such a Knower is required for explaining the possibility of error.

My third point follows directly from the preceding; it concerns the transcendental character of the entire argument. The point of such an argument, one must remember, is not to offer a touchstone for determining when we have made a mistake in a particular case, but rather to specify the conditions which make error as such possible. If error, any error, is actual, then the conditions for its possibility cannot themselves be merely possible but must be actual as well. It is for this reason that Royce claims the actuality and not just the postulation of the Absolute Knower. About this feature of the transcendental argument, Royce was right; the point goes all the way back to Aristotle's claim that the actual cannot be accounted for solely on the basis of possibility.

Whatever difficulties there are in Royce's position, I think he should be defended against one misunderstanding of which some of his critics, including James, were guilty. Royce makes no claim, as James seems to have thought, that the knowledge of the Absolute Knower is available to us to be used as a standard for judging particular judgments. James's famous exclamation, "I say, Royce, damn the Absolute!" was prompted by the commonsensical idea that it does us no good in the way of knowing to know that the Absolute Knower knows it all, because that knowledge is inaccessible to us. But here James missed the point—and this would remain true even if Royce's entire argument were fallacious. The Absolute reached in the argument is an implicate, a condition necessary for explaining error and the truth which makes error possible. The parallel with Kant's *Critique of Pure Reason* in this regard is instructive. The *Critique* tells us what knowledge of an object means and the conditions which make it possible, but the *Critique* by itself does not enable us to determine the material truth or falsehood of this or that judgment. So it is with Royce's argument; it tells us what an error is and why an Absolute Knower is required if the fact of error is to be made intelligible, but that account itself does not provide us with any formula for ascertaining in a given case whether we have made an error or not.

Absolute Idealism, Community, and Interpretation

One thing remained constant throughout Royce's philosophical career: his commitment to idealism as the only satisfactory metaphysics. "A doctrine," he has written in *The Spirit*, "remains, in the metaphysical sense idealistic, if it maintains that the world is, in its wholeness, and in all of its real constituent parts, a world of mind or of spirit."[6]

The shape of that idealism, however, did not remain fixed. Even if we allow, as I think we must, that there is continuity between his earlier and later thought as regards what may be called the "social principle" and the reality of community, his conception of the spiritual reality was altered both in response to criticism and as a result of the influence of Peirce's theory of interpretation. The dropping of the language of the Absolute in his last writings is not the least of these alterations. I shall select three focal points at which Royce showed concern to rework his ideas in an effort to do justice to certain features of experience which, as it seemed to some, had

6. Royce, *The Spirit of Modern Philosophy*, p. xiv.

been subordinated by his uncompromising idealism. These points are the status of the self and the reality of finite individuals; the recognition of time as a real order allowing for novelty; and the solution to the problem of the One and the Many. In considering each of these points in turn, I shall have to simplify matters somewhat because of the extensiveness of the relevant discussions, but I trust that I shall not distort Royce's views in the effort.

To begin with and remaining on a commonsensical level, the most obvious uneasiness about Royce's Absolute was expressed in the fear that its all-encompassing unity meant the disappearance of individual finite selves endowed with some measure of autonomy. James gave expression to this uneasiness when he described Royce's world as a "block universe" whose grade of unity is so tight that there seems to be no room for possibility, indeterminacy, contingency, and creativity. In short, for James, such a world could have no open future. Apart from his more rhetorical pages in which he celebrated the completed unity of the one Self, Royce never envisaged the Absolute as undifferentiated, and, in fact, it is one of his major criticisms of mysticism that it so often results in an undifferentiated immediacy wherein everything finite is absorbed. Royce, it is clear, rejected such a view, but it remains to be seen how well he succeeded in doing justice to individual selves within the confines of his absolute idealism.

In his Gifford Lectures, *The World and the Individual*, Royce set forth a novel theory of being, the fundamental thesis of which is summed up in the formula "To be is to be the fulfillment of a purpose." According to this view, what there is represents the will or purpose of the Absolute Self who intends this world and no other; every being in it must be seen as this individual and no other, since all belong to one and the same system. The idea that will or purpose defines individuality is of the utmost importance because it figures largely in Royce's conception of the individual self as an overarching purpose or plan. The self, in the end, is a task to be performed, calling into play the active powers of each individual. There can be no doubt that Royce envisaged for each individual the need to identify himself or herself in some form of contrast to other selves, the world, and God. Each will have, says Royce,

> the really deep and important persuasion that he *ought to possess* or create for himself . . . some one principle, some finally significant contrast, whereby he should be able, with an unified and permanent meaning, to identify that portion of the world's life which is to be, in the larger sense, his own, and whereby he should be able

to contrast with this, his larger Self, all the rest of the world of life.[7]

Individuals, then, are such that they are identified by the projection of and the persistent effort to realize a purpose providing the unity and identity essential for selfhood. In my own language, I refer to this aspect as the expression of "what I mean to be." That we are here dealing with something undeniably individual is clear; Royce continues,

> Now this purpose, I maintain, is indeed your own. As nobody else can share it, so nobody else can create it; and from no source external to yourself have you derived it.[8]

That is a strong declaration of uniqueness and individuality.

There is, however, the other aspect of his idealism noted above; the whole of being represents the realized purpose of the Absolute Self so that we have not to do merely with what I mean to be, my purpose, but with what "I was meant to be" from the standpoint of that Self who intended me and no other. How are these two aspects to be brought together? Here Royce meets a problem by no means unknown to the Western philosophical, no less than the theological, tradition. In my view, although he did seek to bring both the "I mean" and the "I was meant" into some form of unity, he cannot solve the problem on the basis of his Absolute. The reason is that a completed and fully determinate self or object is what the Absolute now possesses, and if this is so, it is difficult to see in what sense it can be said that my individual purpose as it now stands before me has not been derived from any source external to myself. If, of course, Royce means that the Absolute Self is not external to me in the sense that two beads on a string are external to each other, well and good. But what holds me apart now from that completed self which the theory demands and cannot do without? The problem is endemic to an idealism which allows the real no tenure apart from will and mind and is therefore forced to identify that real with a totality or completion of meaning and knowing. Short of this completion, we have nothing at all. That is the perennial problem of absolute idealism.

Having suggested why I believe Royce cannot reconcile the two aspects ultimately, let me call attention to the great strength of what we may refer to as his proximate solution. Long before Sartre, and

7. Josiah Royce, *The World and the Individual,* 2 vols. (New York: Macmillan, 1899–1901), 2:274.
8. Ibid., p. 294.

even Marcel, Royce had the idea of the self as a plan or project, an essentially ethical task. He never wavered on the basic point that the self is not a datum given to direct perception, nor is it some combination of conceived universals. The self is a living unity extending over time, and the unity is provided by a purpose to be realized. Unlike Sartre, however, who identifies the self with freedom, Royce saw the role of destiny, of Providence in religious terms, and the need to acknowledge the existence of factors and conditions in the makeup of an individual that cannot be put down to freedom alone. If the world is not just so much brute fact but is intended as the fulfillment of a purpose, then I must find myself already endowed with capacities, talents, interests answering to what "I was meant to be." In short, whatever freedom I have to realize what "I mean to be" must be limited. Nevertheless, these capacities and endowments, Royce contends, do not organize and direct themselves—to do that is a task to be carried out by me and no other.

From my standpoint as this individual there is a life-plan to be framed and pursued, and neither task can be performed by anyone else. Again, from that standpoint I am not to regard my completed and fully determinate self as all there in advance. But, as I have pointed out, if the argument from error stands, there is no way in which Royce can avoid the necessity of the completed object if he is to have any object at all. This is the root of his problem. In fairness, however, I should say that Royce would have pointed in reply to his ingenious theory of the Actual Infinite set forth in the supplementary essay to *The World and the Individual,* where the totality is said to be found in the form or purpose generating all its members and not in a *seriatim* completion ending with a final term. I cannot discuss this here, beyond saying that it points in the direction of an open end to the world process which Royce was to stress more and more later on.

I shall telescope the remaining two points—time as a real order allowing for novelty, and the conception of community as the final solution to the problem of the One and the Many—since they are intimately connected. Of crucial importance was Royce's discovery of Charles Peirce's theory of signs and interpretation. Royce gladly acknowledged his debt to Peirce in this regard, but he assumed sole responsibility for the special applications of the theory to problems in the philosophy of religion and especially to the task of reinterpreting Christianity in terms of what he called the essential Christian ideas. To anticipate those applications, I shall mention the two relevant for our purposes. One is Royce's fastening upon the connection between time and the open-ended nature of the

interpretative process; and the other is the double claim that interpretation is unique and not reducible to other cognitive forms, and
that it is especially suited for the achievement of understanding between selves and consequently for the realization of communities of
persons.

Peirce had argued as a general thesis that all thought takes
place through the medium of signs which have the distinctive
triadic character of (a) pointing to an object, state of affairs, or
anything we can intend; (b) embodying some meaning, qualification, or determination of that thing; and (c) addressing themselves
to a potential reader or mind capable of interpreting what the sign
means through the use of other signs. There is a more exact
formulation of sign-functioning as a triadic relation of sign, object,
and interpretant, but that might prove more confusing than
enlightening for our purposes. Royce sought to bring out the
peculiar features and role of interpreting signs by contrasting
interpretation with the two basic faculties of the human mind
bequeathed by Kant's analysis in *The Critique of Pure Reason*—
perceiving and conceiving. *Perceiving* has as its object a thing,
datum, complex of fact which is present to us and apprehended
directly. *Conceiving* aims at defining the universal and repeatable
characteristics of things and their structures and relations. Royce
was well aware that, while Kant had held that only a synthesis of
the two can lead to knowledge, a debate has continued from Plato
to Bergson and beyond as to whether one of the two is fundamental and the other derivative. More important, however, than the
resolution of this problem is the assumption that the dichotomy
presented is exhaustive and that there is no other cognitive
process. Royce denied this assumption in a most telling way. Not
only are perceiving and conceiving self-limiting processes—the
former comes to rest in the presence of the datum and the latter
has done its work when the ideal type of the fact has been
determined—but neither taken alone is equal to the task of
interpreting signs. Consider his example of the weathervane.
Perceiving the device as an object present and describing it by
means of concepts are both possible for someone who does not
know how to read it, that is, to interpret the meaning of the device
as a sign indicating the direction of the wind. Unless one understands that the vane is a sign and knows what the position of its
movable part means, one can do no more than look at the object
and describe its features; one cannot interpret. Interpretation,
moreover, is not self-limiting, because every reading of a sign takes
place through an interpretation which is itself a sign addressed to

a future interpreter. The process is essentially social, since every sign is a sign of a mind that was, and is addressed to a mind that is yet to come upon it.

Adopting Peirce's earlier claim that the self is not the proper object of either perceiving or conceiving since it is essentially a conversation of interpreted meanings, Royce declared that interpretation is the only appropriate cognitive process whereby selves come to know themselves and each other. This notion is at the root of the doctrine of community, illustrated at an elementary level in the process of translation and then extended by Royce to include religious, moral, political communities based on traditions extending over long periods of time. When translators confront a text in a given language, they encounter the signs of another mind; in translating this text into another language they produce a second set of signs addressed to a future mind; and interpreters say, in effect, to that mind: "What I say to you is what the text says to me." There is thus a linkage of meaning, via the office of the interpreter, between three minds—the writer of the text, perhaps long gone, the present interpreter, and the future mind who, in reading the interpretation, becomes related to a mind in the past.

It should now be evident that through the doctrine of interpretation, Royce is attempting to provide a solid foundation for a real time-order. Seen from the standpoint of an individual, the present self interprets the past self to the future self. I recall today that some weeks ago I promised to return a book at some determinate time in the future. The reference to both memory and anticipation led Royce to consider the ability of otherwise distinct selves to extend themselves in both directions by identifying themselves with certain events in the past as part of their own history, and by identifying themselves with certain hoped-for events forming part of a future not yet actualized. Such ideal extensions are the substance of what he called communities of memory and communities of hope. The community comes into being when many distinct selves find themselves accepting as part of themselves and their own biography a common past and a common hoped-for future. The experiences, persons, and events, for example, which form the substance of religious communities, are preserved in the sacred literature of the community, available as signs to everyone present to interpret them. When one identifies oneself with this past and regards it as belonging to one's own history, he or she is at once linked through spiritual bonds with all other selves making the same identification. In commemorating the deliverance from Egypt, for example, the members of the Jewish community give thanks to the Lord for delivering *us* from bondage. Each individual, in saying "we" and "us," is making an identification with that common heritage which all share. The same phenomenon is evident in national communities; consider that in his Gettysburg Address, Lincoln did not say "the forefathers," or "some forefathers," but "our forefathers," a clear expression of the identification by all participants of themselves with a tradition shared by all.

We cannot follow Royce's extended application of the doctrines of interpretation and community to what he called "the problem of Christianity" and his account of the social dimension of religion supremely exemplified by the Beloved Community. However, let me bring the discussion to a close by defining more exactly the nature of community as Royce saw it, and how it serves to relate the One and the Many. To begin with, Royce, like Aristotle and Hegel, regarded community as a distinct type and level of being,[9] not to be understood in terms of adding or summing individuals. Royce repeatedly insisted that if one thinks of a one, and another, and another, and so on, it will not be possible to arrive at a community, but only a collection. Understanding what a community is depends on seeing, first, that genuinely distinct individuals are required, and, secondly, that these individuals become linked to each other in virtue of the fact that they are all linked to the same third reality. For the existence of a community, three conditions are required: the power of the individual to extend his or her life in time; a number of distinct selves capable of communicating with each other; and the inclusion by the ideally extended selves of some events which are for all of them identical.

The first condition depends on Royce's thesis that the self is no datum either of perception or conception, but a life which is interpreted and interprets itself over a course of time in accordance with purposes and reasons determining what that life shall include and how it will be identified. As regards the second condition, the existence of individuals in communication, Royce was emphatic, in his own words, "that a community does *not* become one, in the sense of my definition, by virtue of any reduction or melting of these various selves into a single merely present self, or into a mass of passing experience."[10] The point is crucial and often overlooked. Suffice to say here that were there

9. This does not mean, as nominalists and individualists invariably suppose, that a community is something that still continues to have some sort of being even if there were no members! This conception misses the point.

10. Josiah Royce, *The Problem of Christianity* (Chicago: University of Chicago Press, 1968), pp. 255–56.

not many there would be no problem of how to relate them to the One. Anyone who supposes that Royce wants to absorb individuals into a community has misunderstood him.

The third condition is in many ways the most important because it points to the unifying spiritual bond enabling us to say that though there are many members, there is but one body. Insofar as all members acknowledge as belonging to their own past a heritage of faith, of deeds, of insights, they form a community of memory such that each member knows about all the others the fact that they are identified with the same past he or she acknowledges. And so with the community of hope engaged in accomplishing some goal—what Royce usually called a cause in performing deeds aimed at helping to realize that goal. Each individual knows that the others accept as part of themselves that hoped-for future and are committed to the common task of contributing to its realization. The Many are One in virtue of their relation to the common third reality, but they remain many since this very relationship contributes to their own fulfillment as individual persons. One loses one's life in the cause, only to find it again through individual but cooperative endeavor with fellow beings unified by a bond of love and loyalty.

Recognition of the discursive and temporal character of the process of interpretation, and of the dynamic life of communities through their members in history, no longer made it necessary for Royce to adhere to the *totum simul,* or "all at once" conception of consciousness characteristic of his earlier thought. A dynamic development of life and spirit in a historical order has now taken precedence over the previous conception of a completed Absolute. And, in fact, as I have noted, that term disappears and is to be found, if at all, only in the faint echo of an Ideal Interpreter which, if my memory serves me correctly, makes but one appearance in the pages of *The Problem of Christianity.* Instead, we have a new orientation in Royce's thought leading into a possibly creative future. At the end he was expressing the hope that the historical process would move in the direction of realizing a community of all humanity in which spiritual ties of understanding, loyalty, and devotion would prove strong enough to overcome the conflicts and divisions among people which lead ever and again to those two distorted forms of human relations—collectivism and individualism. The former is a One without a real Many, while the latter is a Many without a real One. Royce's vision of community points to a form of life transcending these distortions because it is a unity of a One and a Many which allows for both without sacrificing either.

8

The Value of Community:
Dewey and Royce

"The Value of Community: Dewey and Royce" stemmed from my interest in the fact that both thinkers, despite their very different approaches to philosophy and their different outlooks, focused attention on the reality of communities and the important roles they play in modern life. As Dewey repeatedly insisted, we must get rid of the idea that the social dimension is something "ideal" and not actual. Royce for his part was attempting, in the tradition of Aristotle and Hegel, to show that community is a distinctive level of being and can never be understood as a collection or as the "sum" arrived at by taking this individual and another individual and so on without end.

Both saw the problems arising from the vastness and near invisibility of our national community and hence the need for communities on the local level. Dewey revived the Jeffersonian idea of "face to face" relationships between people as represented by the town meeting and saw this institution as an integral part of a democratic system. It is important in this regard to note that one of Dewey's fundamental ideals about education is that the school should itself be a community in which individuals learn to cooperate, listen as well as speak and share their experiences with one another. He was convinced that if young people are not introduced to the values of a community at the beginning of their lives, they are not likely to understand what participating with others means in later life.

Royce advocated his "wise provincialism" as a way of preserving both the variety in American life styles and outlooks and originality in thought which he thought was endangered by a homogeneity in opinion resulting from everyone reading the same newspapers. Royce thus anticipated in 1902 some of the problems we have come to see in the powerful influence of the mass media.

It is also of interest that both Dewey and Royce were impressed by a book entitled The Crowd *written by the French psychologist Gustave Le Bon. This book deals with what came to be called "mob psychology" and it focused for both thinkers the problem of distinguishing the informed public opinion needed in a democracy from mob "thinking" which for Royce was no thinking at all. Each arrived at the same idea that a community, its thought and action, are not to be confused with that of a mob that stifles individuality and demands conformity to the slogans of the moment. This essay appeared in* The Southern Journal of Philosophy, *vol. 12, no. 4 (1974), pp. 469–479. It is reprinted with the permission of the Editor, Department of Philosophy, Memphis State University, Memphis, Tennessee 38152.*

Although the philosophies of Royce and Dewey are clearly divergent in their motives and aims, one cannot but be struck by the fact that the two, in contrast with the thought of James, come together in emphasizing the *social* character of experience. The point at which this convergence makes itself most forcibly felt is in the ideas of community, communication and communion. Both thinkers believed and articulated their belief in the importance of community as a repository of value and both laid stress on its essential role in the resolution of ethical problems. The basic aim of this essay is to call attention to some of their ideas concerning community in relation to the dimension of value in man's experience. Since, however, the topic is a large one and is the subject of discussion at numerous points in the works of these two most prolific writers, the marking out of limits is absolutely essential. In the case of Dewey, emphasis will fall on the contribution of community to the establishment and preservation of democracy as a *moral* ideal, which indeed it was for Dewey from first to last. In the case of Royce, attention will be focused primarily on the role of what he called the "wise provincialism" as a means of restoring the individual in the midst of a vast, impersonal, national society which levels life to uniformity and mediocrity. In both cases, the contemporary significance of their ideas becomes evident when one bears in mind the fact that they were rooted in life and experience on the American scene and represent, as Dewey would have said, philosophical reflection not on the problems of philosophers, but on those of men.

Dewey regarded the development of reflective thinking as one of the most important aims of education, largely because of the crucial role played by such thinking in the debate, discussion and persuasion essential for conducting the affairs of a free society. The primary task of the school in this regard is to provide a framework in the form of a *community of dialogue*, which, as Dewey repeatedly emphasized, is the precursor of all logic. "The problem of securing diffused and seminal intelligence," Dewey writes, "can be solved only in the degree in which local communal life becomes a reality."[1] And, as two recent writers have said, Dewey was pointing to the school as one of the "few remaining institutions in American society which could provide children with a rich sense of dialogue and community."[2] The erosion of older communal forms such as the extended

1. *The Public and Its Problems,* Chicago: The Swallow Press, 1927, pp. 217–18.
2. "Dewey on Education and Schooling," G. E. Axtelle and J. R. Burnett in Jo Ann Boydston, Ed. *Guide to the Works of John Dewey,* Carbondale, Ill.: Southern Illinois University Press, 1970, p. 269.

family, the local neighborhood and the church through the impact of urbanization, industrial specialization and the mobility which leads people to scatter, has made the community provided by the schools more important than ever before. Time and again, Dewey argued that the roots of a vital democracy are found in just those "face to face" associations which the complexity and impersonality of modern technological society make it increasingly difficult to sustain. The school, he believed, should at the outset of life be a living example of the sort of community that an ideal democracy would be. Writing in 1899 in *School and Society,* Dewey declared:

> The introduction of active occupations, of nature study, of elementary science, of art, of history; the relegation of the merely symbolic and formal to a secondary position; the change in the moral school atmosphere, in the relation of pupils and teachers—of discipline; the introduction of more active, expressive, and self-directing factors—all these are not mere accidents, they are necessities of the larger social evolution. It remains but to organize all these factors, to appreciate them in their fullness of meaning, and to put the ideas and ideals involved into complete, uncompromising possession of our school system. *To do this means to make each one of our schools an embryonic community life,* active with types of occupations that reflect the life of the larger society, and permeated throughout with the spirit of art, history, and science. When the school introduces and trains each child of society into membership within such a little community, saturating him with the spirit of service, and providing him with the instruments of effective self-direction, we shall have the deepest and best guarantee of a larger society which is worthy, lovely, and harmonious [italics added].
> (*Ibid.* 270)

Returning years later to the same theme of the school as a center of community and communication, Dewey referred to class recitation, not as the exhibition of the mastery of materials, but as "the social clearing house, where experiences and ideas are exchanged and subjected to criticism, where misconceptions are corrected, and new lines of thought and inquiry are set up."[3] Dewey's intention throughout is that patterns of community established in the school as the larger democratic community writ small, as it were, maintain themselves as the continuing basis for social life long after formal schooling has ceased. In the light of his intention, it is not difficult to see why an educational system geared not to the formation of community, but, on the contrary, oriented towards competitiveness

---

3. *The School and Society,* Chicago: The University of Chicago Press, 1915, p. 49.

and contention, will provide no foundation for life in a pluralistic society whose very existence is dependent on the harmonizing of divergent interest and aims.

In a discussion of the meaning of Jeffersonian democracy, Dewey cited the controversial issue of states rights versus federal power in order to call attention to Jefferson's belief in the need to keep the units of political organization small enough to allow for direct communication. The underlying problem was of constant concern to Dewey and not only as regards the political sphere but in connection with the entire fabric of society. "Whatever else is reasonably settled or is unsettled," he wrote, "it is certain that the ratio of impersonal to personal activities in determining the course of events has enormously increased."[4] And he went on to underline the numerous developments both in American life and in the life of the industrialized nations that have had the effect of replacing personal exchange by impersonal forces operating on such a scale that those who are affected by them find it almost impossible to discover from what source they emanate. These developments have not only manifested themselves in more regions of human life than was true when Dewey was writing in 1939, but the pace of the expansion has accelerated beyond what he could easily have imagined. Things have gone far beyond the replacement of the small shop by the gigantic manufacturing plant, and the replacement of the village by the great urban center; numerous enterprises such as the publishing of serious books, for example, are now controlled from corporate centers so remote that those in power are almost certain to be more informed about the manufacture of goods and appliances than about the publisher's art. The basic problem focused by Dewey, however, remains. "The point," says Dewey,

> is the intervention of an indefinite number of indefinitely ramifying conditions between what a person does and the consequences of his actions, including even the consequences which return upon him. The intervals in time and space are so extensive that the larger number of factors that decide the final outcome cannot be foreseen. Even when they can be anticipated, the results are produced by factors over which the average person has hardly any more control than he has over those which produce earthquakes. (*Ibid.* p. 58)

For attacking this problematic situation, which Dewey called "one of the most serious of present problems regarding democracy"

---

4. *Freedom and Culture*, New York: G. P. Putnam's Sons, 1939, p. 57.

(*Ibid.* p. 159), he insisted on the need for a return to the "face-to-face associations" implied in Jefferson's advocacy of smaller units of communication. There is a difference, he claimed between a society and a community; the former points to the fact that nothing exists in isolation—electrons and atoms included—but a "community adds the function of communication in which emotions and ideas are shared as well as joint undertakings engaged in" (*Ibid.* p. 159). Democracy ultimately depends on vital attachments and stable loyalties which can be formed and nurtured only through local agencies of communication and cooperation. As Dewey had claimed in *The Public and Its Problems*, "Democracy must begin at home, and its home is the neighborly community" (p. 213). He was, of course, not unaware that large social agencies cannot be confined to the local scene, but it was his belief, nevertheless, that the creation and preservation of communities in which communication has the best chance of being direct and personal, represent an important counter-force within a democratic system to the ever-increasing development of impersonal organizations. The proof both of the reality of the problem and of the need to deal effectively with it through the fostering of community is dramatically provided by the negative case. As Dewey rightly perceived, the power of the totalitarian leader resides chiefly in his ability to create, among those whose support he seeks, the sense that he is establishing a new personal solidarity and community among people even if he has to exploit their latent hatreds, prejudices and hostilities to do so. But if this is the case, it is all the more imperative that the problem be recognized for what it is, so that human capacities for community will come to be directed towards causes and ideals that enhance and harmonize life with life as over against those which aim at discord, domination and oppression.

According to Dewey, all of our actions bear upon them the mark of the community to which we belong, and the difficulty we often meet in discerning this mark stems from the fact that everyone belongs to many groups. Dewey repeatedly rejected the idea that morals "ought" to be social, on the grounds that this judgment implies some other and extra-social basis for morality. In his view, morals *are* social and this fact must remain central for any theory concerned with the appraisal of human conduct. On the other hand, in stressing the essentially social character of morality, Dewey wanted to avoid a typical misunderstanding which says that evil action is "individualistic" and good action "social." Such a conception is a mistake because all action is in a social matrix and, as Royce pointed out, much illiberal and purely selfish action stems from the fact that membership in highly specialized groups teaches the individual to discern his own interest clearly and endows him with the passion to pursue it in a single-minded way. For Dewey, the special significance attaching to the social character of conduct depends, first, on the quality and degree of our perception of "ties and interdependencies" and, second, on "the use to which they are put."[5] His own example of self-seeking through the command of money and economic power serves to clarify the point. "Money," he says, "is a social institution; property is a legal custom; economic opportunities are dependent on the state of society; the objects aimed at, the rewards sought for, are what they are because of social admiration, prestige, competition and power." (*Ibid.*) If, he continues, we condemn the money-making man it is not because he has withdrawn from society into himself; on the contrary, he is acting from habits and concrete aims established under social influences. All depends on how the individual uses his social relationships and perceives his connections with others; if he uses them entirely for his own inequitable advantage in the form of economic power, we are justified in pronouncing him egotistic; nevertheless both his conduct and our disapproval of it "are facts within society" (*Ibid.* p. 318) precisely because his unjust advantage figures as a social asset.

How seriously Dewey took the web of social connections and dependencies within which all action takes place can be seen in his appeal, at the end of *Human Nature and Conduct,* to the whole community of life as an ultimate sustaining power.

> Infinite relationships of man with his fellows and with nature already exist. The ideal means . . . a sense of these encompassing continuities with their infinite reach. This meaning even now attaches to present activities because they are set in a whole to which they belong and which belongs to them. Even in the midst of conflict, struggle and defeat a consciousness is possible of the enduring and comprehending whole. To be grasped and held this consciousness needs, like every form of consciousness, objects, symbols . . . Religion has lost itself in cults, dogmas and myths. Consequently the office of religion as sense of community and one's place in it has been lost . . . Religion as a sense of the whole is the most individualized of all things, the most spontaneous, undefinable and varied . . . every act may carry within itself a consoling and supporting consciousness of the whole to which it belongs and which in some sense belongs to it . . . Within the flickering incon-

5. *Human Nature and Conduct* (New York: Modern Library Edition, 1922), p. 317.

sequential acts of separate selves dwells a sense of the whole which claims and dignifies them. In its presence we put off mortality and live in the universal. The life of the community in which we live and have our being is the fit symbol of this relationship. (*Ibid.* pp. 330–32)

Community and Democracy

There can be little doubt that the most important and, at the same time, the most comprehensive function of community and shared experience in Dewey's view is that of serving as a foundation for democracy as a mode of life. This topic in all its aspects is obviously too large to be dealt with adequately under present circumstances. Several basic points, however, can be underlined. In his discussion of the "Democratic conception in education,"[6] Dewey proposed as a measure of the value of any form of social existence, two criteria based on observation of the traits exhibited by actual communities. "Now in any social group whatever," he wrote, "even in a gang of thieves, we find some interest held in common, and we find a certain amount of interaction and cooperative intercourse with other groups." (*Ibid.* p. 83) These two features, the common interest and the degree of interaction with others, are to serve as a standard for evaluating community life. Curiously enough, instead of proceeding to classify and appraise dominant interests defining different groups as such, Dewey refers instead to "how numerous and varied" the interests of a given group actually are as if number and variety were sufficient bases for appraisal. True to his own demand that reflective thought always be specific and retail rather than wholesale, Dewey sets out to assess the criminal organization in these terms. The ties of such a group are said to be few in number and ultimately reducible to one, that of plunder. As a consequence, the group is isolated from other groups and thus is cut off from the interchange through which the values of life are to be learned. By contrast, a family group lives in and through many shared interests—material, intellectual, esthetic—and, far from being an isolated unit, enters into multiple relations with other groups of an educational, commercial and political sort.

That Dewey did not mean to rest his case on this rather simplified example becomes clear in the sequel. We are to apply the criteria indicated to a despotically governed state for the purpose of

6. *Democracy and Education* New York: The Macmillan Company, 1916 (Paperback edition, 1961, pp. 81ff.)

seeing how such a state appears when it is set over against a democratic community. To begin with, Dewey does not agree that there is no common interest standing between the ruler and those subject to him in a totalitarian regime because those in command "must make some appeal to the native activities of the subjects, must call some of their powers into play." (*Ibid.* p. 84) The interest appealed to, however, is largely that of fear which, according to Dewey, has its positive side in caution and circumspection, but in this case, fear is *isolated* because it is directed merely to the hope of material comfort, so that other interests and activities of the subjects are left untouched. Consequently, there is no appeal to many and varied interests, and no mutual exchange between the members of the group. The development of a large number of common values requires free sharing and this is precisely what the division into a privileged and a subject class makes impossible. Both groups suffer, though the evils are likely to be more tangible in the one case than in the other. In Dewey's view, the more activity is confined by rigid class lines, the more "action tends to become routine on the part of the class at a disadvantage, and capricious, aimless, and explosive on the part of the class having the materially fortunate position." (*Ibid.* p. 85) Dewey's analysis at this point closely parallels that of Royce who maintained that no cooperative enterprise can be sustained without "interpretation" or some basic understanding on the part of the individual of the meaning of the total activity in which he is engaged. Attacking efficiency as too narrowly conceived by "scientific" management in production, Dewey points out that it "is reduced to a mechanical routine unless workers see the technical, intellectual, and social relationships involved in what they do, and engage in their work because of the motivations furnished by such perceptions." (*Ibid.*) This is an important point since it serves to counteract the general tendency to suppose that the "practicalism" we associate with pragmatism means no more than "efficiency" to the total neglect of the human factors involved, social and emotional. Where more interests are involved than are possible in a two-class structure, and especially reciprocity of interests, social goals and the human values associated with them become matters of everyone's concern.

The second criterion, namely, the degree of isolation and exclusiveness characterizing a group in relation to other groups, is determined by a group having, as Dewey says, interests "of its own" such that the pursuit of these interests precludes interaction with other groups. The essence of the "anti-social" is isolation and fear of involvement with others because of the possibility of having to alter fixed ideals, private beliefs and customs through contact with "outsiders" and those who do not "belong."

As should be obvious, the criteria stated and used as a means of measuring the validity of a totalitarian system, are intended by Dewey to point on to democracy. From that standpoint, there must be first not only more numerous and varied "points of shared common interest," (*Ibid.* p. 86) but also a greater recognition of mutual interests in the resolution of problems related to social control. The second requirement involves open interaction between social groups and the need for change in social habits depending on the demands of the new experiences and situations which such interaction imposes upon us. The extent of Dewey's reliance on the communal and the social as primary values can be seen in his extended conception of democracy. "A democracy," he writes, "is more than a form of government; it is primarily a mode of associated living, of conjoint communicated experience." (*Ibid.* p. 87) Really to perceive the significance of his deeds and activities, an individual must see them in their relations to and impact upon others. "The extension in space," says Dewey, "of the number of individuals who participate in an interest so that each has to refer his own action to that of others, and to consider the action of others to give point and direction to his own," means the overcoming of the divisions—race, class, nation—which narrow vision and work in the opposite direction from the aims of true education.

Royce and Provincialism

Since much has been written about Royce's doctrine of community and a considerable part of that has focused on the significance of community for religion, it might prove fruitful to concentrate on another feature of his social theory of reality, one concerned with ethical, cultural and political values. A constant theme in Dewey, as we have seen, is the problems arising from the fact that associations become too large, too invisible and impersonal so that the "face-to-face" community is lost. Royce likewise was concerned with this issue and he discussed it under the title of "provincialism" and the contribution to be made, within the confines of a large federal system of government, by lesser communities that are alive, present, and visible to their members.

Let us begin by considering, first, what Royce understood by provincialism, and, second, what social and political problems he believed it could help to resolve. The paper on which the following account is largely based was written in 1902 and therefore speaks to a situation vastly different from our present one; on the other hand, no one can avoid being struck by the prophetic character of some of Royce's comments, especially his perceptive citation of what would today be called the "mass media" as the creator of a homogeneity of opinion which stands opposed to both originality and individuality. Provincialism is meant to denote both the customs and social tendencies characteristic of a "province" and the pride or conviction about these customs and manners which the inhabitants of a province display especially when confronted with new and other customs coming from the outside. As to what a "province" is, Royce points out that, although there is "no easy way of defining how large a province may be,"[7] we all suppose that a province—a county in England, a canton in Switzerland, the New England area in America, the Rhineland in Germany—represents some part of a nation as opposed to the nation as a whole. We often, Royce continues, go on to contrast the provincial with the "metropolitan" on the assumption that the smaller towns and cities belong with the province, while the great urban centers are more *representative* of the interests of the larger whole to which they belong. He rejects this assumption on the ground that great cities, too, have their interests, customs and even dialects, and the inhabitants are frequently as indifferent to the customs and habits of those from the "provinces" as the inhabitants of towns and lesser cities generally are to the ways of outsiders. Royce, therefore, goes back to his original contrast as the central one and states his position in the following way:

> For me, then, a province shall mean any one part of a national
> domain, which is, geographically and socially, sufficiently unified
> to have a true consciousness of its own unity, to feel a pride in its
> own ideals and customs, and to possess a sense of its distinction
> from other parts of the country. (*Ibid.* p. 61)

Accordingly, provincialism as a form of consciousness, will embrace the love and pride which the inhabitants of a province have for the customs and ideals which define their identity. With provincialism thus defined, the question is, what are its forms and what role does Royce assign to it in the social organization of human life? Stated in its most general form, Royce's thesis is that, "in the present state of the world's civilization, and of the life of our own country, the time has come to emphasize, with a new meaning the intensity, the pos-

7. *Race Questions Provincialism and Other American Problems,* New York: The Macmillan Company, 1908, p. 59.

itive value, the absolute necessity for our welfare, of a wholesome provincialism, as a saving power to which the world in the future will need more and more to appeal." (*Ibid.* p. 62)

The first point to notice is that Royce's reference to a "wholesome" provincialism implies its distinction from some other type which is either destructive of human society or in other ways undesirable. And this is indeed Royce's view. Referring to the sectionalism that made itself felt with such force both before and after the Civil War, Royce insisted that devotion to the national unity demanded the "condemnation of certain powerful forms of provincialism" (*Ibid.* p. 63) and he did not hesitate to acknowledge the evils of sectionalism and its capacity for creating disunity. He contended, nevertheless, that there is a "wise" or "higher" provincialism, dedicated to the preservation and extension of human community, which has a social function not capable of being exercised by the nation as such. This provincialism is not to stand in opposition to national unity, but rather to develop along with it as a means of sustaining individuality and independence of spirit. There are, Royce believed, three evils or distortions of social life which the higher provincialism is needed to combat. Each of these problematic tendencies is still evident at present, but their form and proportions have greatly altered since Royce's day.

The first problem concerns the initiation and incorporation of newcomers into some form of community which is small enough to be visible. Those for whom it is essential to have a sense of belonging to and participating in a society of other individuals with similar interests and concerns, may be people coming to America from other countries, or they may, in a spatially mobile society, be people moving from one region of the country to another. In either case, Royce thought it important that a visible community be available and he saw provincial loyalty as performing a most significant function at just this point. Though one's loyalty should be ultimately to the national community, it is too large and impersonal, standing in need of the creative force of smaller social units to bring many individuals to an awareness of their acceptance and participation in a democratic society. It is to be doubted whether our large urban areas can, as such, provide the needed community, for it seems that newcomers to these areas, especially those who belong to minority groups, are apt to find there no community apart from that provided by the segregated groups of their fellows, a fact which does nothing to establish faith in the openness of a democratic society. On the other hand, it is quite possible that members of ethnic groups which for a variety of reasons, have not been made to feel at home in American life would rather face the anonymity of the metropolis than a provincial community whose loyalty may be such as to exclude them from participating in it. The problem, nevertheless, to which Royce was pointing is still real enough, but it is now so vast and complex that a proper treatment would involve the full resources of the social studies. Royce seems to me to be correct in his stress on the need for intermediary communities of the sort he described, if we are to preserve what Dewey called the face-to-face type of association. But it is not clear that the provincial loyalties he espoused do not in the end express themselves in the form of sectional interests—political and economic—so powerful that they can readily work against the general welfare which Dewey was attempting to underline in his conception of the public.

The second problem with which the higher provincialism is to contend is what Royce called the "leveling tendency" in modern civilization. In words little short of prophetic, when one considers that they were written in 1902, Royce defined this tendency as "that aspect of modern civilization which is most obviously suggested by the fact that because of the ease of communication amongst distant places, because of the spread of popular education, and because of the consolidation and of the centralization of industries and of social authorities, we tend all over the nation, and, in some degree, even throughout the civilized world, to read the same daily news, to share the same general ideas, to submit to the same over-mastering social forces, to live in the same external fashions, to discourage individuality, and to approach a dead level of harassed mediocrity." (*Ibid.* p. 74) We know at present the utter truth of these words, better, no doubt than Royce could have known it himself. He had studied the human capacity for imitation and he saw it as an internal force working together with the external agencies of the press, the corporation and the demands of social conformity, for the establishment of ever greater uniformity in American life. What is needed, he maintained, is a counter-tendency aimed at *variety* so that some initiative and a spirit of independence are preserved. Here again provincialism is invoked as a way of counteracting impersonal social organization and the drift towards a state of affairs in which the reach of freedom extends not beyond the freedom of each person to be exactly like all the others. On the other hand, it would be a major oversight to ignore the fact that the problems of mediocrity and uniformity have been major concerns of thoughtful Americans in recent years. And indeed a topic for further and fruitful discussion would be the extent to which the desire of the younger generation to overcome the vastness and impersonality of social conformism not only through individual freedom of expression but by creating small groups based on special and generally neglected interests represents anything like what Royce had in mind when he recommended his wise provincialism.

The third of the questionable tendencies which the higher provincialism is to combat is, as Royce says, closely connected with the second, and it represents a more complex and subtle aspect of social organization than the first two. The problem has generally to do with the spirit of the crowd or what has come to be called "mob psychology" and Royce's attention was directed to it by a book entitled, "The Crowd" written by the French psychologist Gustave Le Bon. It is not without interest that Dewey also made reference to this study in his own thinking about the public. Royce thought of the mob not only in terms of the physical presence of a crowd of people in one place bent on accomplishing some immediate aim, but also, and even more importantly, in terms of the psychological conditions which determine people to *think* as a mob even though they are widely separated in space. "It is enough," says Royce, "if the newspapers, if the theatre, if the other means of social communication, serve to transmit the waves of emotional enthusiasm which creates mob opinion." (*Ibid.* p. 95) At the root of Royce's concern over the mob-spirit was his awareness that in a society aiming to be free and to maintain popular government, it is extremely difficult to avoid domination by what is essentially mob-thinking, which is to say, imitation and enthusiasm and not really thinking at all. It was Royce's contention that not all thought and opinion associated with groups need be of this type. He envisaged another type of social group—the small community—composed of those who "respect one another's individuality, who criticize each other constantly, and earnestly, and who suspect whatever the crowd teaches." (*Ibid.* p. 87) The crucial difference between such groups and the mob, is that, precisely because of the individual interchange they involve, these groups can arrive at opinions which are wiser than those held by the individual members. Conversely, in the case of the crowd, where imitation of, and enthusiasm for, an opinion or interest of one individual prevails, the result is invariably more stupid than any of the individuals participating. It is difficult, Royce pointed out, to imagine human language, for example, ever arising out of the mob-spirit; on the contrary, the efforts of individuals to communicate with other individuals stand as the only basis for the origin of human speech and Royce was quite right in his claim that the funded experience and insight which finds expression in the language of a provincial group will surpass that of

151

any individual members. Groups, moreover, sensitive to individuals and their variety rather than their uniformity are best fitted to create social products of lasting importance—the system of Roman law, for example—which surpass the experience and thought of any individual. He might well have cited the efforts of the conventions through which the American Constitution came into being as models of the sort of community of interacting individuals that forms a counter force to the mob-spirit.

The upshot of this discussion is Royce's proposal that, because of the vastness of national unities and the consolidation of social forces which drive towards uniformity, conformity and the dead weight of mob-thinking, we must find refuge and renewal in smaller communities in which the individual can regain his self-consciousness and dignity. Once again, the community must restore the individual.

9
Creativity in Royce's Philosophical Idealism

"Creativity in Royce's Philosophical Idealism" aims to bring out certain important features in his thought which were overlooked largely because of the specter of his Absolute and James's claim that Royce had a "block universe" within which there is no room for freedom and creativity. The fact is, however, that Royce's idealism is not of a piece with the sort of rationalism associated with a Hegel, a Bosanquet or a Blanshard, because it is a voluntarism through and through and has for its central idea the primacy of individual will and purpose.

Here Royce offers some justification for the well-known comment about the American mentality made by his student, George Santayana, in the "Genteel Tradition in American Philosophy." There Santayana spoke of two mentalities symbolized by the colonial mansion on the one side and the skyscraper on the other; the "American Will," he wrote, "inhabits the skyscraper; the American Intellect inhabits the colonial mansion." And, he continued, the will, the inheritor of the future, is all "aggressive enterprise," while the latter is all genteel tradition by which he meant the stale beliefs and standards of the fathers. It is clear that Santayana thought of the "real" America as the will in the skyscraper and not the intellect in the mansion; one senses this judgment when he cites Mark Twain, Walt Whitman and William James as those who left the genteel tradition behind. Although Santayana found both the shape and the general drift of Royce's philosophy uncongenial, he should have seen how great an importance Royce attached to the will even if he did not suppose that the skyscraper is its only home.

I seek to bring out the importance of the creative act in his thought by singling out three points where it figures most prominently. The first concerns studies he had made about the nature of imitation in the learning process; the second has to do with his concept of the individual as a creative will that defines what that individual "means to be or become;" the third is about the logic of interpretation and the creative ingenuity of the interpreter. All three are to be seen as expressions of will guided by particular purposes.

Stated briefly, through being able to imitate a model— duplicating a paper cutout which a teacher makes, memorizing words spoken by a teacher and the like—the individual becomes aware of the power to follow a plan or procedure and produce a copy. Very soon thereafter, the child finds that he or she is capable of variations that go beyond the model thus evoking a sense of being able to create something new that is no mere copy. The discovery of the power to innovate is at the same time the discovery of the will that is at the center of the person. From this starting point, Royce went on to develop the insight that one has a "will of one's own" with the thought that we have both to learn what it is and indeed to "create" it since it is not presented to us full-blown, as it were. This idea led him on to the theory of the self as a projected life-plan that expresses what an individual self "means to be" or to become through the exercise of a will that is "mine" and no other. Creativity is at the center of the process for if I am to become what I mean to be, I cannot merely repeat myself but must go beyond where I was before in much the same way that the child goes beyond the model. The logic of interpretation involves the same creative advance; to take but one illustration, the act of comparison so essential to both the sciences and the humanities requires that we view two items to be compared as related to each other in some respect, that is, to a third term. How fruitful and illuminating any comparison will be depends entirely on discovering the appropriate third terms. These are not simply "given" to us, but require insight, ingenuity and more often than not the ability to hit on a novel idea. Much of what has been written by philosophers in recent years about creativity draws its inspiration from Whitehead and process philosophy and that is, of course, justified, but Royce, despite the bad image that plagues his thought, had much to contribute on the topic and it is now time to recover what he had to say. This chapter appeared in Contemporary Studies in Philosophical Idealism, *edited by John Howie and Thomas O. Buford, Cape Cod, Mass.: Claude Stark Company, 1975. It is reprinted with the permission of the editors.*

It may seem strange to be considering the sources of creativity and novelty in Royce's metaphysics in view of the long-standing belief, largely established by the critical attitude of William James, that Royce believed in a "block universe" presided over by an Absolute which leaves no room for finite freedom and creativity. While there is no need to deny that in the earliest expressions of his position Royce could speak of the Absolute as possessed of *"totum simul"* knowledge and of individuals as "drops" in an ocean of Being, the fact remains that Royce's theory of reality is first, last, and always a voluntarism embracing the primacy of individual will and purpose. This feature of his thought has often been missed entirely or has been dropped from sight by those who, correctly noting that the form of his philosophy belongs to the systematic strain in modern rational idealism, have nevertheless failed to take seriously the central place accorded to the individual will in his scheme of things. Royce's is not an idealism of knowledge and logical determination alone; it is an ethical idealism in which being is defined in terms of purpose and the resolve to be, or the desire to shape life in accordance with a chosen plan. Moreover, in his view, the world disclosed by theoretical knowledge—the world of description—though perfectly real, is abstract in the sense that the full scope of reality includes as well the world of free individuals and the social relations in which they stand. Whatever necessity attaches to the world of nature expressing itself in lawful form is seen by him as both abstract and relative vis-à-vis freedom and individuality.[1] I mention these considerations at the outset lest distorted views of Royce's position have established the presumption that creativity and freedom are alien to his thought.

Before proceeding directly to Royce's own position, I would like to cite several important features characterizing what I would consider a viable conception of creativity under any circumstances. And since for want of space I shall be concentrating in my treatment of Royce on creativity in relation to the self, I shall frame my own conception accordingly. A fuller treatment would, of course, have to include an account of creativity in all natural processes as is done, for example, in Whitehead's thought; and while I do not say that Royce left nature out of account,[2] the fact that he frequently understood it exclusively in terms of what it would have to be in order to be known or to be the expression of the divine knowledge and will led to the neglect of other features.

Creativity in relation to persons should be understood primarily as a constructive response. I purposely use the term "response" in order to distinguish the activity from that of a "reaction" which is provoked or evoked in situations where a preceding action determines in large part what the reaction will be. By contrast, response entails acknowledgment of a situation as having a certain pervasive quality; it involves appraisal, appreciation and judgment. Response, in short, is a critical affair involving logical, ethical, esthetic and other factors which guide and structure the activity. To this extent, creativity as constructive response is quite different from habitual reaction which, when it is successful, is almost exclusively repetitive of past patterns of behavior. Creativity in response means the realizing of novelty in the form of a relevant contribution to some projected aim or goal. Kant saw this point very clearly in his *Critique of Judgment* where he connected purposive behavior in man, artistic expression, and organic development in nature with judgment, itself a creative process which cannot be entirely reduced to rule, even if some rules are required for critical judgment. The

---

1. Royce, *The World and the Individual* (New York: Macmillan, 1901), vol. 2, 72.
2. Royce, "The Interpretation of Nature," in *The World and the Individual,* vol. 2. Royce's account is remarkable for its emphasis on the factor of time-span in the analysis of natural processes.

point is that the judgment of a singular case requires appeal to a general rule, but the actual application of that rule to the case at hand is not to be uniquely determined by an endless hierarchy of interpolated rules. Judgment is impossible without a creative element, and that is precisely why we think of "good" judgment as a worthy talent.

Creativity must be distinguished from certain phenomena which are frequently associated with it in the popular mind but which are really quite antithetical to it. Creativity excludes bare repetition both in fact and in intent, because repetition involves no constructive contribution on the part of the one who responds, and therefore no novelty. Creativity excludes chaotic novelty unrelated to either form or plan. A mere succession of the different, as in a series of changing colors presented one after the other, no matter how striking, shocking, arresting these different items may be, does not of itself constitute creativity. Creativity excludes irrelevant innovation unrelated to a plan or form; the merely novel is not by itself an embodiment of creative response. Creativity, by contrast, requires the *significant novel*, which always means a constructive contribution to the realization of a good. Royce, in my view, fulfills all these conditions in his conception of the free individual whose task it is to create his will, find a life plan, and then seek to realize it in his own unique way.

In order to present Royce's view as clearly as possible, I shall select from his many writings three topics which seem to me best to represent the creativity theme. First, there is the concept of imitation, which figures largely in ethics and social philosophy and leads to the conception of the creative act which transcends its model. Second, there is the metaphysical concept of the individual who, as creative will, is called upon to fill his place in the social order of persons in his own unique and induplicable way. Third, there is the logic of interpretation, embracing the will to interpret, which expresses itself in creative activity aimed at establishing communities of understanding for mediating conflicts inimical to human welfare. Thus the spheres of ethics, metaphysics and logic serve to exemplify the creative aim at the center of Royce's thought. As was previously mentioned, creative action is essentially connected with will and with the voluntaristic cast of Royce's idealistic theory of being.

Since each of our three topics directs attention to a particular manifestation of will, it will be helpful to specify what Royce meant by the term. He understood will in a sense broader than that made familiar by the traditional faculty psychology. For Royce, will is virtually synonymous with the individual himself—it means his life-plan, his interest or involvement with that life-plan, the finite purposes and series of acts which realize these lesser purposes within the life-plan, and the *nisus* toward self-realization characteristic of a free individual. The scope of will in Royce's view is well illustrated in the following:

> I am a will, a will which is not there for the sake of something else, but which exists solely because it desires to exist.[3]

> My whole inner life is, namely essentially, my will. I long, I desire, I move, I act, I feel, I strive, I lament, I assert myself. The common name for all this is my will.[4]

The ultimacy of will for Royce is seen in his insistence that it finds justification in itself and, consequently, that it may serve ultimately as the justification of everything that is. Royce's constructive idealism—in his language, the Fourth Conception of Being—clearly expresses the point. According to this view, *to be is to be the fulfillment of a purpose,* whatever exists finds its being in manifesting the will of a divine self such that all finite individuality has its uniqueness in the fact that this or that being and no other represents the realization of the divine purpose. As we shall see, there is a certain tension in Royce's thought centering on the relation between *what I was meant to be* in accordance with the divine purpose and *what I mean to be* in accordance with my own will. Royce was not unaware of the problem, and sought to deal with it in his account of the human person and his place in the world of being. For the moment it is sufficient that the breadth of his concept of will be understood.

Self-consciousness, Imitation and Creativity

Regardless of the attempts that have been made to subordinate Royce's metaphysics and to deal with his views on this or that topic by omitting his theory of being, the fact remains that such attempts run counter to Royce's own frequently expressed intention. What Royce has to say about the self, its nature and knowledge of itself, its moral tasks, its freedom and its destiny cannot be made intelligible apart from his fundamental contention that the self is not a substance, that it is not "any single and unambiguous fact of con-

---

3. Royce, *The Spirit of Modern Philosophy* (New York: Houghton Mifflin & Co.; and Cambridge: The Riverside Press, 1892), p. 253.
    4. Ibid., p. 252.

sciousness"[5] such as might be apprehended in one perception. It is to be understood primarily as an ethical concept, a time-spanning intended purpose or life-plan which in seeking to realize we are at once distinct from our fellow human beings and related to them at the same time. The dual relational character here involved stems from Royce's social theory of self-consciousness which explains how the empirical, individual ego comes into view.[6] According to this theory, we come to an awareness of ourselves as realities distinct from other selves precisely through the process of contrasting our ideas, our deeds, and our plans with the ideas, deeds, and plans of others. In an early paper, "Some Remarks on the Anomalies of Self-Consciousness,"[7] Royce declared:

> If a man regards himself, as this individual Ego, he always sets over against his Ego something else, viz.: some particular object represented by a portion of his conscious states, and known to him as his then present and interesting non-Ego.[8]

Considered as alone and apart from such contrasts I do not grasp myself; my own self as this individual comes into view only as I find myself in some contrast relationship involving another who listens to me, who contradicts me, who interrupts me or approves of what I have done: in short, all the familiar relations of social intercourse. Later in *The World and the Individual,* Royce expressed the point thus:

> I affirm that our empirical self-consciousness, from moment to moment, depends upon a series of contrast-effects, whose psychological origin lies in our literal social life, and whose continuance in our present conscious life, whenever we are alone, is due to habit, to our memory of literal social relations, and to an imaginative idealization of these relations.[9]

Here Royce is speaking of the fully developed, emergent self-consciousness which is the product of social training and interaction with the non-ego. We must, however, attend to his account of the details manifest in the process through which this consciousness comes to be, for among those details is the concept of imitation which plays a major role in understanding the creative act.

5. Royce, *The World and the Individual,* vol. 2, p. 265.
6. In what follows, I shall not stress the relations to other selves because here I want to stress the *rise* of self-consciousness.
7. Royce, *Studies of Good and Evil* (New York: D. Appleton, 1898), p. 169ff.
8. Ibid., p. 180.
9. Royce, *The World and the Individual,* vol. 2, p. 260.

Royce begins by distinguishing acts which may be regarded as essentially instinctual—eating, sleeping, crying, and the enjoyment of "physical well-being"—from acts which are essentially imitative in character. When the child plays at being a horse or a doctor, or when he acts in the fantasy of some interesting hero, he is seeking to follow a model presented to him from beyond himself. He is more or less vividly aware of shaping first his conduct and later his ideas in accordance with those of another person. Such shaping Royce regards as the initial move in the direction of self-consciousness in contrast with being simply a creature of natural impulses and passions. The special significance of imitation in this initial stage is that the child acquires ideas about the meaning and intent of the acts he imitates, and comes to view this meaning and intent as belonging to the mind and consciousness of the person he imitates. He perceives what the other person does, and he listens to directions, explanations, suggestions as to how to follow the other in what he does—speaking, using implements, performing physical exercises, or whatever—and as the process advances and imitation becomes a reality, the child finds itself now aware of a basic contrast marking a boundary between two sets of contents. On the one hand, there are the perceptions of the acts performed by the model, together with the gradually discovered meanings which they have for the one who performs them; these contents appear as uncontrollable and as belonging to the other person so that the child has to wait for them to be performed. On the other hand, there is the set of perceptions of the imitative acts themselves which the child has been able to perform, and these perceptions are accompanied not only by enjoyment but also by the discovery of new powers, the sense that he can do the imitative deeds, that they are controllable and do not emanate from a source beyond himself. Thus arises the contrast between ego and non-ego, drawn, in this instance, on the basis of the discovery of one's capability or capacity to perform; the non-ego appears in the form of the presented which is merely accepted and cannot be controlled. In whatever terms the disclosed ego may come to be understood, one point remains firm: in Royce's view, the social character of self-consciousness, far from entailing any merging or submerging of the individual into an impersonal or alien other, serves the function of awakening individual consciousness in the form of an awareness of skills, talents and powers which we ourselves can express. As he put it later in *The Philosophy of Loyalty*, through imitation we learn how to possess and carry out our own self-will; "we learn speech first by imitation; but henceforth we love to hear ourselves talk."[10]

Imitation, however, though a primary channel leading to the marking of a boundary between ego and non-ego, does not of itself account for the forms of creative self-expression which, for Royce, constitute the life of the free individual. Imitation, in the form in which it leads us to reproduce an act or some feature of our model, places us in a position where we can distinguish our reproductive act from the model given to us; by itself, however, imitation means no more than conformity and habitual adjustment to the customs and conventions of society. Obviously such habitual activity always forms some part of our self-conscious life, both in thought and action; however, in Royce's view, social conformity fails to solve the problem faced by the morally autonomous individual of finding unity and directionality in realizing himself, and it also cannot account for the creative response in which I do not merely repeat myself but surpass my former state in a novel act.

With regard to the first of these problems, I can do no more than indicate the bare outline of Royce's proposed solution; I want chiefly to emphasize the second topic, the creative act in relation to the model. Royce envisaged the task of answering such questions as, For what do we live? What is our duty? What are we to value and what to reject? in terms of a paradox expressing an impasse which no one can avoid. On the one hand, following Kant, Royce held that we are morally autonomous beings who must have our own plan of life and who cannot accept as the reason for our duty any external authority such as is represented by social conformity.[11] On the other hand, his claim is that no one can discover a life-plan if he confines his quest merely to his own individual consciousness. "I have," he says, "no inborn ideal naturally present within myself,"[12] and the conclusion drawn is that, apart from social training of the sort discussed in connection with the process of imitation, we do not know our own will. The problem is that the will we can discover through social training frequently represents no more than routine conformity, something which Royce describes as quite different from "ideal life." Social training, moreover, heightens the sense of the importance of having one's own way and of rebelliousness, all

10. Royce, *The Philosophy of Loyalty* (New York: Macmillan, 1908), p. 34.
11. Ibid., chap. 2, esp p. 30ff. I believe that in this analysis Royce did not sufficiently attend to the difference between finding a life-plan and justifying it or discovering a reason or ground for its claim upon us. The discussion in the text, however, can be carried on without making a special issue of the distinction.
12. Ibid., p. 31.

of which may result in nothing more significant than the discovery of clever ways for an individual to outwit others and obstruct the social process without any corresponding self-fulfillment. And yet, Royce insists, it is only through such social training that we learn of our own will, or rather that we become aware of having a will of our own. "To learn your own will,—yes, to create your own will, is one of the largest of our human undertakings."[13] This assertion brings us to the heart of our concern. Our own will is not "given," as it were, apart from ourselves; it does not already exist, needing only to be discovered. That will must, in some sense, be created by each of us, and yet it will not be "created" *de novo* out of nothing since it will be a function both of our own powers, talents, and capabilities and of the social causes and opportunities that may present themselves in our situation. There is here a tension similar to one we shall meet in the next section: we are faced with the problem of "finding" our wills and we are also called upon to "create" them. The first suggests a discovery and acceptance of something already given; the second suggests a bringing forth of something novel. The two come together for finite, that is, human freedom, in the awareness that creativity in finding our purpose in life is a creative synthesis of both features; we discover our actual capabilities and capacities through the self-knowledge that arises from social intercourse, and we form our life-plan as that which is to unify these talents so as to perform the creative acts aimed at carrying out that plan.

I turn now to the account Royce gives of the creative or free act in relation to its model. This account takes us back to the idea of imitation, and requires in addition a second concept not previously mentioned in our discussion, the concept "between." This concept, as Royce reminds us, had been given quite extensive logical treatment in the chapter entitled "The Linkage of Facts" in *The World and the Individual*,[14] though not every part of the concept is relevant for describing the activity of the self. In order to help in understanding Royce's position, two preliminary comments are in order. First, Royce had a faith in the direct application to metaphysics of such logical concepts as "between," "self-representative system," "least upper bound," etc., which was no less infinite in extent than the unending system of interpretation with which his philosophy comes to completion. In principle, there can be no objection to this attempt to achieve clarity and precision of thought vis-à-vis noto-

13. Ibid.
14. Royce, *The World and the Individual*, vol. 2, 76ff.

riously difficult problems. But there is a liability involved: in applying these generalized concepts to the concrete, to the self, for example, Royce frequently modified this meaning and the result is often confusing. Second, and more important, Royce had an annoying tendency to restate, summarize, and reformulate what he had said before. Again, this practice is unobjectionable, or rather would be if he had not so frequently made changes both in meaning and emphasis in the course of the restatements. The use, for example, of such logical concepts as "between" and "well-ordered series" for elucidating the activity of the self appears in at least four distinct places in *The World and The Individual*, each time with modifications which make it difficult to be sure that one has grasped his meaning. Therefore, in order to focus the issues for our discussion, I shall pass over the restatements and express in my own way what I take to be Royce's view in accordance with the following chapters of the Gifford Lectures: "The Linkage of Facts," "The Human Self" and "The Place of the Self in Being."

To begin with, Royce sets out to distinguish clearly between the world as it is disclosed from the standpoint of science—the world of description—and the world of purposive and creative individuals who express themselves in novel acts—the world of appreciation. Science begins with discrimination involving comparison and differentiation. Every discrimination requires the specification of a difference which holds the discriminated items apart; comparison is thus not dyadic but triadic because "between any two objects of the world there is always another to be found."[15] The function of intermediaries is itself dual because intermediaries both link items and hold them apart. A red object and a green object differ with respect to their color, but are the same in being colored. For Royce, the entire procedure of science is to be understood as the process of finding series of terms such that every discrimination means finding what is "between" the discriminated items and thus indicating the sort, degree and direction of their difference. In short, the relation "between" establishes directionality in the world because we come to see the between as a stage to be passed through in a process of development. The series thus generated by discrimination is not well-ordered as is the natural number series, for example, because in them there is no immediate "next" but always a third to be discovered "between" the discriminated items. We need to preserve this concept of "between" for the later analysis of imitation and creative activity. At this juncture, Royce wants simply to employ

15. Ibid., p. 88.

the distinction between (a) well-ordered series in which there is an immediate "next" and (b) the series of discriminations in which there is no "next" but always a "between," for distinguishing the activity of scientific knowing from the apprehension of the world as it is experienced by the self which has a unique life of its own.

The decisive difference between the worlds is that in the world of description there is nothing about its objects that requires us to investigate them in one order rather than another, whereas in the world of purposive activity, there is a necessary order. We may begin with physics or anthropology as far as the objective world is concerned, since it is "anybody's world"; the only requirement for science is that we employ methods which result in a convergence of one scientific truth. But if we introduce the concept of purposive activity, all is changed. A purpose and its realization require a determinate succession of events which has an irreversible direction; no plan can be realized unless we know what is to come next in the order of activity. The world of description is but one aspect of a larger reality; there is in addition the knowledge which we as individuals have of the world—the meaning which it has for us as persons—and the volitional processes which we initiate in it. For Royce there is, in addition to the discriminatory processes resulting in facts and their serial arrangement—discoveries which might have been made as readily by anyone as by anyone else—a world of creative activity. In expressing ourselves in purposive deeds, we no longer have the sense that another might have done the same thing. On the contrary, when we project a plan and set out to realize it through action, we have the vivid sense of bringing forth something individual and unique, something not to be duplicated elsewhere by anyone else. Royce was prepared to interpret science itself as a purposive activity when viewed from the standpoint of the scientist himself. To link facts in objective series is to describe the world, but the activity of doing this is, for the individual thinker, an activity which occupies a particular place in that order which is the expression of himself. Stated in logical terms, the world of purpose and of persons is a world of self-expression taking the form of a discrete series in which each act is followed by a *next* without intermediaries. In Royce's view, I repeatedly proceed from one act to the next, and thus, through a recurrent operation, produce novelty because I always proceed to a new act. Insofar as the process of discrimination is my own activity and belongs to my own life, then, I am aware of my conceptual acts as succeeding without intermediaries, even though the logical process of discrimination as I carry it on requires the finding of intermediaries.

On the basis of the two distinct types of series, Royce believed that he had found a clear way of discerning the world of impersonal, universal knowledge on the one hand and the world of unique, creative persons on the other. A word of caution is, however, in order at this point. In the initial discussion of the difference between the worlds of description and appreciation to be found in "The Linkage of Facts" and in the treatment of purposive self-expression in the "Supplementary Essay," the impression is given that the well-ordered series formed by a recurrent operation is alone required for understanding purposive activity, while the series formed by discrimination and the "between" relationship belongs uniquely to the process of gaining scientific knowledge of nature. This impression is not in fact correct; further on in his account of the self and its place in the system of reality, Royce makes it clear that both types of series are involved in purposive action and that the between relationship figures essentially in a certain type of creative act which has imitation at its base. I shall not consider what is behind this apparent shift beyond pointing out that in the later treatment Royce was attempting to connect the two types of series in the interest of showing that reality has the character of selfhood.[16] To that analysis we may now turn.

Royce begins with a distinction between two kinds of activity possible for finite beings; for the sake of convenience, we may call them *direct* and *exploratory*. When we are in possession of a purpose and feel that our knowledge of the situation is adequate, we proceed to act directly and in a determinate way. This type of activity, though recurrent, has its own element of novelty and it marks the life of the self who knows what his life-plan is. On the other hand, there are those who are as yet unable to act in a direct way and who therefore are experimenting or exploring, a process which Royce describes as the search for a new object "between" any pair of objects that have already been discriminated. The search for the between, itself a kind of activity which may be recurrent, is connected by Royce with the phenomenon of imitation. As we saw, imitation was described in the paper on self-consciousness as an essentially reproductive affair in which the child repeats the activity of the model. Here two new features are added which at once introduce the possibility of creative novelty. Imitation is now seen to

16. I further abstract from Royce's ultimate metaphysical thesis that according to the true view of reality which transcends our ignorance, the two worlds of description and appreciation become one, and what there is must be viewed as one well-ordered series expressing the absolute self.

depend, first, on discriminating between acts performed by another and one's own acts, and second, on an interest in modifying what one has done in the past in the direction of what is done by the model. In short, to imitate is to construct an act which stands between my previous acts and the acts of the model, and this standing between is precisely what holds the new act apart from both my former conduct and the conduct of the model. "I never merely repeat his act,"[17] says Royce, and this means that imitation is "a kind of experimental origination, a trial of a new plan, the initiation of a trial series of acts."[18] The process of finding new intermediaries is seen by Royce as identical with the growth of the self. The results of imitative activity themselves become established and lead in turn to recurrence or repetition, the sign that the will has found its purpose. But we must distinguish between the will on the lookout, so to speak, and the will that has discovered itself. The latter acts directly in well-ordered fashion, while the former is engaged in a process of trial and error, seeking by mediation to discover what one has to do. For Royce, both processes have novel results, although it is clear that he regarded the discovery of the act which lies between my past behavior and my model as "the principal source of the novel forms of self-expression."[19] Action which is a direct and definite form of self-expression, and which has become habitual or recurrent, nevertheless brings forth novel results in accordance with the nature of the circumstances. Royce was fond of comparing this sort of activity with the recurrent operation of counting which leads to the number series and to an endless wealth of new theorems about that series. The activity which is indirect, tentative, and aimed at discovery is non-recurrent with respect to any given experiment, and it is essentially a process of adaptation through novel forms of response which are not "given" in advance but must be discovered and embodied in what is essentially a creative act.

Being Myself As A Task

The second topic I have selected for its bearing on the creativity theme, although it involves Royce's metaphysics, is actually more concrete than the preceding discussion, and in addition it has the advantage of familiarity. That Royce's purposive idealism represents a type of absolutism is well known, as are also the difficulties,

17. Royce, *The World and the Individual*, vol. 2, 311.
18. Ibid.
19. Ibid., p. 314.

real or alleged, which an absolute idealism must face when the question of the reality of the finite individual is posed. It was precisely these difficulties which William James, himself an indefatigable defender of the individual, had in mind when he uttered his famous challenge—"I say, Royce, damn the Absolute!" I cannot undertake to set forth in any detail either Royce's conception of the Absolute Self or his theory of individuality. It is possible, however, to explain what he meant by the claim that the self is an ethical category carrying with it a task, and to show how he proposed to characterize the uniqueness of the individual in an idealistically conceived world where that individual is already understood as in some sense the expression of the divine will. As was suggested previously, the problem is to relate what an individual "was meant to be" from the standpoint of the Absolute Self to what that individual "means to be" from the standpoint of his own purposive will.

In accordance with Royce's conception of Being as that which fulfills a purpose, the world and all its contents, selves and things, must be viewed as "the expression of one determinate and absolute purpose, the fulfillment of the divine will."[20] The world in its wholeness is therefore unique, and every one of its proper parts is unique in virtue of its being distinguished from all the rest. Thus far we have the familiar doctrine that given one unique individual, an infinity of others can be defined through relations to that given individual. The question that interests us is: What does this doctrine mean in the case of the individual self or person? For an answer, we must return to Royce's conception of the self.

The crucial feature of that conception is that the self is not a substance and is not a single, unambiguous fact of consciousness; the self is a complex unity of life extended over a temporal interval and unified by a purpose which serves to identify that self in distinction from all the others. Such a fixed and finished characterization, though correct in outline, is nevertheless misleading because it leaves out of account the distinctively ethical dimension of what Royce means by a self. In any present we can become aware of some portion of ourselves—thoughts, feelings, hopes, fears, plans, deeds—and in so doing we become further aware of a past through which we have lived and a future through which we expect to live. In short, the present is but a fragment of a larger self which we feel that we ought to be able to identify as enduring and as distinctively ourselves in contrast to all other individual selves and to the Absolute Self. This principle of identification or time-spanning unity is

20. Ibid., p. 292.

not simply "given" to us from without, but appears to us as something which we *ought* to be and which, in the end, we must create. After a man has discovered that the self is not exhausted in the present or passing experience, he will seek to identify himself in some other way. He will have, says Royce,

> . . . the really deep and important persuasion that he *ought* to *possess* or create for himself, . . . some one principle, some finally significant contrast, whereby he should be able, with an unified and permanent meaning, to identify that portion of the world's life which is to be, in the larger sense, his own, and whereby he should be able to contrast with this, his larger self, all the rest of the world of life.[21]

My being as a self, then, comes to me as a task to be performed, as a purpose to be fulfilled such that in fulfilling it I am at the same time expressing the divine will in human form. My task, in the end, is to be an individual and unique self in contrast both to other selves and to God. Here Royce resolves the tension between what I was meant to be and what I mean to be. I was meant to be a unique, individual self, and I ought to mean to become that self by finding a life-plan or ideal for myself which remains as my steady intention throughout my temporal span. Reference to God or the Absolute Self, far from leading, as has often been thought, to a dissolution of finite selves or to their mystical blending in one Individual, actually has the opposite effect. The divine purpose is realized only to the extent that an individual becomes a unique self by finding his own purpose in a life-plan. Each self, to be sure, remains in relation to all other finite selves and to God, but it belongs to each individual's intent, says Royce, "always to remain other than" his fellows in virtue of a plan which no other can realize.

The question now arising is this: Has Royce forgotten, in this strong emphasis on unique individuality and the otherness of selves to each other, all that was previously said about the social origin of self-consciousness, about social training, and about the linkage of persons brought into being through the myriad social interactions of daily life? Royce's answer takes the form of admitting that we are all dependent on the world surrounding us insofar as we are defined in general terms. "Your temperament," he says, "you derived from your ancestors, your training from your social order."[22] Indeed all opinions as definable ideas can be shared with other selves.

21. Ibid., p. 274.
22. Ibid., p. 293.

What cannot be derived from other lives, however, is the unique character of the individual, that character which represents his own way of expressing his will to be a self. Referring to the individual's purpose, Royce writes:

> Now this purpose, I maintain, is indeed your own. As nobody else can share it, so nobody else can create it; and from no source external to yourself have you derived it.[23]

In his explanation of man's relation as a self to the world of description, Royce goes even further and maintains that all causal explanation is confined to types and to describable, general characters of events, so that the self as an individual eludes such explanation. The individual is said to be "the indefinable aspect of Being"[24] and this means that my being as this individual who is nobody else in God's world is causally inexplicable. This inexplicability, however, is not that of any given fact or event, because being this individual is never divorced from my intent and resolve to be this individual, which means that it is ultimately my *will* that transcends the world of description. In short, being a self remains a task given to my creative will. I am this individual insofar as I mean to be so and see my purpose as my own. Ultimately, however, this purpose is not only my own, because it is also God's purpose for me; nevertheless, only I and no other can carry it out.

Interpreting and Mediating as Creative Endeavor

Our third topic, though it has prefigurations in Royce's earlier works, properly belongs to the last phase of his work—the philosophy of interpretation and community. I shall attempt to make clear what I take to be the creative and constructive features of the interpretative enterprise both as it figures in the realm of logic and knowledge and in an endless number of practical, social situations where some form of mediation is called for. As we shall see, we are once again concerned with the will, but now with the will to understand, to mediate and overcome conflict, and ultimately with the will either to create community between multiple individuals or to bring to clear consciousness already existing bases for community which have become obscured or forgotten.

23. Ibid., p. 294.
24. Ibid., p. 325.

The background for Royce's theory of interpretation is to be found in Peirce's theory of signs[25] and in his account of the triadic relations involved in all sign-reading activity. In accordance with the philosophical discussions taking place in the early decades of this century concerning the respective nature of and connections between perception and conception, Royce liked to set interpretation off against both as a distinctive process which is not reducible to either, nor to their bare conjunction. We may clarify this point by citing Royce's own example of the weather vane and its function as a sign. His main contention is that someone may perceive a weather vane and note that it consists of a certain arrangement of pieces of metal rotating on a vertical axis about a pair of crossed horizontal axes, and he may set about conceiving or describing this object by means of the most exact concepts you please, but that in neither activity has he yet encountered the weather vane as a sign which must be read. To read it he must know that the weather vane is a purposeful device, that the positions of its arrow have a meaning and that he must assign the appropriate meaning to the positions he observes. This example is, of course, a simple and obvious one, but it illustrates the fundamental fact that the being of a sign is to be read or interpreted. For Royce, all signs are signs of minds and are addressed to minds which alone are capable of reading them. The signs may be spoken words in conversation, they may be the behavior of persons to be understood, they may be texts to be deciphered, interpreted, or translated from one language into another, or they may be deeds to be interpreted: in all cases, however, the logical structure of the process remains the same. Three terms are always involved: there is the interpreter,[26] the object or sign to be interpreted, and the person to whom the interpretation is addressed. The interpreter always says, in effect, to the one he addresses, What I say to you is what the sign said to me, i.e. what it means, and the process is, in principle, endless, since the interpretation is itself expressed as a sign which needs to be read and so the process continues. The process, moreover, is a creative one in the sense that in reading signs I am attempting to pass beyond the enclosed circle of my own ideas and experience in order to enter into the thought and experience of another mind. In reading a

25. See John E. Smith, *Royce's Social Infinite* (New York: Liberal Arts Press, 1950) for a full account.

26. To avoid confusion, it is essential to notice that the "interpreter" here means both the one who interprets and the idea or meaning through which he interprets.

passage from Homer, for example, I must have the will to understand what he meant with the aid of an essentially living reason. To do so requires sympathy, insight, and ingenuity. I may have to consider in some cases what he might have meant, or could have meant, in the light of other knowledge concerning him and the period in which he lived. While interpretation aims at grasping and expressing the same meaning expressed in the original signs, the process is more subtle than that of finding synonymous expressions in a dictionary. Interpretation is not in fact reducible to the application of strict rule. Rules of grammar and syntax will, of course, be assumed, but beyond that I must be guided by my will to understand and by my desire to enter into the experience of another.

Royce saw the process of interpretation as especially fitted for the attainment of self-knowledge and the understanding of others. Wherever interpreting succeeds, a community of understanding is created; two distinct minds are now brought into a unity in virtue of their becoming related to the same third term. Royce's extensive analyses of communities based upon memory, or the acknowledgment by many distinct selves of common items which belong to their respective pasts, and upon hope based on the anticipation of some goal to be realized and with which all members identify themselves, depend on processes of interpretation where the many members all come to attach the same meanings to the signs involved.

Royce also understood the process of comparison, which he regarded as fundamental for the extension of knowledge, as akin to that of interpretation because it is essentially a triadic affair requiring creative ingenuity on the part of the thinker in supplying the missing third terms. To make instructive comparisons, for example, between two biological forms, two paintings or symphonic compositions, two economic systems, two pieces of creative writing, it is necessary to find relevant and interesting "thirds" or respects by means of which the two forms can be compared. The finding of these respects represents a creative activity. Comparisons do not make themselves nor are they made, as seems so often to be assumed, merely by making an exhaustive description of each form to be compared. What is required is the proposal of a significant common term as in the following example: If we show a person an ordinary ring strip made of paper and also a Moebius strip and ask him to compare them, he will have to introduce some idea, however vague, of a feature in accordance with which the comparison can be made. Let us suppose that he is not a mathematician and is forced to rely on direct perception; he will almost certainly concentrate on the shape. One is "round" he will say, and the other has a "twist" in it, and surely they differ in this respect at least. Such an answer is so far correct, but it is not very precise or particularly instructive. But now suppose that we ask him to introduce a more interesting, less obvious, and perhaps more fruitful respect for comparison. Perhaps he can say more exactly what he meant by the vague idea of shape. If he is able to translate this idea into, for example, the number of sides or edges determining a figure's shape, he will have a new basis for comparison. With this idea on the ground, he can now make a more precise comparison: one strip has two sides and two edges and the other has but one side and one edge. A more exact comparison has resulted, but only because the thinker has hit upon a significant respect which was not "given" but had to be introduced as a creative act. All comparison requires the same ingenuity, and thinking in this view is an endlessly creative process.

Interpreting or mediating was for Royce not only a matter of knowledge in the narrower sense but also a highly practical activity aimed at the overcoming of conflict and the harmonizing of competing claims. The mediating function involved is an offshoot of Royce's concept of community, and it represents an attempt to unify the diverse in some specific and practical way. In a curious little book entitled *War and Insurance,* Royce called attention to certain situations in which individuals are related in a merely dyadic way so that they constitute what he described as "dangerous pairs" because of the possibilities for conflict latent in their relationship. Examples of such pairs are buyer and seller, plaintiff and defendant, insured and beneficiary, employer and employee, and all the familiar examples of related individuals whose interests are to some degree opposed such that the advantage of one means the disadvantage of the other. In Royce's view, these dyads must be transformed into triads or rudimentary communities of interpretation. Mediation of some kind is required, whether in the form of an actual mediating individual or in the form of a containing system which will make it possible for each member of the pair to have access to the means of understanding the other, his rights and obligations in the particular situation. The task of the mediator is to interpret one member of the pair to the other. In some cases the tensions resulting from misunderstanding will be overcome through further knowledge and insight which dispel illusion and prejudice. In others, the conflict may be more severe, requiring mediation going far beyond any mutual understanding. In those cases, the mediator must appeal to a system of law established for the purpose of determining the nature and extent of just claims and their satisfaction. In Royce's view, all forms of mediation exhibit essentially the same phenomenon, namely, the transformation of a dyadic relationship—the claim of A, for example, merely counterbalanced by the opposed claim of B—which is a source of conflict, into a triadic one where a third term is interpolated between A and B for the purpose of containing their potentially dangerous clash of interests.

Mediating of the practical sort here in question is a creative affair in at least two respects. First, the mediator must have the will to interpret, and he must express it in the form of a penetration into two distinct selves; and if he is to succeed he will need whatever measure of creative imagination he has at his disposal. Second, the mediator is attempting to create a community of understanding where none existed before, by bringing into a new relationship two individuals, interests, claims, etc., previously related in an external and dyadic way. Royce frequently saw the interpreter as filling the role of a peacemaker who aims at linking together what would otherwise pose a constant threat of conflict if left unreconciled.

There are other facets to Royce's philosophy which have been left largely untouched. I believe, however, that the topics I have selected provide some insight into the creative freedom of the individual which played so large a part in his thought from the early papers to *The Problem of Christianity.*

10
Signs, Selves and Interpretation

"Signs, Selves and Interpretation" is an application of what I regard as the resources to be found in Peirce's original theory of signs and interpretation and Royce's further development of the subject for gaining some insight into the nature of the self, its self-consciousness and relations to other selves. Peirce provided a matrix for meaningful discourse and communication with the theory of signs and the triadic process of interpretation from which Royce took hints and arrived at what I think is the most fruitful line of thought about the self. Royce was right in his claim that the self is no datum of the sort that Hume could not find, and still less is it a "bundle" of perceptions, but rather a certain kind of meaning that takes the form of a dominant purpose persisting through the thoughts and deeds which contribute to the realization of that purpose. The dominant purpose, or life-plan—what I mean to become—is the source of the unity and continuity of the self and its experience and also of identity in the sense that I can always pick myself out from all others as the one who has willed my life-plan, a plan that could not be willed by anyone else. The dominant purpose that defines the self finds its root in what I call a "center of intention" which stands for the person who means this or that idea or experience to be communicated to the other, or, in the context of action means to do this or that deed required for realizing some purpose. Here I am construing in my own way what Royce was saying when he claimed that in communication between two persons neither self is a datum of perception for the other and neither self is for the other merely a collection of abstract characters expressed through concepts. It is for this reason that interpretation must be made central: it cannot be understood in terms of some ill-defined "combination" of percepts and concepts but only through the triadic relation required for reading signs, which is precisely what we are doing when we attempt to understand each other in any situation. Interpretation, in short, is the sort of meaningful process through which to express our center of intention and to enter into the center of the other. The illustration in the text about the understanding and misunderstanding that took place between Hamlet and Ophelia is a clear case of the interpreting process. This process is, of course, not a merely "intellectual" affair since we encounter each other as embodied and located which means, among other things, that words will not be the only signs involved. There will be in addition, gestures, facial expressions, bodily movements and past behavior not to mention tone of voice and the subtleties

of emphasis. It is important to notice that in all this there is no need to become involved in the so-called problem of "other minds." That problem, if it ever was a real problem, is resolved by the very existence of signs since these are in the nature of the case vehicles of meaning that stem from minds intending to express an idea. A problem would arise only on the fantastic supposition that any individual could legitimately regard all the signs in existence as "mine."

This chapter appeared in Contemporary American Philosophy, Second Series, Ed. John E. Smith, London, 1970, pp. 312–328, and is reprinted with the permission of the publisher Allen & Unwin/Unwin Hyman, part of HarperCollins Publishers.

Towards the end of the last century and therefore some decades before the 'linguistic revolution' in philosophy had taken place, C. S. Peirce was developing his theory of signs and analysing the process of interpretation through which signs are read or understood. At the same time Royce had taken note of Peirce's essentially logical analyses of signs and their relations both to their objects and interpretants, in the hope of extending Peirce's results to include a theory of the human person and the communities to which he or she belongs. There is much that is of relevance for contemporary philosophy in the proposals set forth by both thinkers. Therefore, I shall develop, under the rubric of 'the theory of interpretation', two basic themes; *first,* an account of the nature of sign functioning and the process of interpretation along lines first suggested by Peirce, and *second,* the application of the idea of interpretation to the problem of self-knowledge and the nature of human community along lines first marked out by Royce. Against this background, I shall further develop the self-knowledge theme in my own way in the hope of throwing some light on the important but elusive problem as to the nature of the self.

I. Signs and Interpretation

Before proceeding to Peirce's theory, it is necessary to avoid a certain confusion that invariably arises whenever the term 'interpretation' is used. This confusion is due to the fact that the term, though it can and should be used in a technical sense, has a widely known ordinary connotation according to which an 'interpretation' is made to stand in contrast with a 'fact'. We are all familiar, for example, with situations in which we say, 'We were not provided with the "facts" of the case; all we received were "interpretations".' Such a locution clearly implies an opposition between a recital or description of what is the case—the facts—and some further determination or account of these facts which aims at 'interpreting' them or saying what they 'mean'. The opposition implied in an ordinary use of the term 'interpretation' is, to be sure, not without some foundation in experience. If we consider, for example, a witness testifying in a court of law to events at the scene of a crime, he might say, 'I saw the defendant *running* down the street, and I also saw that he was *very angry.*' It would normally be thought that testifying to the running is the report of a fact open to sense perception and we would not ordinarily claim that the witness was giving an 'interpretation' (unless, of course, *any* statement made by anyone is to be called an 'interpretation', in which case the term would have no differential meaning at all).

On the other hand, where the witness says he 'saw that' the defendant was 'very angry' we would normally say that he was interpreting in so far as being angry is not, like the phenomenon of running, something that can obviously be seen, but is rather to be apprehended by interpreting some sign such as a facial expression, a cry, or a gesture. From the standpoint of reciting the facts of the case, the running is just what it is; it is not a sign of something else (although it may be *taken to be* a sign for certain purposes), whereas the facial expression, the cry or the gesture are taken as signs revealing a certain emotion, state of mind or disposition. If the witness merely described the behaviour as he saw it, without 'interpreting', then the assertion about anger would not have been made and a report on the facial expression, the cry, the gesture would constitute exact parallels to the running. The point at this juncture is not to settle once and for all the question of the relation between 'fact' and 'interpretation', but rather to call attention to the confusion resulting from the uncritical contrast between the two implied in ordinary uses of 'interpretation'. Since 'fact' must be put down to objective states of affairs, to what is the case, to what is actually there to be encountered, 'interpretation', taken as the antithesis of fact, will be made to appear as no more than an accretion, a contribution of the mind, stemming from the interests and predilections of the one who interprets. Such a consequence is unfortunate on two counts; first, it identifies interpretation not as the unique cognitive act which it is, but rather as an opinion or conjecture about matter of fact, and second, to oppose interpretation to fact is to obscure the sense in which critical interpretation is based on and is responsive to the facts of the case.[1] In what follows the meaning

1. The foregoing paragraphs presuppose that the term "interpretation" is *not* to be understood as referring to every activity involving thought, concepts and language, but only to the special activity of reading signs. For even if, as has been

of 'interpretation' as a technical term will be made clear; at the outset, however, it is essential that connotations attached to the term in ordinary use be not allowed to cloud the issues.

In developing what he called 'a new list of categories' Peirce was struck by the peculiarity of a certain type of object which he called a *sign*. In addition to the immediate qualities and the abstract characteristics of things, and also to the network of actions and reactions in which the distinguishable items of the world participate, there is a class of items called signs; it is the peculiar feature of these items that they must be understood through a process to which Peirce gave the name of *interpretation*. Signs have the capacity of pointing beyond themselves—the sign is not its own object except in some special cases where a sign is part of another sign—to something else, but this pointing beyond is only actualized when the sign is read or interpreted by a mind or a sign-using animal. In the realm of signs, *to be* is identical with *to be interpreted;* unless a sign is taken as such and interpreted, it is only potentially a sign.

Peirce offered many characterizations of what it is to be a sign: let us consider several of them. In an article on 'Sign' in Baldwin's *Dictionary*,[2] Peirce defined a sign as 'anything which determines something else (its *interpretant*) to refer to an object to which itself refers (its *object*) in the same way, the interpretant becoming in turn a sign, and so on *ad infinitum*'. We may supplement this rather formal definition with some other passages in which Peirce elucidates the meaning of signs. In a paper on 'Meaning' written in 1910, Peirce writes:

> But in order that anything should be a sign, it must represent, as we say, something else, called its *Object*. . . . The sign can only represent the object and tell about it. It cannot furnish acquaintance with or recognition of that object; for that is what is meant in this volume by the object of a sign; namely that with which it presupposes an acquaintance in order to convey some further information concerning it.

---

maintained, there is an element of "interpretation" in the most evident cases of perception, we, nevertheless, must not overlook the difference between perceiving and interpreting as represented respectively by the running and the anger in the previous illustration. The running was just seen; there was no reading of signs. The anger, on the other hand, was not seen; the gestures, etc. were seen and taken as signs which were then interpreted as expressions of anger.

2. Baldwin, James M., ed. *Dictionary of Philosophy and Psychology*, New York, Macmillan, 1901–05; revised edn, 1928, Vol. 2.

The following statement is from an undated manuscript; the passage is important because it brings out the 'realistic' strain in Peirce's theory in its stress on the sign being determined by its object. Peirce writes:

> A sign is a cognizable that, on the one hand, is so determined (i.e. specialized, *bestimmt*) by something *other than itself*, called its object, while on the other hand, it so determines some actual or potential mind, the determination whereof I term the Interpretant created by the sign, that the Interpreting Mind is therein determined mediately by the object.[3]

From these passages we can derive an understanding of the main features of signs and the situation in which they function. Five features are noteworthy. First, the situation in which signs function always involves a triadic relation with three distinct terms related in a definite way. There is the sign itself, its object and the interpretant (i.e. the reading or interpretation) of the sign which refers to the object in the same way as the original sign. When we consider an actual process of interpretation and not merely the logical structure exhibited in interpretation as such, a fourth term is introduced— the interpreter or the sign-reading agent who performs the task. The interpreter or the one who grasps signs as such and attempts to read them, must not be confused with the interpretant which is the interpretation given by the interpreter to the original sign. Some philosophers, operating on behaviourist assumptions, have often silently omitted the interpreter, substituting instead the interpretant which the interpreter proposes as the interpretation of the sign he seeks to read. The fact is, however, that no signs are self-interpreting and the triadic structure of interpretation always presupposes the interpreter in the form of the one to whom the interpretant 'occurs' or by whom the interpretant is proposed.

Second, a sign is always representative in character because it refers to an object other than itself. As representative, the sign does not furnish acquaintance with its object but rather presupposes that the interpreter is already acquainted, if not with the singular object of the sign in question, at least with the type or kind of object involved. If, for example, we say, 'Caesar is dead', the interpreter of the sign 'dead' must be able to think this predicate as characterizing an individual person who lived in the past and whose existence is otherwise known to the interpreter. The sign 'dead' by itself does

---

3. *Collected Papers of Charles Sanders Peirce*, ed. Charles Hartshorne and Paul Weiss, vols. 1–6, Cambridge, Harvard University Press, 1931–1935, vols. 7, 8, ed. Arthur Burks, 1958, 8.177.

not furnish this knowledge. The past experience of the interpreter and the extent of his acquaintance with things therefore come into play in every interpretative process.

Third, to be representative, a sign must be determined by its object, otherwise the referents of signs would exercise no control whatever over the realm of interpretation. On the other hand, if any given sign is to receive an interpretant some mind or other must be determined by that sign to think a certain content about the object to which the sign refers. The object, therefore, determines the thought of the interpreter in mediate fashion, and thus exercises some constraint on the interpreting process. This point is of special importance for the theory of interpretation because it helps us to avoid the quite mistaken notion that an interpretation is a mere superaddition laid over or placed on a set of data as an externally related meaning content. While no interpretation is a 'copy' of presented data, it does not follow that these data will play no part in determining what their correct interpretation should be.

Fourth, implicit in the previous passages is the view that no theory of interpretation can afford to dispense with an interpret*er* or mind. Since it belongs essentially to signs to find interpretants, an actual or possible interpreter is always required. No sign is its own interpretant and every sign is addressed to a potential interpreter. Though natural processes may be, so to speak, self-propelling, the process of interpretation considered apart from the interpreter is not. As will become clear, the fact that interpretation issues in a dialogic process makes it peculiarly apt for throwing light on self-knowledge and the nature of the self. No sign interprets itself, but is always addressed to an actual or potential interpreter capable not only of taking the sign *as* a sign, but also of providing a possible interpretant. Some relation between interpretation and a dialogic process now becomes evident. This fact brings us to the fifth noteworthy feature of Peirce's analysis, namely, the future orientation of interpretation and its procedure *ad infinitum*.

The interpretant of every sign is itself a sign addressed to an actual or potential interpreter—the interpreter may be other than the one who furnishes a given interpretant or it may be the same interpreter at a subsequent time—and thus the process is, in principle, without a terminus. Of course, the context or purpose determining any particular process of interpretation may bring that process to an end as, for example, when a course of deliberation ends in a decision followed by an action, or when it is decided that 'for practical purposes' a given analysis can be terminated because it has reached a point of clarity and precision sufficient for those purposes even if, given other purposes, the process would have to continue. The open-ended character of interpretation mirrors, in this feature, the character of conversation between two selves. Such conversation is essentially a reciprocal interpreting of signs; it is also an inner dialogue which everyone of us carries on whenever we are deliberating, working out a critical theory by considering possible objections, proposing modifications and developing arguments, or when we are seeking some understanding of our own selves, our motives, purposes and intentions.

Before attempting to illustrate more fully the five features of signs and their interpretation contained in the passages cited from Peirce, let us summarize the features themselves. They are:

(1) Sign-reading through interpretation always involves triadic relations (and if we consider the interpret*er*, we introduce a fourth term).

(2) The sign represents its object, but requires that the interpreter be otherwise acquainted with (or have knowledge of) the object.

(3) The sign is determined by its object as is also the interpreter when he supplies the interpretant.

(4) Interpretation presupposes an actual or potential mind.

(5) The process of interpretation is, in principle, without terminus, since every interpretant is a sign addressed to an interpreter.

We may take as a basic illustration of sign functioning and the process of interpretation the situation in which an archaeologist uncovers an inscription which he desires to read. The case is, of course, special but only to the extent that signs in a natural language are involved and the question of 'natural' signs such as smoke, thunder, etc., is not considered. The archaeologist, through his knowledge of ancient languages, is able to identify the inscription as written in hieroglyphics. He now wishes to make the text of this inscription available to someone who reads, say, the English language, but who is unable to read or decipher hieroglyphics. To accomplish his purpose, the archaeologist becomes an interpreter by offering a *translation* of the original inscription in the form of a second set of signs, in this case, the second set will be expressions in English. The second set purports to interpret or to express in English what was expressed in the original inscription cast in hieroglyphics. With regard to (1) the triadic relation exhibited is evident; if the object represented by the signs constituting the Egyptian text was, let us say, the Nile delta, then the interpretants of these signs or the resulting English text would stand related to the Nile delta in exactly the same way as the hieroglyphic signs originally stood to that object. The three terms, sign, object and interpretant, are so related that what the first expresses about the second is identical with what the third expresses about the second.

As soon as the translator discovers the object of the signs before him—the Nile delta—he is able to interpret them accurately only in so far as he is otherwise acquainted with or knows the object in question. Peirce's point here is that the sign does not 'present' but 'represents' its object and in order for the sign to convey information about its object, the interpreter of the sign must be able to apprehend that object as something already known (2). The interpreter does not merely apprehend the sign and produce the interpretant, but he directs his thought to the object and understands it as characterized according to the meaning expressed in the sign that represents it. If the sign is to afford valid representation, it must be determined by its object and the interpreter must be determined in turn by the object when he seeks the proper interpretant. If the element of constraint exercised by the object is omitted, we are led to think of the world as exhausted by sign vehicles and their dictionary equivalents; the objective world disappears. A linguistic idealism results, and it comes to be believed that the interpreter is merely substituting an interpretant for a sign instead of actually thinking the *object* which the original sign represents.

The claim that interpretation presupposes an actual or potential mind raises issues that go far beyond present purposes. It is clear, however, at least in the case of artificial signs as represented by our Egyptian text, that when our archaeologist identifies the text as written in the sacred characters of an ancient civilization, he at once assumes not only that the characters of the text represent the Nile delta, but that the text itself as a set of signs represents an ancient mind or community of minds intending to express a meaning about that delta which he is trying to decipher. He places these signs in a category different from those 'signs' that might have been made by the claws or hoofs of some ancient bird or beast walking over a soft clay surface which later hardened and was preserved. It is not that an interpreter is prevented from seeking the 'meaning' of these latter signs, but he could do no more than search for their *cause*, since the relation of bird or animal to the surface is dyadic in character, a case, in Peirce's terms, of action and reaction, an essentially causal connection. From the reaction or result we infer the action or the cause; the characteristic triad is missing since the signs in question had no *intended* object. There is a claw and the clay surface with its imprint; nothing more. The triad appears, to be sure, when a later interpreter comes upon the scene and seeks to read the sign, but in that case the intended object is *his* intended object, *not* the intended object of the sign. In the case of the hieroglyphic text, however, we ask for the 'meaning' of the signs, referring to the expressions intended by an ancient mind or sign *using* animal.

The need for a mind is even more obvious if we attend to the fact that it belongs to the nature of a sign to be read or interpreted. It is only through interpretation that the being of a sign is realized. This process can be initiated only by someone capable of taking a sign as a sign and of being aware that it requires interpretation. The 'taking as' is an operation characteristic of a mind or sign-using animal. Our archaeologist had first to recognize his text as in fact a set of signs expressing meanings about intended objects; only then could he envisage his task as a translator.

The process of interpretation continues only as long as any sign addressed to an interpreter is actually read and hence is cast into the form of another sign. Unlike perception which terminates in its object, interpretation proceeds *ad infinitum,* since every sign interpreted is a succeeding sign which in turn requires the recursive operation.

As a prelude to considering the bearing of the foregoing account on the nature of the self and of self-knowledge, let us look more closely at the functioning of the interpreter.[4] An interpreter of the sort illustrated above, is essentially a mediator who brings two distinct minds into relation. One who interprets is like a person with coins the value of which he knows in the realm where they are legal tender, but who is trying to discover what value, if any, these same coins have in another domain where other coins are legal tender. Each of us must understand those to whom we are related in terms primarily of our own experience. The question is, what of the experience of the other, what is that like as had by the other and how shall I be understood by him in those terms and how shall he be understood by me in my terms? The point is that I do not start out by knowing either the significance of his experience when interpreted through my own or the significance of my own experience when interpreted through his. The point is that a gulf must be crossed which is the gulf of individuation. It is the contention of this

---

4. As previously indicated, the interpreter is the one who interprets; the interpretants are his interpretations. If we attend only to the latter, however, on the ground that "logical" considerations require no more, we are likely to overlook some of the functions performed by the interpreter as an individual related to other individuals in a concrete situation.

essay that that gulf is bridged by the process of interpretation in which we gradually and with effort come to see what the other means in his own terms and also to what extent our own experience is valid in terms of his experience. I am seeking to discover you not merely as I experience you, but as you experience yourself and vice versa, but each of us is forced to discover the other in terms of his own experience.

To return to our illustration, the mind expressed in the signs of the ancient text has now been interpreted or translated into equivalent signs in the English language to be read by an English reader. The interpreter says implicitly to the English reader concerning his translation, 'What I say to you is what the text said to me', and in this way he brings a contemporary mind into a unity of understanding with a mind long passed away. In performing his task the interpreter does much more than correlate or match terms one-to-one. He must find in the language *into which* he translates the appropriate way of expressing what he takes the signs of the language *from which* he translates to mean.[5] He must, that is to say, interpret or put a construction on the original signs and then discover how to express *that* interpretant in the other language. The familiar claim that the translator always offers an 'interpretation' should be taken to mean that passing from the signs of one language to those of a second is not a process that can be entirely subject to rule; instead it always involves the ingenuity of the interpreter since he has to grasp the meaning of the original signs.

The mediating function of the interpreter lends itself to wide application; interpreters are at work in such diverse contexts as law, diplomacy, political institutions, education, religion and indeed throughout the entire fabric of cultural life. The lawyer represents a plaintiff and interprets his case to the court; a diplomat represents a country and interprets its actions and aims to the representatives of other countries; the priest or pastor represents his religious tradition and interprets its meaning to the members of the community. The underlying motive of all interpreting is the cre-

5. Examples of idiomatic speech bring out the point very nicely. In his *Anthropologie*, Kant, discussing the differences in human capacities from person to person, uses the idiomatic expression, *"Er hat das Schiesspulver nicht erfunden."* A supposedly literal translation would have to be, "He did not invent gunpowder." But if we want to know how we would express in English the meaning that is expressed in the German sentence (with, of course, help from the context) we would have to translate, "He is no genius" or, more colloquially, "He is no great shakes." The latter says accurately in the language *into which* we translate, what has been said in the language *from which* we translate.

ation of communities of understanding in which diverse persons are brought into some form of unity and conflicting claims are made less explosive by being contained within a framework of shared meanings and intelligent discussion.

If interpretation creates communities of understanding between distinct persons, it must be intimately connected not only with interpersonal relations embracing distinct individuals but also with the relations between a person and himself at different times. In short, interpretation is essential for a community of distinct individuals as well as for that peculiar community of relations with ourselves which each one of us represents. Royce was the first one to see this remarkably concrete bearing of Peirce's theory of interpretation. Let us now consider the light which it throws on the nature of the self and self-knowledge.

II. Interpretation, the Self and Self-Knowledge

Royce proposed to extend Peirce's theory of interpretation at two basic points. The one is actually a prelude to the other. First, he argued that interpretation is a distinct and irreducible activity not to be confused with either perceiving or conceiving taken as distinguishable modes of apprehension. Second, Royce held that interpretation is especially suited for understanding certain objects which cannot be identified with either of the objects generally thought to be apprehended respectively by perceiving and conceiving. What Royce had in mind is obvious enough; the individual person and a community of persons represent 'objects' neither of which can be uniquely identified as singular matters of fact, such as particular instances of qualities like 'blue' or 'long' which can be perceived or, again, as objects of conceptual thought such as 'prime number' or 'frictionless system' which are never the object of any perception. Royce's insight may be recast as follows: where two distinct persons confront or encounter each other, neither person is for the other an object of the same sort as a particular instance of a perceptible quality or as something to be apprehended by conceptual thought alone. A person does not fit into either of these categories nor does a community of persons, because both are time-spanning or enduring organic unities peculiar in that they are unified by a *centre of intention* expressing itself through what can be perceived and conceived, without either unity being identical in type with the characteristic objects of either form of apprehension. Royce, therefore, proposed the novel idea that both individual persons and communities of persons are the appropriate objects of *interpretation* which, though dependent upon both perceiving and conceiving, is identical with neither because, through the medium of signs, interpretation reaches back into the centre of intention which is the core of both persons and communities.

The uniqueness of interpretation *vis-à-vis* other activities characteristic of a rational being is best seen in the singular fact that a person confronted by a sign can both perceive it as an object or thing in the world, and also describe it in terms of well-defined recurrent characters without being able to read or interpret it. To take a simple illustration—more complex and subtle examples occur in the domain of human speech, gestures and actions—a person may encounter a metal weather vane on the roof of a barn, he may perceive it through direct encounter and note the position of the arrow in relation to certain metal figures shaped to represent letters of the English alphabet, he may also set out to describe the geometric shape and content of the object before him, all without taking the object as a *sign* and therefore without reading its meaning. Nor will either increasing the accuracy of his perception with instruments or introducing more precise concepts for description alter the situation; a sign is not merely an object among other objects, but rather a representative device whose meaning must be interpreted.[6] The process of interpreting is not identical with that of correlating concepts with percepts in accordance with procedures of empirical verification in which the sensible fact is said to be the 'cash value' of the concept. The point can be illustrated with clarity in a familiar human situation. Consider a person who, like the Biblical Job, has been the victim of an almost uninterrupted series of disasters. His wife has died, his sons have been killed in battle, and he discovers that he himself has a dread disease. In despair, he cries, 'Life is not worth living!' Such an utterance is not a description of his situation nor is the utterance deducible from a description, since another person facing the same tragedies might give them an opposite interpretation. Still less is it an explanation of how the disastrous facts came to be. The exclamation is instead an *interpretation* aimed at reading the meaning of these facts. The victim sees the events as signs to which a meaning can be assigned.

6. If it is said that the sign vehicle can be perceived as an object among other objects, the point may be admitted, but then the sign cannot function as a sign until it is *taken as* a sign and interpreted. If I cannot read Arabic, being confronted with a page from the *Koran* printed in the original language, I can perceive a series of characters written in straight lines across the page, but for me they will *not* function as signs, since I cannot read them, even if I am able to recognize the characters as belonging to the Arabic alphabet.

This meaning is intended as the import of the facts, but is neither a description nor an explanation of them.

To return to Royce's analysis, we must make clear the main purpose behind his having made a special point of distinguishing interpretation from both conception and perception. In his efforts to arrive at a theory of the self and of self-knowledge, Royce was led to reject the two antithetical approaches to the problem which seem to have been taken for granted since the period of Enlightenment. The empiricists, on the one hand sought, like Hume, to apprehend the self through some form of perception, while rationalists like Descartes or Leibniz on the other, appealed to intellectual intuition. Royce's claim is that neither in my own case, nor in that of my neighbour can it be true that the self is identical with a singular perceptual datum or with some abstract character such as that of individuality or personality. He was proposing to abandon both the rationalists' thinking substance and the empiricists' series of passing states possessing the tenuous unity of memory in favour of a new alternative. Suppose the self were the sort of reality to be known and experienced as the appropriate object of interpretation—each person confronts another as a *centre of intention* expressing him or herself through the medium of signs, among which are included not only words, exclamations and gestures, but also actions and abstentions, and even the body itself. In every encounter, every conversation, the participant selves are *directly* present to each other, but no one of us knows the centre of intention of the other in an *immediate* way, i.e. without the reading of signs. Each of us is directly presented in the signs through which we express ourselves, but we are not identical with these signs, since they point beyond themselves back to the core self which is the centre of intention. So convinced was Royce of the necessity for interpretation in all self-knowledge and understanding that he was even prepared to identify the self *as* an interpretation; for him the enduring identity of the self in time is the success with which the present self interprets the past self to the future self.[7] Here I part company with Royce and shall develop the theme of selfhood and interpretation in my own way. I find much that Royce wrote on the topic illuminating and I agree both with his doctrine that the self as such is no simple datum among others, and with his equally emphatic rejection of all

7. A clear, but simple, model of the process is found in the fulfilling of a promise. A promise made belongs necessarily to the past self; when the time of fulfillment approaches, the then present self recalls the commitment and interprets that past to the future self who is to realize the deed specified in the original promise.

attempts (for example, that of William James) to understand the self solely in terms of relations holding between passing thoughts. But I do not believe, as Royce did, that we can legitimately regard the self as identical with an interpretation because the self as centre of interpretation is required as the interpreter. In my view, the self is experienced and known through interpretation, but it is not itself an interpretation. Such an identification would be at once too idealistic and rationalistic in its import. The self is, as I shall suggest, more than a mind; it is a dynamic, organic system of habits, feelings, desires, tendencies and thoughts, unified through plans and purposes framed and projected by what I call a centre of intention. This centre expresses itself through the instrumentality of the body where it is localized for the other person. When another seeks to understand or interpret me, it is my centre which is his target.

Let us consider more closely what happens when two persons engage in discussion, have an interview or hold a dialogue of some sort. We may omit for the present, the philosophers' problem of the existence of other minds—the argument from analogy and all that, in order to look at the situation as we find it. You and I confront each other primarily as living bodies in and through which meanings, purposes, intentions, are being expressed. Each of us, therefore, is *for* the other as a series of signs, words, gestures, facial expressions and, over extended periods of time, deeds and actions, which need to be interpreted. These signs, however, do not appear either as isolated phenomena or as self-sufficient in their own right. As soon, for example, as you say something to me—ask a critical question, contradict what I have just said, propose an alternative view—I find myself supposing that that particular sign or set of signs is expressive of or proceeds from some more complex and fundamental intention. I think of you as 'aiming' or 'driving at' some goal of thought which is not fully expressed in any single expression. I think of you, moreover, not only as having a purposive centre of intention which is not exhausted in the signs you express on any one occasion, but also as a being capable of projecting a purpose or plan which extends to the unity of an entire life. I *presuppose* this unity of aim in your expressions and I attempt to apprehend it through these expressions themselves. It is, in fact, precisely because I presuppose this unity of aim on your part that I take your expressions as signs to be interpreted. I do not begin the other way around, starting with these expressions as *evidence for* the existence of yourself and your mind. In that case, I would be attempting to *explain* your being as an object or phenomenon rather than to *understand* you as a person. Without presupposing the unity of your aim—whether well or ill expressed—I would never have taken your expressions as signs to be interpreted in the first place. In personal encounter, each of us endeavors to apprehend the centre of intention presupposed in the other. The only access we have to that centre is through signs (this is true as well of the internal dialogues we carry on with ourselves in order to clarify our ideas, discover our interests, form plans, etc.), but the signs express that centre; they are not identical with it.

The process of interpreting in which we jointly engage represents an endeavor to bring about a community of understanding, not in the sense that the participants agree at every point in their opinions, evaluations, etc., but rather in the aim of coming to a common understanding of what each of us is saying. Notice, again, that interpretation differs from some related rational processes in which we also engage. When, for example, I seek to interpret what you say and to grasp what you are trying to express in actual conversation and encounter, I am neither *describing* your person, nor *explaining* your behaviour. Were I describing you as a person, I would be considering you not as a subject communicating yourself but rather as an object or the referent of sets of descriptive predicates. I might under such circumstances, record your words and depict your gestures, but I would not be engaged primarily in interpreting both words and gestures in order to penetrate your aim and centre of intention. On the other hand, were I attempting to explain your present state, I would once again be viewing you as an object and seeking to give a causal account of how you came to be what you are, your present constitution, physical, psychological, social, moral, etc. Again, in confronting you with this purpose in view, I would not be seeking to interpret what you say to me as an individual, autonomous subject; on the contrary, I would be viewing you as a 'case', a patient, an instance of a set of general laws said to exercise control over all human behaviour. But in interpreting, where I take your signs as expressive of a more or less clearly focused aim, I am meeting you as a subject, a person, I am seeking to discover what you mean to say and to penetrate your centre of intention. We encounter each other as two subjects seeking to create between us a community of understanding.

Consider as an instructive example, the following concrete encounter between two persons well known in imaginative literature. Hamlet[8] says to Ophelia, 'I never loved you', and Ophelia, both stunned and puzzled, says, 'But, my Lord, you made me believe so.'

8. I am paraphrasing in order to simplify the situation.

We have here a complex encounter and one that is by no means confined to the immediate occasion of the conversation. Each party has in mind a series of past deeds and encounters, gestures, conversations and indeed past interpretations. Each puts an interpretation on that past, an interpretation which is an attempt to sum up or express a unity of purpose and intention defining a single self. Hamlet is now prepared to interpret his past behaviour and to claim that whatever that behaviour appeared to express when it was manifest and whatever interpretation Ophelia put on it, he never was in love with her. Hamlet here assumes the role of interpreter with respect to his own signs; he seeks to say what his past behaviour meant from the standpoint of his present centre of intention. Ophelia, on the other hand, places a different construction on what was, at least in principle, the same set of signs. She not only interpreted Hamlet's behaviour—words and deeds—as meaning that he loved her but also hints at a specific intention on his part to lead her to make the very interpretation at which she did in fact arrive. Ophelia views Hamlet's behaviour, and Hamlet views his own behaviour as the expression of an enduring centre of intention; the problem for both is to discover the proper interpretation of the signs through which that centre expresses itself or is made manifest. Ophelia does not confront Hamlet's behaviour merely as a collection of disparate acts, but rather as having the unity of import and purpose characteristic of an enduring self. This unity is neither a substance to be apprehended in intellectual intuition nor Hume's celebrated bundle of perceptions, nor again is it a series of passing thoughts somehow associated with a body. The self is an organic unity enduring in time; it is a togetherness of a *one*—the centre of intention—and a *many* in the form of the multitude of acts, thoughts, events which mark out the unique temporal history or career which forever identifies not only the Hamlets and Ophelias of the world, but every human person.

The curious fact is that we often understand the many or the detail or the self more clearly than the unity or centre of intention, and yet that detail does not introduce us to the unique individual when it is taken apart from the centre of intention which it expresses. The contents of our lives, the places we visit, the persons we encounter, the music we listen to, the triumphs we enjoy and the tragedies we endure, are events with repeatable structures and when viewed as objective happenings they may be described and explained in generic terms as if they belonged to or expressed either nobody or 'anybody', which is the same. But just as the self is not a bare unity or centre of intention apart from the events in and through which it expresses itself, it is also not a mere collection of detail. The detail as the expression of my centre is what gives individuality and uniqueness to my history. The events of my life may be taken objectively as instances of general kinds, but my centre of intention is individual and unique, not to be taken as an instance.

The self in its concreteness, however, is not to be identified either with the one or the many, but with the togetherness of the two. Since the self is a living creature, that togetherness cannot be understood as a static affair; instead it must be a *unifying* which means a constant recreating of identity in the course of change and development.

What sort of reality can this unifying be and how is it to be understood? Royce's suggestion of a *purpose* is right to the point. The dominant purpose that guides us fulfills the conditions for unifying. What makes us one person in the course or history of our lives is the overarching purpose through which we organize and harmonize the lesser desires, purposes and drives that constitute our life. When we grasp that purpose we grasp what enables us to endure as a unity. And when we seek to understand another, that purpose is our target; we must interpret all the signs expressive of the person in relation to that purpose in so far as we are able to apprehend it.

Interpreting and understanding each other is a difficult affair, not least because of our failures in interpreting ourselves. Contrary to widespread belief, it is not true that we are all in possession of clear interpretations of our own selves and suffer only from lack of insight into the selves of our neighbours. More often than not the situation is precisely the opposite. The measure of distance and objectivity we enjoy in interpreting the signs or behaviour of our neighbour cannot exist in our own case, because the interpreter and the one to be interpreted are one and the same. Hamlet's interpretation of himself has the marks of an *ad hoc* reading of the signs, a reading designed to suit present purposes, whereas Ophelia's interpretation is meant to be based on a slowly and steadily built insight into a fairly stable intention manifesting itself over a period of time.

In the end the great difficulty we encounter in attaining understanding both of ourselves and of others must lead to an acknowledgement that interpreting is as much an art as a science. For interpretation is always a *creative* and therefore risky enterprise.[9] We must pass beyond ourselves and the problematics of our own

9. See "Creativity in Royce's Philosophical Idealism", chapter 9.

experience to the interiority of another. Such an effort will involve us in a greater possibility of error than we are likely to encounter when we deal with another self in terms of description and explanation. And yet interpretation is the only instrument we have for moving from the signs we do encounter to the centre of intention which we never encounter as we encounter the signs that express it. And yet without grasping that centre we are not in communication or community with the other. Every venture in human understanding is an adventure whether we move outwards to apprehend the other or inwards to understand ourselves. Patience, tolerance and love—virtues often in short supply—are required for success, and no doubt this is why finding a truly understanding person is as precious as it is rare.

Overview

11

Receptivity, Change and Relevance: Some Hallmarks of Philosophy in America

In this chapter I single out three features—there are, to be sure, others—which are characteristic of philosophical thinking in America and at the same time stand in some contrast with the practices of philosophers in Britain, Germany and France. I focus on an openness of mind and an experimental spirit that are manifested in a willingness to attempt to understand philosophical ideas from whatever quarter they may come. Secondly, I want to underline the efforts of the classical American thinkers especially to do justice to the reality of change, development and the temporal dimension of existence. Thirdly, there is the need to understand the importance attached to the relevance of ideas themselves, but also to the task of discovering what ideas are relevant, or, as James liked to say, "count" in any attempt to deal with some issue or problem.

As regards receptivity, consider the great interest displayed by American thinkers in the philosophy of existence—Kierkegaard, Heidegger, Sartre, Camus, Unamuno and Buber—in continental Phenomenology, in Wittgenstein and the analytic and linguistic philosophies of Britain and in the logical empiricism of the Vienna Circle whose members, with a few exceptions, came to set up shop in America. I believe that this openness is central to the American vision of how to pursue philosophical ideas and it is a salutary trait, even if it has not always been reciprocated. The insularity of British philosophy is notorious and what better illustration can be found than Ayer's William James Lectures about Pragmatism in which he remains totally unaware of the thorough-going critique made by the Pragmatists of the classical conception of experience and simply assumes that it and its typical problems remain intact. German philosophy still continues the "Kant oder Hegel?" debate and where outside influences enter—earlier on in Horkheimer's Eclipse of Reason, *and more recently in Apel's transcendental semiotics—it is for the purpose of showing that Peirce, for example, is important only because he had roots in Kant's philosophy. French philosophers have never gotten over Descartes and he still casts an appreciable shadow over so innovative a thinker as Sartre. Perhaps we should not lament the absence of a recognizable "national" tradition in philosophy when we consider how restricting that can be, a block to the path of inquiry.*

American thinkers were among the first to recognize the reality of change, to take, as the phrase goes, "time seriously," and to consider the philosophical implications of the theory of evolution. One of the fundamental reasons that the treatment of knowledge and truth at the hands of the Pragmatists met with such resistance both at home and abroad is that they were trying to adjust the traditional conception of the "timelessness" of truth to the facts about the temporal growth of knowledge in the sciences. Rorty sees this very well and makes it central to his interpretation of Pragmatism. In giving up certainty, but not knowledge, the Pragmatists, moreover, paved the way for a better understanding of the relations between philosophy and the sciences; the former is not simply a hopeless muddle of competing "schools" in comparison with the neatness of a steadily advancing scientific progress. No less a thinker than Kant held that where there are "schools" of thought, there is no science, but at present the existence of such differences in interpretation even in the "hard" sciences has come to be accepted and it is not thought to be the end of science.

The importance attached to time, change and growth, however, has not been confined to the sphere of knowledge alone, but extends across the entire culture. Royce showed the role of a remembered past and a hoped for future in the founding of a community and in providing it with an identity in the midst of change. Peirce's theory of evolutionary love points to a process wherein the competitiveness of the "greed philosophy" is to be overcome through cooperation and community. James's "meliorism" is another case in point; his vision of the strenuous life included the responsibility of all of us to attack human ills in every form and to strive to make the world better than we found it. And, of course, Dewey's instrumentalism is rooted in the idea of effecting change so that diagnosing and explaining a problematic situation must be such as to afford guidance in coping with what went wrong.

The classical thinkers, and especially James, may have been over-confident in their belief that the urgent need for the relevant idea or piece of information somehow makes the determination of that relevance easier than it actually is. Their concern, nevertheless, was legitimate and it is now clear that what suspicion there was about encyclopedic knowledge and systems of philosophy was due to a sense that they often furnish no clues to what is relevant for dealing with a specific issue. We see the point illustrated by James's pointing to the encyclopedia on the bookshelf—the symbol of total knowledge—and asking, "When do I say these truths?" One does not go about uttering true propositions about items from "Aardvark" to "Zygote" without any indication of what particular conception or fact "counts" or is relevant to the matter at hand. Despite the fact that certain demands for relevance in thought may prove to have been short-sighted or ill-advised, the concern itself is what kept the American thinkers on the track of the concrete in both thought and action. It also enabled them to detect and avoid the often trivial "puzzles" so dear to professional philosophers and at the same time to turn aside the artificialities of much skepticism. Peirce's warning is right on the target: "Do not claim to doubt as a philosopher what you do not doubt as a man."

This chapter appeared in Two Centuries of Philosophy in America, *Edited and with an Introduction by Peter Caws, APQ Library of Philosophy, 7, Basil Blackwell, 1980, pp. 185–198. It is reprinted with the permission of the Editor of the APQ Library.*

Anyone who has given thought to what might be meant by the phrase "American Philosophy" becomes aware at once of the dilemma which presents itself and which, like all significant dilemmas, resists a neat solution. By "American philosophy," it would seem, we must mean either an identifiable American position, outlook or system of thought, on the one hand, or a mere catalogue, an enumeration of all the types of philosophical thinking taking place on the American scene, on the other. In the first sense we would be pointing to a substantive "American" philosophy analogous, for example, to British empiricism or German idealism, whereas in the second sense, the adjective "American" would have a largely geographical connotation, conveying little more than the place or the environment within which a quite heterogeneous collection of philosophical issues have been discussed and philosophical positions articulated. I am inclined to think that there was in fact an indigenous American philosophy in the first sense to be found in the many-sided development of pragmatism beginning with the early papers of Peirce and continuing through the work of Dewey and Mead. Since, however, that classical development had run its course a decade or so before the middle of the century and was succeeded, on the academic scene at least, by new interests in language, semantics, epistemology and logic introduced through both British and Continental sources, it is no longer legitimate to speak of American philosophy solely in terms of the classical position. In saying this I do not mean to imply that the basic ideas of the pragmatists have simply disappeared; on the contrary, there is at present a new interest in their ideas both at home and abroad. I mean rather to call attention to the fact that so many new interests, positions and approaches have made their appearance in our midst that it is clearly impossible to speak of American philosophy as if it represented one substantive position or tradition. And indeed this is precisely what one should expect in a pluralistic culture such as our own.

In view of these considerations, it seems to me that the only way to do justice to a rather complex situation is to speak about "philosophy in America" with the aim of distinguishing some hallmarks which have become evident on the philosophical scene. In pursuing this aim, we shall be speaking neither of *an* American philosophy nor of an inventory of philosophical positions, but of something closer to a pervasive spirit in philosophical thinking manifesting itself in the interests and concerns of American philosophers and in their manner of approach to philosophical issues.

The hallmarks I have selected, receptivity, change and relevance, represent, I confess, a somewhat mixed bag. The first points primarily to an attitude, a style, a manner of approach; the second is simply a basic and predominant fact about the nature of things which carries with it an entire spectrum of philosophical problems to be resolved; and the third is a fundamental concern about the bearing of thought in all its forms on the problems of human existence, especially a concern for determining what idea or piece of knowledge counts and what doesn't count for the answering of a question or the solving of a problem. In attempting to make clear what I mean by each of these hallmarks, I shall avail myself of some representative illustrations drawn from developments of the past sixty years.

I. Receptivity

American thinkers have ever been open and receptive to points of view other than their own and they have welcomed the many different winds of philosophical doctrine from whatever quarter they have blown. This receptivity, to be sure, has called forth from foreign critics interpretations filled with ambivalence. Some have seen the willingness to enter sympathetically into philosophical positions conceived abroad as a sign of our uncertainty and insecurity stemming from a deep suspicion of the philosophical product grown in America. Both versions of C. D. Broad's notorious comment on this head come to the same conclusion in the end. According to one version, old and dying philosophies come to America for last rites and a proper burial, while according to another, such philosophies are resurrected, as it were, and start a new life as a form of, in Russell's phrase, "transatlantic truth." In both interpretations, the imported position is supposed to be the genuine article on a market that is without a serious domestic rival.

Polemical academic politics aside, however, there is another way of looking at the receptivity displayed by American thinkers; it calls attention to a broadly empirical outlook on the world, including the world of thought, and represents what Dewey called the experimental spirit, a refusal to be encapsulated in one position while remaining heedless of all others. This positive interpretation of receptivity which bespeaks a genuine concern for understanding what philosophers in other places are saying and not a desperate attempt to fill a philosophical void, is dramatically illustrated by the treatment accorded by American thinkers to the philosophy of existence in its own development from Kierkegaard to Sartre. And, as I shall suggest, this treatment is even more dramatic when it is compared with the corresponding response to American pragmatism in some other parts of the world. The selection here of the philosophy of existence as an example is not meant to ignore the manifestation of the same receptivity on the part of American philosophers to the phenomenological movement, both German and French, or to the linguistic philosophies and the philosophies of analysis originating in Britain. Anthony Quinton has given a brief resume of the latter development in an article which appeared in *Times Literary Supplement* of June 13, 1975.

American thinkers began their engagement with the philosophy of existence through the study of Kierkegaard in the 1930s and in the intervening years many have followed the pursuit of *Existenz* through the numerous writings of Heidegger, Sartre, Camus, Marcel, Unamuno and others. Consider that, before the position could be understood and appropriated, translations of the principal works had to be prepared involving several foreign languages, unfamiliar styles of thought, and obscurities so formidable that even our best translations of the major works are still interlaced with words and phrases from the original languages. *Existenz* and *Dasein*, for example, are by no means adequately represented in their meaning by the English term "existence" and consequently we have had to add them to the language. With the texts themselves in hand, commentaries and interpretation were forthcoming, and in the end the various forms of existential philosophy came to exert a powerful influence not only upon philosophy itself, but upon psychiatry, literature and theology on the American scene. Neither mere curiosity nor casual interest will explain the persistent and laborious thought and scholarship which have been expended in the attempt to understand and come to terms with the complex issues—being, freedom, thought, time, anxiety, death—forming the substance of the existential outlook. I cannot attempt to explain the many motives behind the reception of this type of philosophy in America; obviously there were cultural, psychological, and religious factors at work along with philosophical considerations in the entire development. In my view, the underlying directive force, however, in the appropriation of existentialism was the attitude of receptivity, the openness to fresh experience and novel ideas rooted in the sense that no one standpoint encompasses everything and therefore that intellectual life and growth demand a willingness to penetrate the thought and experience of others no matter how strange and discontinuous they may be in relation to familiar patterns of thought.

The receptivity here manifested stands in sharp contrast to the insularity frequently displayed by philosophers in foreign parts in the face of American pragmatism. Let us take note of the fact that this position had its beginnings more than a century ago in Peirce's papers of the 1870s and in James's essay "Philosophical Conceptions and Practical Results" of 1898, and that it developed continuously in a voluminous literature through at least the 1940s and 1950s. In 1956 Sidney Hook, in *American Philosophers at Work*, complained that America has remained a largely undiscovered country on its intellectual side, especially its pragmatic philosophy. The striking fact is that, until recently, the situation had not changed much both on the Continent and in Britain. With a few exceptions, there has not been a major concern to understand pragmatism in its basic doctrines and motives after the fashion of the concern of American philosophers to plumb the depths of existentialism (and one could of course add the philosophies of analysis and the types of phenomenology as well). And the attention which pragmatism is now beginning to receive abroad shows not so much an interest in coming to grips with the basic ideas of the pragmatists as an attempt to accommodate them for other purposes. Thus Ayer, in *The Origins of American Pragmatism*, disregards, for the most part, the pragmatists' critique of classical British empiricism and the primacy of epistemology, and treats these thinkers as if they were seeking to answer all the questions about perception and the external world associated with British philosophy since Hume. Current interest in Peirce on the Continent, moreover, tends, in accordance with familiar trends, to focus almost entirely on his logic to the exclusion of those more adventurous features of his thought represented by tychism, synechism, scholastic realism and panpsychism. Such selective or differential interest is *something less* than what I have been describing as receptivity.

I cannot leave this topic without mentioning two more immediate indications of receptivity as a hallmark of the American habit of mind in contrast to what is characteristic in other philosophical quarters. In February of 1976 news was received of the death of Professor Michael Polanyi, a scientist and philosopher whose roots were firmly established in the European tradition of thought. I find it highly significant and illustrative of the point I am making that there appeared in the obituary published by the *New York Times*, February 24, 1976, the following sentence; "Professor Polanyi was a visiting professor at 14 universities, and his work as a chemist and his philosophic writings *were perhaps better known in the United States than in Europe.*" This judgment is undoubtedly true and the reason for it is not difficult to find. Abroad he was earmarked as a scientist and not as a philosopher but in this country, regardless of labels, many philosophers were interested in and receptive to his attempts, admittedly dark in places and sometimes out of focus, to describe the role played by the scientist himself and his assumptions in the conduct of actual inquiry. His conception of tacit knowing evoked interest among us and, without allowing the fact that he was not ticketed as a professional philosopher to stand in the way, we were anxious to give him a hearing and to understand what he had to say about the logic of the scientific enterprise and the place of science in human society.

My final comment on receptivity takes the form of a personal anecdote. In 1955 I was invited as a guest of the *Philosophisches Seminar* at the University of Heidelberg and in the course of my stay it was suggested that I might give a talk or two there and at the neighboring University of Mainz. I soon divined, however, that there was little interest in my speaking about Dewey or Royce or the then current situation in American philosophy; instead I ended by giving some talks, in German, on *"Der Raumbegriff bei Kant"!* I remember thinking at the time that whereas I might have delivered some fresh ore, I was condemned to carrying coals to Newcastle.

II. Change

In citing the basic fact of *change* as a matter of special concern to American philosophers, I want to begin by calling attention to a difficult problem which first made its appearance with the doctrine of evolution in the last century and has made itself felt in every domain of life since that time. In considering the influence of Darwinism on philosophy, Dewey laid the greatest emphasis on change and development as ultimate facts and generic traits of existence. Peirce, James, Whitehead and countless others were to reinforce this emphasis, reminding us that we must, as the phrase goes, "take time seriously." That this is no simple injunction or one that is easy to follow can be readily seen. For two millennia the great majority of philosophers of the Western tradition sought to explain whatever change and temporality they acknowledged in terms of reality which is essentially timeless and does not change. The results were invariably the same; either time and change were demoted to the sphere of appearance, or basic and pervasive facts about each were ignored or distorted in the interest of preserving the explanatory scheme. The revolution in thought which took place in connection with the introduction of the evolutionary viewpoint in the last century may be seen as the exact reversal of a pattern of thinking which is as old as the paradoxes of Zeno. Whatever the fundamental purpose of these paradoxes was, they make abundantly clear that certain static or fixed elements were thought adequate for representing ultimate fact with the result that motion and change become impossible, unintelligible or both. The evolutionary conceptions of the past century precisely reversed this relationship; change, growth and development in time were established as the ultimate facts and the fixed or unchanging was seen as either a limiting case or totally abstract in character.

The critical point at which the fact of change became a major philosophical issue was in connection with the theory of truth and knowledge and consequently with the interpretation of science. Truth, it had long been argued, must have a timeless character and have a tenure which transcends change. Consequently, knowledge, if it is to be knowledge of such truth, must itself share in a similar superiority to both time and change, which is the principal reason for the frequent identification of knowledge with certainty in a large segment of modern philosophy. The curious fact, however, is that while many philosophers were developing theories of truth entailing its timeless and certain character, natural scientists were emphasizing the tentativeness, the fallibility, and the contingency of their own conclusions; they were emphasizing the fact that the warrant for their assertions is limited to the available evidence and therefore that the possibility of revision in the future cannot be ruled out in advance. The situation, however, was highly ambiguous because many of the philosophers who conceived of truth and knowledge in terms essentially timeless were simultaneously assuming that the sciences represent the most reliable knowledge we have. The discrepancy, moreover, is not removed merely by insisting on the distinction between a theory of the nature of truth and a specification of the tests of truth, because the two cannot remain unrelated and if the former is understood as a timeless affair we are faced with the same problem all over again because the tests of truth will necessarily be involved in contingency and fallibility.

American philosophers since the days of Peirce have been wrestling with this perplexing problem of bringing philosophical thinking into accord with the facts of an historically conditioned and self-corrective inquiry. How is it possible to take seriously the facts of change and fallibility in the knowing situation and at the same time avoid a relativism which suggests that in essence we have no knowledge at all? Russell laid hold of the issue many years ago when he deplored the fact that in the Index to Dewey's *Logic* he could find no entry under "Truth," but only the directive to consult "Warranted Assertibility." As a believer in the thesis that present and given fact is the causal and commanding condition for the truth of the proposition which asserts it, Russell was totally dissatisfied with Dewey's approach and placed it at once in that suspect category of "Transatlantic Truth" through which he had wittily described James's theory of truth as set forth in *Pragmatism*. That the central issue is not an idle one can be seen from a number of developments on the contemporary scene; the discussion about foundationalism in knowledge, the argument about observation and the theory-dependent character of observational, descriptive terms, and the many-sided controversy about the proper interpretation of the course of the development of scientific knowledge. It would be fair to say that all these discussions find essential roots in the recognition of the facts of time and change and the need to incorporate them consistently into a theory of human knowing.

It is important to notice that the classical pragmatists, each in his own way, addressed the problems posed by the need to take time and change seriously into account with respect to existence generally, but especially in connection with knowledge, and it is not without significance that some of their ideas on this head are being revived on the current scene. In view of this fact, it is pertinent to recall some central points. I shall mention three; first, the focus on inquiry as an actual process aimed at the finding of critical conclusions; second, the thesis that the warrant for these conclusions is a combined function of evidence and of the normative structure controlling the critical or experimental process by which they were reached; and third, the belief that knowing is the answering of questions under existential conditions and that every warranted answer represents a community of agreement among those qualified to judge unaccompanied by actual grounds for doubting the answer within the confines of the evidence available at a given time. It is, of course, obvious that no critical account of these notions can be attempted here, but a brief resume of each will serve the purpose at hand which in this case is to illustrate the grappling with the problem of change as a hallmark of philosophical thinking in America.

As regards the first topic, Peirce, James, Dewey and Royce each in a different vein were at one in approaching the nature of knowing via analyses of actual inquiry, including both particular techniques appropriate to particular subject matters and the logical structure of inquiry as such. In each case an attempt was made to determine, in the words of James, "what knowing is known as" and thus to avoid purely dialectical conceptions with little or no foundation in the facts about actual inquiry. Accordingly, Peirce developed the theory of the three types of reasoning in inquiry—abduction, deduction and induction—showing how the first initiates the process in the proposal of hypotheses, how the second functions in the derivation of consequences, and how the third figures in testing through sampling and other experimental procedures. James called attention to the process whereby new fact—the discovery, for example, of radioactivity—is married to old truth and broadly based theory so as to preserve a maximum of continuity and a minimum of dislocation. Royce taught for many years a seminar on methods in the sciences and sought to elucidate the distinctive roles of the mechanical, historical and statistical models in scientific research. And Dewey in his *Logic, The Theory of Inquiry* aimed at producing a comprehensive account of empirical method exhibiting the functional role of logical forms in the directed process of reaching warranted assertions. The important point in all this is that decades before the revolutionary impact of introducing the history of science into the philosophical discussion, all these thinkers had acknowledged the crucial fact that inquiry is a temporal process taking place under historical conditions and that no account of it is adequate which ignores these facts and concentrates exclusively on the supposedly atemporal or purely logical features in it. As recent discussion makes plain, this lesson has now been learned, if not so well learned that the impact of change, as perceived by some interpreters, becomes overwhelming and threatens both the objectivity and continuity of scientific thought. But that is another topic.

The second sign previously mentioned which points to the willingness to acknowledge the facts of temporality and change and to deal directly with the ensuing problems is found in the thesis that knowledge is an outcome of a temporally conditioned process and that the warrant for this outcome resides in the self-correcting, critical method through which it was reached. This claim, as Peirce and Dewey well understood, raises serious questions concerning the validity of the thesis, maintained in modern thought by rationalists and empiricists alike, that knowledge must have "foundations"—to use the current term—in the sense of being rooted ultimately in some *incorrigible* item—clear ideas, ultimate data of sense, ultimate premises—which provides a guarantee for whatever further claims to knowledge may be built on that foundation. Peirce, it will be recalled, specifically objected to this thesis as based on an "exploded" conception of logic going all the way back to Aristotle's belief that if man is to have knowledge at all there must be first premises which are prior and better known than any propositions derived from them. The attempts of Peirce and Dewey to replace this view by a logic of inquiry which rests not on the incorrigible but on what is not actually doubtful *in situ* and on the condition of the available knowledge at the time subject to the critical control of empirical test, are, of course, well known.

The problems they envisaged and sought to resolve are being discussed at present under the rubric of foundationalism and antifoundationalism. The central issue can be expressed by means of a familiar figure which, though like all such devices it breaks down in the end, is nevertheless illuminating. For the foundationalists, the ship of knowledge, though it sails the seas of inquiry, has an anchor which is in some sense always taking hold on all its voyages—even if the anchor chain is of an infinite length—and the ship arrives at no destinations beyond the reach of the anchor and its chain. The opposing view holds that the ship of knowledge has no anchor but it does sail in the sea of inquiry and whenever it arrives at a destination it does so as the explicit result of having been guided by sound navigational principles and operations. I am not, of course, suggesting that the situation is anything like this simple; I am merely attempting to call attention to the recognition by the non-foundationalists of the temporal character of the knowledge process and its control by the logic of inquiry in comparison with conceptions of truth which abstract from the process through which it is gained in order to uphold some form of incorrigibility.

Closely related to the foregoing, and a third sign of the sensitivity of American philosophers to the fact of change and its consequences, is the idea, again proposed by Peirce and much in evidence at present, of knowledge being a function of a critical community of investigators whose activity results, at least on some occasions, in a convergence of opinion which represents the answer to some question under investigation by many inquirers. This conception of a funded result of inquiry was, of course, a direct response to the problem posed by the development of knowledge under historical conditions and the need to revise or even discard to some degree previous conclusions as erroneous. Certain facts about asymmetries in nature—for example, the existence of incongruous counterparts—have long been known, but for a long time it was assumed that this fact had no empirical consequences. At the present time, it is known, in contrast to earlier opinion, that these differences in spatial orientation are not vacuous, but are the source of different behavior patterns in both physical and organic systems. In order to avoid having to say that previous generations of scientists "knew" what later turned out to be either false or only

partly true, the proposal was to interpret the intersubjectively cor-
roborated results of research as *convergent opinion* which represents
coming as near the truth as actual inquiry has been able to come *at
a given time.* That such an opinion may be in need of modification,
correction or even replacement at *some subsequent time* is a presupposition of the entire process of inquiry. In not calling the opinion
which has turned out to be either false or in some degree incorrect
by the name of "knowledge" taken in some simple and unqualified
sense, we at the very least avoid the paradox wherein it turns out
that large numbers of people "knew" what was not true.

The view of scientific knowledge as a convergence of opinion
within a determinate community of inquirers has not been without
its critics, but whatever difficulties it presents I feel constrained to
point out two criticisms which seem to me invalid. Years ago Russell
raised the critical query as to why Peirce thought there is an "ideal
limit" to which scientific belief tends, and more recently others have
followed this up, claiming that Peirce never showed that there *must*
be a convergence. But such criticism misses the point by ignoring
the empirical context of Peirce's view. If one attends to Peirce's
many illustrations from the history of science, one sees that he was
basing the theory on the evidence of what actually happens when
there is general agreement on the answer to some question. What
Peirce had in mind is nicely illustrated by Polanyi's example of the
periodic table. The general acceptance of the validity of that arrangement of the elements and the theory on which it is based is set
in high relief by the anomalies in it. As Polanyi points out, these
anomalies led no one to reject the table but rather to seek further
explanation of the discrepancies. To ask for a *must be* proof of such
agreement is to ask for the very foundationalism Peirce was rejecting and at the same time to betray the fact that one is not much of
an empiricist after all. Whatever "must be" there is about Peirce's
ideal limit is more like the assertion that a thrown die *must* come up
6 at some time or other than it is like the proposition that every
prime number *must* have some successor which is prime.

The criticism which says that the community-of-inquirers-
seeking-convergence conception cannot provide a guarantee against
conventionalism or a large-scale conspiratorial hoax is based
on a misunderstanding of what is involved. The convergence is far
from being some sort of democratic referendum because the
requisite opinions are under the constraint of public evidence together with logical and experimental canons of inquiry. In comparing the situation with that of an insurance company, Peirce argued
that just as no company can accept a single risk where failure would

bankrupt the entire operation, the scientific community cannot accept the opinion of any investigator whose personal interest in the outcome of the inquiry exceeds his commitment to finding the truth.

III. Relevance

In coming to my final hallmark of philosophical thinking in America, a word of caution is in order. By "relevance," I do not mean concern for some short-run utility in thought or the demand that thinking be under the constraint of an immediate program for action; I mean something closer to what Whitehead meant by "importance," what James meant by the idea that counts, or what Susan Stebbing had in mind when she wrote that excellent little book entitled *Thinking to Some Purpose*. Running throughout American thought from one end to the other like a scarlet thread visible at every point in a fabric has been a persistent belief that thought must have an orientation in terms of purposes which serve as principles of selection for relevance. The idea is illustrated to the utmost in the conception of intelligence as problem-solving where the task is to discover not how much we know but precisely what items in our store of knowledge count or have relevance for dealing with the problem at hand. It seems clear that the characteristic American suspicion of conceiving of the aim of philosophy as that of arriving at one comprehensive system of reality wherein all parts are internally related to each other stems from the sense that under these conditions finite terms and situations would become difficult to define, and thinking would find itself lost because deprived of a principle of selection or limitation. Every determination makes a "difference" in the total mapping of the whole, but the remaining problem is what particular determinations count for the resolution of a particular problematic situation *within* the totality? It is precisely this consideration which James had in mind when he pointed to the encyclopedia on his book shelf as representative of a totality of knowledge and then asked, "When do I say these things?" What determines my judgment that a given item of knowledge is relevant whereas another may be ignored? The pragmatists may have been too sanguine in their belief that this question is answered in and through the demands imposed by a problematic situation, especially since we cannot suppose that all problems present themselves with the obviousness characteristic of such standard examples as those of finding my way out of a forest or of removing some physical obstacle which thwarts a habitual response. But underneath the belief in the selective function of the problematic lurks another belief, namely that if knowledge is ever to function in the resolution of human perplexities and especially in the meeting of human needs and the overcoming of obstacles to the advance of civilization, not only must there be a purpose or aim invoked, but it must be one which stands in addition to the purely theoretical purpose of mirroring the entire universe in thought. Relevance becomes a desideratum at the point where it is seen that while every single fact must stand related in myriad ways to an infinite environment which is, on the occasion of abstracting that fact, suppressed, nevertheless not all of these relations will count in the same way and to the same degree when our interest in and concern for that fact is something other than knowing it from a theoretical standpoint.

There are, to be sure, many facets to the entire topic of relevance; I am concentrating on but one, the feature of purposive selection in achieving an intellectual aim, and I would like to offer an example which is particularly well suited for making clear what is meant. Ornithology is a branch of knowledge which had rudimentary beginnings several millennia ago but, like numerous other sciences, it was developed on a sophisticated taxonomic basis only in the past three centuries. The bird population of the world, though not as numerous as the insect, is still staggering in its numbers and an accurate mapping of the many families and species plus their characteristics, distributions and relations to the environment has been the monumental task of scientists in many countries since the seventeenth century. A science of this sort naturally relies heavily on observation and at many levels and for different purposes. The most accurate descriptions of individual specimens will, of course, be possible only under conditions where, as the expression goes, the bird is in the hand. Under these conditions the anatomy, musculature, plumage, etc., of every known species can be exhaustively determined and recorded, resulting in the vast record which contains our scientific knowledge of these feathered creatures. Other features of the kingdom of the birds—their nesting, feeding, reproduction, migration, etc.,—will have to be investigated by other and more laborious forms of observation involving patient cooperation with natural conditions beyond human control.

Now suppose the idea should occur to someone—as it did to Roger Tory Peterson—that it should be possible to construct a *field guide* to the birds of a geographical region which would enable a person with ordinary powers of observation and memory to make *identifications* of individual birds and flocks of birds perching, hopping and on the wing in fields, meadows and swamps with no equipment save binoculars. Notice that the conditions are definite, but quite different from those obtaining when a given bird is in the hand or when the behavior of pairs or groups of birds is being observed under such limited conditions of control as can be imposed when one studies the birds in their natural habitat. Only those identifying marks will be of service which can be seen or heard under field conditions and hence a principle of selective relevance is indicated. Obviously not everything known about the species likely to occur will be relevant. The size in centimeters of the lower mandible, the color of the roof of the mouth plus all the anatomical information about the bird no matter how accurate and detailed will be of no avail whatever for accomplishing the purpose at hand. What will be needed instead is a list of *identifying features* characteristic of the birds themselves and their known habits— wingbar colors, tail feather colors, bill and eye-ring colors plus characteristic songs, flight patterns discernible in the field, characteristic trees frequented by certain types of birds, etc.—plus a selection of *comparative features* enabling the observer to distinguish similar species from each other. From the available store of information making up the scientific record, there must be chosen the items which *count* or contribute to the purpose at hand. We have to be able to say, in the case before us, that, barring accidents and strays, such and such a species is the *only* one in the area which is larger than a robin and shows clearly a white rump patch when it takes to flight.

Although the foregoing illustration may seem to be far removed from more recondite philosophical topics, it represents quite precisely one aspect at least of that concern for selective relevance in thought which has ever been at the center of philosophical thinking in America. This concern has often been confused with the belief that all thought is for the sake of action, whereas the truth of the matter is otherwise. The essential contrast is not between thought and action but between our theoretical knowledge on the one side and the human purposes which should determine what items among that knowledge are relevant for these purposes and how that knowledge should be used. If this concern for the difference which thought and knowledge make in human life is being *practical*, then American philosophers have always exhibited the trait.

Index

Absolute, the: Royce on, 123–25; as totality, Hegel on, 112–13

Abstraction(s): criticism of, guidelines for, 116; dual character of, 108; meaning of, 105–8; partiality of, 112; positive aspect of, 108; problem posed by, 109–11; way of dialectical recovery of whole and, 111–13; way of functioning or instrumentalism and, 113–16

America, philosophy in, 193–207; change in, 199–205; receptivity in, 196–99; relevance in, 205–7

Analytic philosophy, plurality of experience and, 73–74

Anti-foundationalism, 202–3

Appreciation, world of, Royce on, 162–63

Art, experiential roots of, Dewey on, 33

Art as Experience (Dewey), 33

Ayer, A. J., verifiability theory of meaning of, 94–95

Baldwin, James M., on "sign," 176

Barrett, William, on odyssey of reason, 40

Bergson, Henri, 63

Between: in process of development, Royce on, 161–63; search for, imitation and, 164

Boyle, Robert, 48

Bradley, F. H., on metaphysics, 94–95

Broad, C. D., 196

Camus, Albert, 197

Carnap, Rudolf: conception of logical analysis of, 95–97; on existence and factual truth, 68

Change in American philosophy, 199–205

Classical empiricism, James's critique of, 72–73

Clifford, W. K., James on, 61

Cognitive relations, conjunctive relations and, 79–80

Communication: "leveling tendency" of, 150–51; "mob psychology" and, 151–52

Community, communities, 5; communication and, 141–43; democracy and, 145–47; of dialogue, Dewey on, 140; of hope, 135, 137; of memory, 135, 137; requirements for, 135–37; Royce's doctrine of, 135, 136–37; of understanding, successful interpretation and, 170, 183; value of, 139–52

Comparison, process of, interpretation and, 170–71

Conception: interpretation distinguished from, 183–84, 185; Kant on, 134; Royce on, 134

Conjunctive relations in experience, 77–81

Creativity: being one's self and, 164–65; as constructive response, 155; imitation and, 164–65; interpretation and, 170–72; mediation and, 172; in Royce's philosophical idealism, 153–72

Critical philosophy, development of: linguistic turn in, 89; pragmatic turn in, 97–101; reflexive turn in, 89, 90–93

Critical standpoint, reflexive turn in philosophy and, 92–93

Critique of Judgment (Kant), creativity and, 155–56

Critique of Pure Reason, The (Kant), perceiving and conceiving in, 134